BEST OF

Betty Crocker®

2013

BEST OF Betty Crocker®
2013

For more great recipes and ideas, go to bettycrocker.com

PUBLISHED BY
Taste of Home Books
Reiman Media Group, LLC
5400 S. 60th St., Greendale WI 53129
www.tasteofhome.com

Printed in the U.S.A.
1 3 5 7 9 10 8 6 4 2

Taste of Home® is a registered trademark of Reiman Media Group, LLC

The trademarks referred to herein are trademarks of General Mills, Inc., or its affiliates, except as noted.

Yoplait is a registered trademark of YOPLAIT MARQUES (France) used under license.

All recipes were originally published in different form by Betty Crocker® Magazine, a trademark of General Mills, Inc.

International Standard Book Number (10): 1-61765-111-7
International Standard Book Number (13): 978-1-61765-111-3
International Standard Serial Number: 1947-234X

General Mills, Inc.

EDITORIAL DIRECTOR: Jeff Nowak
ASSISTANT MANAGER, MARKETING SERVICES: Christine Gray
COOKBOOK EDITOR: Grace Wells
EDITORIAL ASSISTANT: Kelly Gross
DIGITAL ASSETS MANAGER: Carrie Jacobson
RECIPE DEVELOPMENT AND TESTING: Betty Crocker Kitchens
PHOTOGRAPHY: General Mills Photography Studio

Reiman Media Group, LLC–Editorial

EDITOR-IN-CHIEF: Catherine Cassidy
EXECUTIVE EDITOR/PRINT & DIGITAL BOOKS: Stephen C. George
CREATIVE DIRECTOR: Howard Greenberg
EDITORIAL SERVICES MANAGER: Kerri Balliet
SENIOR EDITOR/PRINT & DIGITAL BOOKS: Mark Hagen
EDITORS: Ellie Martin Cliffe, Krista Lanphier
ASSOCIATE CREATIVE DIRECTOR: Edwin Robles Jr.
ART DIRECTOR: Jessie Sharon
CONTENT PRODUCTION MANAGER: Julie Wagner
LAYOUT DESIGNER: Nancy Novak
CONTRIBUTING LAYOUT DESIGNER: Matt Fukuda
COPY CHIEF: Deb Warlaumont Mulvey
CONTRIBUTING PROOFREADER: Victoria Soukup Jensen
EDITORIAL ASSISTANT: Marilyn Iczkowski

Reader's Digest North America

PRESIDENT: Dan Lagani

PRESIDENT, BOOKS AND HOME ENTERTAINING: Harold Clarke
CHIEF FINANCIAL OFFICER: Howard Halligan
VICE PRESIDENT, GENERAL MANAGER, READER'S DIGEST MEDIA: Marilynn Jacobs
CHIEF CONTENT OFFICER, MILWAUKEE: Mark Jannot
CHIEF MARKETING OFFICER: Renee Jordan
VICE PRESIDENT, CHIEF SALES OFFICER: Mark Josephson
VICE PRESIDENT, CHIEF STRATEGY OFFICER: Jacqueline Majers Lachman
VICE PRESIDENT, MARKETING AND CREATIVE SERVICES: Elizabeth Tighe
VICE PRESIDENT, CHIEF CONTENT OFFICER: Liz Vaccariello

The Reader's Digest Association, Inc.

PRESIDENT AND CHIEF EXECUTIVE OFFICER: Robert E. Guth

COVER PHOTOGRAPHY
PHOTOGRAPHER: Jim Wieland
SENIOR FOOD STYLIST: Kathryn Conrad
SET STYLING MANAGER: Stephanie Marchese

Front Cover Photographs, clockwise from top: Praline-Pumpkin Cake, p. 196; Red Pepper-Filled Appetizer Hearts, p. 25; Double-Layer Peppermint Fudge, p. 244; Cobb Salad Wraps, p. 150; Bacon-Pepper Mac and Cheese, p. 80
Back Cover Photographs, clockwise from upper left: Mexican Chocolate Cheesecake, p. 197; Maple and Mustard-Glazed Chicken, p. 113; Strawberry Truffle Brownies, p. 342; Roasted Red Pepper Dip, p. 27

table
OF CONTENTS

336

128

23

260

109

165

42

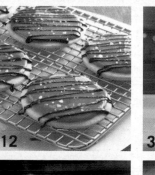

11

312

35

9

8

43

With Betty Crocker You Can Expect the Best—
315 RECIPES YOU'LL LOVE FOR LIFE!

In kitchens across America, Betty Crocker has been a friend to family cooks for generations. You know you can count on her kitchen-tested recipes to bring a smile to every face around the table. This year, she's done it again, with 315 savory and sweet dishes, plus hundreds of tried-and-true tips that will make your time in the kitchen better than ever.

In addition to all of the classic meals and delightful desserts you'd expect from this new collection, Betty's bringing even more to the table! For the first time, we're sharing Gifts from the Kitchen (starting on p. 313), our favorite items perfect for packing up and gifting at any time of year.

Plus, with more people than ever paying attention to food labels, we've put together a bonus chapter of Gluten-Free Goodness (turn to p. 329), rich, satisfying desserts nobody will want—or need—to pass up. In addition, each recipe in the book comes complete with Nutrition Facts for your peace of mind.

SAVE TIME WITH ICONS

We know that, in homes across the country, cooks' time is at a premium, so you'll find at-a-glance icons throughout this book. They'll help you make quick work of locating dishes that fit your family's lifestyle and schedule.

The **EASY** icon means the hands-on time for the recipe is just 15 minutes or less, so anyone can multitask while getting a hearty dinner on the table.

On-the-go families will appreciate the **QUICK** icon, which means the recipe takes 30 minutes or less, start to finish. With these super-fast meals, you'll never need to resort to drive-thru food.

Our **LOW FAT** icon denotes the dishes that boast all the flavor but a fraction of the fat. When it comes to entrees, a serving in this category contains 10 or fewer grams of fat, while side dishes and desserts have just 3 or fewer grams.

p. 142   p. 310

p. 54

FUN-TO-MAKE, FUN-TO-EAT FOOD

We selected every dish in this latest collection with your enjoyment in mind. Whether you're preparing a holiday feast (start with Enticing Entrees, p. 41), a summer picnic (turn to Hot Off the Grill, p. 107) or a weeknight meal (see Meals-in-One, p. 73), you'll find a memorable menu here.

At Betty Crocker, we know family cooks like you add one ingredient to every dish they share: love. And *Best of Betty Crocker* is the perfect place to begin. You'll be proud to serve the recipes you've made, and your loved ones will be delighted to indulge!

BREAKFAST&BRUNCH

p. 9

20

8

6

brunch casserole

Prep Time: 20 Minutes
Start to Finish: 9 Hours 20 Minutes
Servings: 8

- 2 boxes Betty Crocker® Seasoned Skillets® hash brown potatoes
- 1-1/2 lb bulk spicy pork sausage
- 2 medium red bell peppers, chopped (2 cups)
- 8 medium green onions, chopped (1/2 cup)
- 1 cup shredded Cheddar cheese (4 oz)
- 1 cup shredded pepper Jack cheese (4 oz)

- 2 cups milk
- 1/2 teaspoon salt
- 1/2 teaspoon pepper
- 6 eggs

Chopped fresh cilantro, if desired

1 Spray 3-quart casserole dish with cooking spray. In 4-quart bowl, cover potatoes with 10 cups boiling water. Let stand 3 minutes. Drain well; return potatoes to bowl.

2 In a 12-inch skillet, cook sausage over medium heat 5 minutes. Add bell peppers; cook 4 minutes, stirring frequently, until sausage is no longer pink and peppers are tender. Drain. Add sausage mixture to potatoes in bowl; stir in onions and 1/2 cup of each of the cheeses. Spread into the baking dish.

3 In a medium bowl, beat milk, salt, pepper and eggs until blended. Pour over sausage-potato mixture; sprinkle with remaining 1/2 cup of each cheese. Cover; refrigerate 8 hours or overnight.

4 Heat oven to 375°F. Uncover baking dish. Bake 50 minutes or until light golden brown and cheese is melted. Let stand 10 minutes before serving. Sprinkle with cilantro.

Nutritional Info: 1 Serving: Calories 628; Total Fat 40g (Saturated Fat 16g); Sodium 1812mg; Total Carbohydrate 39g (Dietary Fiber 4g); Protein 26g. Exchanges: 2-1/2 Starch, 3 High-Fat Meat, 3 Fat. Carbohydrate Choices: 2-1/2.

Betty's Kitchen Tip

Try different types of cheeses in this recipe. Swiss and Gouda work well, but you can also experiment with cheese blends, such as Colby-Jack or mozzarella and provolone.

classic hot brown

Prep Time: 20 Minutes
Start to Finish: 20 Minutes
Servings: 6

1/4	cup butter or margarine
1/4	cup Gold Medal® all-purpose flour
1/4	teaspoon salt
1/4	teaspoon freshly ground pepper
2	cups milk
2	cups shredded Cheddar cheese (8 oz)
6	slices Texas toast, lightly toasted
18	oz oven-roasted turkey breast slices
12	slices tomato
6	tablespoons shredded Parmesan cheese
3	slices bacon, crisply cooked, crumbled

Paprika

1 Set oven control to broil. In a 2-quart saucepan, melt the butter over medium-low heat. Stir in flour, salt and pepper. Cook and stir until smooth and bubbly. Gradually add milk, stirring constantly until mixture boils and thickens. Stir in Cheddar cheese until melted. Remove from heat.

2 Spray 13x9-inch pan with cooking spray. Place toast slices in pan. Top each slice of toast with 3 oz turkey, 2 slices tomato, 1/3 cup cheese sauce and 1 tablespoon Parmesan cheese.

3 Broil with tops about 6 inches from heat, 3 to 4 minutes or until lightly browned. Top evenly with bacon; sprinkle lightly with paprika.

Nutritional Info: 1 Serving: Calories 541; Total Fat 26g (Saturated Fat 16g); Sodium 822mg; Total Carbohydrate 31g (Dietary Fiber 2g); Protein 44g. Exchanges: 1-1/2 Starch, 1/2 Low-Fat Milk, 1/2 Vegetable, 4 Very Lean Meat, 1 High-Fat Meat, 2 Fat. Carbohydrate Choices: 2.

Betty's Kitchen Tip

You can purchase turkey from the deli or use packaged sliced turkey breast found with the luncheon meats. Consider swapping turkey for sliced baked ham, as well.

southwestern scramble biscuit cups

Prep Time: 25 Minutes
Start to Finish: 40 Minutes
Servings: 6 (2 biscuits each)

Biscuit Cups

2	cups Original Bisquick® mix
1	tablespoon chili powder
1/4	cup milk
1/4	cup butter, melted
1	egg

Scramble

5	eggs
1/4	cup milk

1/2	teaspoon salt
1/4	teaspoon pepper
1	tablespoon butter
1/4	cup chopped red bell pepper
1/4	cup chopped onion
1	jalapeño chile, seeded, finely chopped
1	cup shredded pepper Jack cheese (4 oz)

1 Heat oven to 350°F. Generously grease bottoms and sides of 12 regular-size muffin cups with shortening or cooking spray.

2 In a medium bowl, stir all biscuit cup ingredients until a soft dough forms. Divide dough into 12 equal pieces. Press 1 piece into bottom and up side of each muffin cup. Bake 8 to 10 minutes or until light brown.

3 Meanwhile, in large bowl, beat 5 eggs, 1/4 cup milk, the salt and pepper; set aside. In 10-inch nonstick skillet, melt 1 tablespoon butter over medium heat. Cook bell pepper, onion and chile in butter 3 to 5 minutes, stirring occasionally, until tender. Add egg mixture to vegetables. Cook 1 to 2 minutes, stirring occasionally, until eggs are loosely set. Gently fold in cheese.

4 Remove biscuit cups from oven. Using back of spoon, press puffed crust into cup to make a deep indentation. Spoon egg mixture into cups.

5 Bake 10 to 15 minutes or just until eggs are set. To remove from pan, run a thin knife around biscuit cup and lift out.

Nutritional Info: 1 Serving: Calories 400; Total Fat 25g (Saturated Fat 12g); Sodium 980mg; Total Carbohydrate 30g (Dietary Fiber 2g); Protein 14g. Exchanges: 1-1/2 Starch, 1/2 Low-Fat Milk, 1 Medium-Fat Meat, 3-1/2 Fat. Carbohydrate Choices: 2.

Betty's Kitchen Tip

Serve these biscuit cups with a dollop of sour cream and salsa. Wear rubber gloves when seeding and chopping jalapeños to protect your skin from irritation.

cheesecake pancakes

Prep Time: 30 Minutes
Start to Finish: 8 Hours 30 Minutes
Servings: 5 (3 pancakes and 3 tablespoons syrup each)

- -

Pancakes
1	package (8 oz) cream cheese
2	cups Original Bisquick® mix
1/2	cup graham cracker crumbs
1/4	cup sugar
1	cup milk
2	eggs

Strawberry Syrup
1	cup sliced fresh strawberries
1/2	cup strawberry syrup for pancakes

- -

1 Slice cream cheese lengthwise into four pieces; place on ungreased cookie sheet. Cover; freeze 8 hours or overnight.

2 Brush griddle or skillet with vegetable oil or spray with cooking spray; heat griddle to 375°F or heat skillet over medium heat.

3 Cut cream cheese into bite-size pieces; set aside. In large bowl, stir Bisquick mix, graham cracker crumbs, sugar, milk and eggs with whisk or fork until blended. Stir in cream cheese.

4 For each pancake, pour slightly less than 1/3 cup batter onto hot griddle. Cook until edges are dry. Turn; cook other sides until golden brown.

5 In small bowl, mix strawberries and syrup; top pancakes with strawberry mixture.

Nutritional Info: 1 Serving: Calories 580; Total Fat 26g (Saturated Fat 12g); Sodium 830mg; Total Carbohydrate 75g (Dietary Fiber 2g); Protein 11g. Exchanges: 2 Starch, 2-1/2 Other Carbohydrate, 1/2 Low-Fat Milk, 4-1/2 Fat. Carbohydrate Choices: 5.

Betty's Kitchen Tip

Top this decadent breakfast with your favorite type of fruit or offer a variety of berries, nuts and flavored syrups.

silver dollar pancake and sausage sandwiches

Prep Time: 20 Minutes
Start to Finish: 20 Minutes
Servings: 4 (2 sandwiches each)

QUICK

1 cup Original Bisquick® mix	4 slices (3/4 oz each) American cheese, cut into quarters
1/2 cup milk	1 cup real maple or maple-flavored syrup, heated
1 egg	
2 teaspoons vegetable oil	
1 package (9.6 oz) frozen fully cooked pork sausage patties, thawed	

1 In medium bowl, stir Bisquick mix, milk, egg and oil until blended.

2 Heat griddle or skillet over medium heat or to 375°F. Grease griddle with additional vegetable oil if necessary (or spray with cooking spray before heating). For each pancake, use about 1 tablespoon batter. Cook pancakes until bubbly on top, puffed and dry around edges. Turn and cook other sides until golden brown. Keep warm.

3 In the same skillet, heat sausage patties about 3 minutes. Turn; top each patty with 2 cheese quarters. Cook 3 to 4 minutes longer or until thoroughly heated and cheese is melted.

4 To serve, place 1 cheese-topped sausage patty on each of 8 pancakes; top each with second pancake. Serve with syrup.

Nutritional Info: 1 Serving: Calories 720; Total Fat 38g (Saturated Fat 14g); Sodium 1020mg; Total Carbohydrate 75g (Dietary Fiber 0g); Protein 19g. Exchanges: 1-1/2 Starch, 3 Other Carbohydrate, 1/2 Low-Fat Milk, 1-1/2 Medium-Fat Meat, 5-1/2 Fat. Carbohydrate Choices: 5.

 Kitchen Tip

Serve these sandwiches with hash browns for a hearty breakfast. Planning a sleepover for your child and friends? Put these cute breakfast sandwiches on the menu!

chopped vegetable pancakes

Prep Time: 30 Minutes
Start to Finish: 30 Minutes
Servings: 4 (3 pancakes each)

- 2 tablespoons butter
- 2 medium carrots, shredded (1-1/2 cups)
- 2 stalks celery, chopped (1 cup)
- 1 medium red bell pepper, chopped (1 cup)
- 1 medium yellow onion, chopped (1/2 cup)
- 2 cups fresh baby spinach, chopped
- 1 cup Original Bisquick® mix
- 2 eggs
- 3/4 teaspoon salt
- 1/4 teaspoon pepper
- 1 cup tomato pasta sauce, warmed

1 In 12-inch nonstick skillet, melt butter over medium-high heat. Cook the carrots, celery, bell pepper and onion in butter 2 to 3 minutes, stirring frequently, until crisp-tender. Add spinach; cook and stir 1 to 2 minutes until wilted. Cool slightly.

2 In medium bowl, stir Bisquick mix and eggs. Add vegetables, salt and pepper; stir well.

3 Wipe the same skillet with paper towel. Spray skillet with cooking spray; heat over medium heat. For each pancake, use 1/4 cup of batter; flatten slightly with a spatula. Cook until golden brown, about 1 to 2 minutes on each side. Serve with pasta sauce.

Nutritional Info: 1 Serving: Calories 340; Total Fat 16g (Saturated Fat 6g); Sodium 1240mg; Total Carbohydrate 40g (Dietary Fiber 4g); Protein 8g. Exchanges: 1 Starch, 1 Other Carbohydrate, 2-1/2 Vegetable, 3 Fat. Carbohydrate Choices: 2-1/2.

Betty's Kitchen Tip

Savory pancakes can be enjoyed any time of day—breakfast, lunch or dinner!

puffed-pancake brunch casserole

Prep Time: 15 Minutes
Start to Finish: 1 Hour 5 Minutes
Servings: 10

EASY

Heather Markowski
Valatie, NY
Better with Bisquick® Recipe Contest

1/4 cup butter	1 package (2.1 oz) precooked bacon, chopped
2 cups Original Bisquick® mix	2 cups shredded Cheddar cheese (8 oz)
2 cups milk	1/4 teaspoon salt
8 eggs	1/4 teaspoon ground mustard
1 cup shredded Swiss cheese (4 oz)	Dash ground nutmeg
1 lb cubed cooked ham (about 3 cups)	

1 Heat oven to 375°F. Spray 13x9-inch (3-quart) glass baking dish with cooking spray. Place butter in dish; place in oven until melted, about 10 minutes.

2 In a medium bowl, mix Bisquick mix, 1 cup of the milk and 2 of the eggs with whisk until tiny lumps remain. Pour over butter in baking dish. Layer with Swiss cheese, ham, bacon and Cheddar cheese. In a large bowl, mix remaining 1 cup milk, remaining 6 eggs, the salt, mustard and nutmeg. Pour over casserole.

3 Bake uncovered 35 to 40 minutes or until golden brown. Let stand 10 minutes before serving.

Nutritional Info: 1 Serving: Calories 460; Total Fat 30g (Saturated Fat 15g); Sodium 1430mg; Total Carbohydrate 19g (Dietary Fiber 0g); Protein 29g. Exchanges: 1 Starch, 1/2 Other Carbohydrate, 3 Medium-Fat Meat, 1/2 High-Fat Meat, 2 Fat. Carbohydrate Choices: 1.

Betty's Kitchen Tip

A platter of mixed fresh fruits of the season is a tasty and nutritious accompaniment for this hearty breakfast dish.

green tea-honey nut granola

Prep Time: 15 Minutes
Start to Finish: 1 Hour 30 Minutes
Servings: 16 (1/2 cup each)

EASY

6	cups Honey Nut Clusters® cereal
1/2	cup cashew halves
1/2	cup pecan halves
1/4	cup packed brown sugar
1/2	cup strong brewed green tea (2 bags per 1/2 cup hot water)
2	tablespoons honey
1/2	cup chopped dried mangoes or apricots
1/2	cup sweetened dried cranberries

1 Heat oven to 300°F. Spray 15x10x1-inch pan with cooking spray. In a large bowl, mix cereal, cashews and pecans.

2 In a 1-quart saucepan, heat brown sugar, tea and honey over medium heat 3 to 4 minutes, stirring constantly, until brown sugar is melted. Pour over cereal mixture; toss until well coated. Spread in pan.

3 Bake 45 minutes, stirring well every 15 minutes. Bake 10 to 15 minutes longer or until crisp and glazed. Stir in mangoes and cranberries. Cool completely, about 15 minutes. (Mixture will crisp as it cools.) Store tightly covered at room temperature.

Nutritional Info: 1 Serving: Calories 179; Total Fat 5g (Saturated Fat 1g); Sodium 124mg; Total Carbohydrate 33g (Dietary Fiber 2g); Protein 2g. Exchanges: 1 Starch, 1/2 Fruit, 1/2 Other Carbohydrate, 1 Fat. Carbohydrate Choices: 2.

Betty's Kitchen Tip

Replacing foods containing saturated fats with unsaturated fats from ingredients such as nuts may help lower blood cholesterol. Since fats are high in calories, keep portions small.

pumpkin butter

Prep Time: 40 Minutes
Start to Finish: 40 Minutes
Servings: 48 (1 tablespoon each)

LOW FAT

. . . .

3	cups canned pumpkin (not pumpkin pie mix)
1-1/2	cups packed brown sugar
1/2	cup granulated sugar
1	tablespoon fresh lemon juice

1	teaspoon vanilla
1/2	teaspoon ground cinnamon
1/4	teaspoon ground allspice
1/8	teaspoon salt

. . . .

1 In a 4-quart saucepan, mix pumpkin, brown sugar, granulated sugar and lemon juice. Heat to simmering over medium-low heat, stirring occasionally to keep mixture from sticking to bottom of pan. Simmer uncovered 30 minutes, stirring often, until mixture coats back of spoon. Remove from heat; stir in vanilla, cinnamon, allspice and salt. Cool completely.

2 Pour into storage containers; cover tightly. Store in refrigerator.

Nutritional Info: 1 Serving: Calories 40; Total Fat 0g (Saturated Fat 0g); Sodium 9mg; Total Carbohydrate 10g (Dietary Fiber 0g); Protein 0g. Exchanges: 1/2 Other Carbohydrate. Carbohydrate Choices: 1/2.

Betty's Kitchen Tip

A spiced fruit butter like the one here tastes delicious when spread over nearly any bread-based item, including waffles, scones, biscuits and toasted English muffins.

streusel-topped banana-chocolate snack cake

Prep Time: 15 Minutes
Start to Finish: 2 Hours
Servings: 12

1-1/2　cups Original Bisquick® mix
　1/2　cup Gold Medal® whole wheat flour
　1/2　cup packed brown sugar
　　2　ripe medium bananas, mashed
　　　　(about 1 cup)
　1/2　cup milk
　　1　teaspoon vanilla
　1/2　cup semisweet chocolate chips

Streusel Topping

　1/4　cup packed brown sugar
　1/4　cup Gold Medal® whole wheat flour
　1/4　teaspoon ground cinnamon
　　2　tablespoons cold butter or margarine

1 Heat oven to 425°F. Grease bottom and sides of 9-inch square pan with shortening or cooking spray.

2 In a large bowl, stir Bisquick mix, 1/2 cup flour, 1/2 cup brown sugar, the bananas, milk and vanilla. Gently fold in chocolate chips. Pour into pan.

3 In a medium bowl, mix 1/4 cup brown sugar, 1/4 cup flour and the cinnamon. Cut in butter, using pastry blender (or pulling 2 table knives through ingredients in opposite directions), until mixture is crumbly. Sprinkle topping evenly over batter in pan.

4 Bake 17 to 20 minutes or until a toothpick inserted in the center comes out clean. Cool on cooling rack.

EASY LOW FAT

Nutritional Info: 1 Serving: Calories 110; Total Fat 3g (Saturated Fat 1.5g); Sodium 105mg; Total Carbohydrate 19g (Dietary Fiber 1g); Protein 1g. Exchanges: 1/2 Starch, 1 Other Carbohydrate, 1/2 Fat. Carbohydrate Choices: 1.

Betty's Kitchen Tip

For a more rustic version, stir in chocolate chunks or chopped chocolate bars instead of chips. Cut the coffee cake into smaller squares for portable party-size bites.

cinnamon banana butter

Prep Time: 35 Minutes
Start to Finish: 45 Minutes
Servings: 128 (1 tablespoon each)

LOW FAT

4 cups mashed bananas (about 8 bananas)	4-1/2 cups sugar
1/3 cup fresh lemon juice	3 teaspoons vanilla
1 package (1-3/4 oz) fruit pectin	1/2 teaspoon ground cinnamon

1 In a 4-quart saucepan, mix bananas, lemon juice and pectin until pectin has dissolved. Heat to boiling over medium heat, stirring constantly. Stir in sugar. Heat to a full rolling boil, stirring constantly; remove from heat. Stir in vanilla and cinnamon.

2 Immediately ladle jam into 8 sterilized 1/2-pint jars, leaving 1/2-inch of headspace. Wipe rims of jars and seal immediately. Process in boiling water bath 10 minutes.

Nutritional Info: 1 Serving: Calories 34; Total Fat 0g (Saturated Fat 0g); Sodium 0mg; Total Carbohydrate 9g (Dietary Fiber 0g); Protein 0g. Exchanges: 1/2 Other Carbohydrate. Carbohydrate Choices: 1/2.

Betty's Kitchen Tip

Make a peanut butter sandwich extra-special by adding a smear of this spiced butter, or use it as a filling between cake layers.

chocolate pancakes
with maple-pear sauce

Prep Time: 20 Minutes
Start to Finish: 20 Minutes
Servings: 3 (3 pancakes and about 1/2 cup sauce each)

1	cup Bisquick Heart Smart® mix
3	tablespoons unsweetened baking cocoa
2	tablespoons sugar
1	teaspoon ground cinnamon
2/3	cup chocolate milk
1/4	cup fat-free egg product
2	ripe pears, peeled, thinly sliced
1/4	cup maple-flavored syrup

1 In a medium bowl, stir Bisquick mix, cocoa, sugar and cinnamon. Stir in milk and egg product until blended.

2 Heat griddle or skillet over medium heat or to 375°F. Grease griddle with vegetable oil if necessary (or spray with cooking spray before heating). For each pancake, use slightly less than 1/4 cup batter. Cook pancakes until bubbly on top, puffed and dry around edges. Turn and cook other sides until golden brown.

3 Meanwhile, in a medium microwavable bowl, heat the pears and syrup on High 2 minutes or until mixture is hot and pears are tender. Serve sauce with pancakes.

Nutritional Info: 1 Serving: Calories 400; Total Fat 4.5g (Saturated Fat 1g); Sodium 430mg; Total Carbohydrate 83g (Dietary Fiber 6g); Protein 8g. Exchanges: 2-1/2 Starch, 3 Other Carbohydrate, 1/2 Fat. Carbohydrate Choices: 5-1/2.

Betty's Kitchen Tip

Chocolate doesn't always mean a food will be overly rich or sugary. These pancakes have just a hint of sweetness. The slightly bitter cocoa flavor is complemented by the sweet pear sauce.

waffle bake with blueberry topping

Prep Time: 20 Minutes
Start to Finish: 9 Hours
Servings: 8

10 frozen waffles	1/4 teaspoon ground nutmeg
5 eggs	1 bottle (12 oz) blueberry syrup
1-1/2 cups half-and-half	1 tablespoon cornstarch
3/4 cup packed brown sugar	1 cup frozen or fresh blueberries
1 teaspoon vanilla	Whipped topping, if desired

1 Spray 13x9-inch (3-quart) glass baking dish with cooking spray. Arrange waffles in baking dish. In large bowl, beat eggs, half-and-half, brown sugar, vanilla and nutmeg with electric mixer on medium speed until well blended; pour over waffles. Cover; refrigerate 8 hours or overnight.

2 Heat oven to 350°F. Uncover the baking dish; bake 35 to 40 minutes or until knife inserted near center comes out clean and waffles are light golden brown.

3 Meanwhile, in a 2-quart saucepan, mix syrup and cornstarch until cornstarch is dissolved. Heat mixture to boiling over medium-high heat, stirring constantly. Cook 3 to 5 minutes or until thickened. Stir in blueberries; cook until thawed.

4 Cut waffle bake into 8 servings; pour about 1/3 cup hot blueberry syrup over each serving. Garnish with whipped topping.

Nutritional Info: 1 Serving: Calories 470; Total Fat 13g (Saturated Fat 5g); Sodium 380mg; Total Carbohydrate 79g (Dietary Fiber 2g); Protein 8g. Exchanges: 2-1/2 Starch, 2-1/2 Other Carbohydrate, 2-1/2 Fat. Carbohydrate Choices: 5.

Betty's Kitchen Tip

For a complete breakfast, serve with bacon or sausage and fresh fruit, such as Strawberry-Blueberry-Orange Salad (p. 19).

strawberry-blueberry-orange salad

Prep Time: 15 Minutes
Start to Finish: 15 Minutes
Servings: 8 (1/2 cup each)

1/4	cup mayonnaise
3	tablespoons sugar
1	tablespoon white vinegar
2	teaspoons poppy seed
2	cups fresh strawberry halves
2	cups fresh blueberries
1	orange, peeled, chopped

Sliced almonds, if desired

1 In a small bowl, mix the mayonnaise, sugar, vinegar and poppy seed with a wire whisk until well blended.

2 In a medium bowl, mix strawberries, blueberries and orange. Just before serving, pour dressing over fruit; toss to combine. Sprinkle with almonds.

Nutritional Info: 1 Serving: Calories 120; Total Fat 6g (Saturated Fat 1g); Sodium 40mg; Total Carbohydrate 15g (Dietary Fiber 2g); Protein 1g. Exchanges: 1 Fruit, 1 Fat. Carbohydrate Choices: 1.

Betty's Kitchen Tip

Experiment with other favorite summer fruits, such as peaches and raspberries or kiwi and blackberries. Toasted sliced almonds will lend extra crunch and enhance the flavor.

overnight lemon coffee cake

Prep Time: 15 Minutes
Start to Finish: 9 Hours 10 Minutes
Servings: 15

EASY

1/2 cup butter or margarine, softened	1-1/2 teaspoons baking powder
1 cup granulated sugar	1/2 teaspoon salt
2 eggs	1/4 teaspoon baking soda
2 containers (6 oz each) Yoplait® Original 99% Fat Free lemon burst yogurt	3/4 cup packed brown sugar
	3/4 cup chopped pecans
2 teaspoons grated lemon peel	1/2 teaspoon ground nutmeg
2-1/3 cups Gold Medal® all-purpose flour	

1 Spray bottom only of 13x9-inch pan with cooking spray. In a large bowl, beat butter and granulated sugar with an electric mixer on low speed until light and fluffy. Add eggs, one at a time, beating well after each addition. Add the yogurt, lemon peel, flour, baking powder, salt and baking soda; beat on low speed until smooth. Spread batter in pan. Cover and refrigerate at least 8 hours but no longer than 16 hours.

2 In small resealable plastic bag, mix brown sugar, pecans and nutmeg. Refrigerate.

3 When ready to bake, let coffee cake stand at room temperature while heating oven to 350°F. Uncover coffee cake; sprinkle with brown sugar mixture.

4 Bake 30 to 40 minutes or until toothpick inserted in center comes out clean. Cool 15 minutes. Serve warm.

Nutritional Info: 1 Serving: Calories 300; Total Fat 11g (Saturated Fat 4g); Sodium 220mg; Total Carbohydrate 44g (Dietary Fiber 1g); Protein 4g. Exchanges: 2 Starch, 2 Fat. Carbohydrate Choices: 3.

Betty's Kitchen Tip

Can't wait? You can bake the coffee cake right away. Just sprinkle it with the topping, and reduce the baking time to 25 to 30 minutes. Make an orange version of this coffee cake with orange yogurt and grated orange peel.

PARTY PLEASERS

p.23

25

36

39

buffalo chicken bites with blue cheese dipping sauce

Prep Time: 25 Minutes
Start to Finish: 55 Minutes
Servings: 40

Chicken Bites

1	egg white
1/3	cup hot Buffalo wing sauce
1	lb boneless skinless chicken breasts, cut into 40 (1-inch) pieces
3/4	cup Original Bisquick® mix
3	tablespoons cornmeal
1	teaspoon salt

1/2	teaspoon pepper
	Vegetable oil

Dipping Sauce

3/4	cup crumbled blue cheese (3 oz)
6	tablespoons sour cream
6	tablespoons light mayonnaise
3	tablespoons milk

1 In a medium bowl, mix egg white and Buffalo wing sauce. Stir in the chicken. Cover; refrigerate 30 minutes.

2 Line cookie sheet with waxed paper. In a large resealable food-storage plastic bag, place Bisquick mix, cornmeal, salt and pepper. With slotted spoon, remove one-fourth of chicken pieces from bowl and add to bag; seal bag and shake to coat. Repeat with remaining chicken pieces. Tap off excess Bisquick mixture and place chicken on a cookie sheet.

3 In a small bowl, mix the dipping sauce ingredients until well combined. Cover; refrigerate until serving time.

4 In a 10-inch nonstick skillet, heat vegetable oil (1/4 inch) over medium-high heat 2 to 4 minutes. Cook chicken bites in oil in batches, about one-third at a time, 3 to 4 minutes, turning once, until golden brown. Drain on paper towels. Serve chicken with dipping sauce.

Nutritional Info: 1 Serving: Calories 60; Total Fat 4g (Saturated Fat 1.5g); Sodium 210mg; Total Carbohydrate 3g (Dietary Fiber 0g); Protein 3g. Exchanges: 1/2 Lean Meat, 1/2 Fat. Carbohydrate Choices: 0.

Betty's Kitchen Tip

Buffalo chicken bites can be breaded ahead of time and cooked just before serving. Prepare through step 2; refrigerate until cooking time.

cheesy bacon burger bites

Prep Time: 50 Minutes
Start to Finish: 50 Minutes
Servings: 28

7	slices bacon
28	fancy toothpicks
28	cherry tomatoes
3	leaves romaine lettuce, cut into 28 (1-1/2-inch) pieces
1/2	cup Original Bisquick® mix
1	lb ground beef
1	egg
1/4	cup mayonnaise
1	teaspoon Worcestershire sauce
1/4	teaspoon salt
1/4	teaspoon pepper
2	oz Cheddar cheese, cut into 1/4-inch cubes (about 1/2 cup)

1 In 10-inch nonstick skillet, cook bacon over medium heat, turning often, until browned but not overly crisp. Drain on paper towels. Discard all but 1 tablespoon drippings. Cut each bacon slice into 4 pieces.

2 On each toothpick, thread 1 tomato half, 1 bacon piece and 1 lettuce piece; set aside.

3 In large bowl, mix remaining ingredients except cheese. Fold in cheese. Shape tablespoonfuls of mixture into meatballs; flatten slightly to resemble hamburgers.

4 In the same skillet, heat the bacon drippings over medium-high heat. Cook the burgers in drippings 2 to 3 minutes on each side or until meat is no longer pink. Insert 1 toothpick into each burger; serve immediately.

Nutritional Info: 1 Appetizer: Calories 70; Total Fat 5g (Saturated Fat 1.5g); Sodium 130mg; Total Carbohydrate 2g (Dietary Fiber 0g); Protein 4g. Exchanges: 1/2 Medium-Fat Meat, 1/2 Fat. Carbohydrate Choices: 0.

Betty's Kitchen Tip

Spice up our mini cheeseburgers by using pepper Jack cheese instead of Cheddar and hot pepper sauce instead of Worcestershire sauce. For traditional flavor, serve Cheesy Bacon Burger Bites with ketchup and mustard for dipping.

creamy artichoke appetizers

Prep Time: 35 Minutes
Start to Finish: 1 Hour 10 Minutes
Servings: 48

3 cups Original Bisquick® mix	1 jar (7 oz) roasted red bell peppers, drained, diced
1-1/2 cups shredded mozzarella cheese (6 oz)	1 tablespoon Dijon mustard
2/3 cup water	1 tablespoon Worcestershire sauce
2 tablespoons vegetable oil	2 teaspoons garlic powder
1-1/2 cups mayonnaise	2 cans (14 oz each) Progresso® artichoke hearts, drained, chopped
1-1/2 cups grated Parmesan cheese	

1 Heat oven to 375°F. Spray 15x10x1-inch pan with cooking spray.

2 In a large bowl, stir the Bisquick mix and mozzarella cheese until thoroughly combined. Stir in the water and oil until dough forms; beat vigorously 20 strokes. Let stand 8 minutes.

3 Using hands dipped in additional Bisquick mix, press dough into the bottom and up the sides of the pan. Bake 9 to 11 minutes or until crust is puffed and top edges are just starting to brown.

4 Meanwhile, in a medium bowl, mix all remaining ingredients except artichokes. Stir in artichokes. Evenly spread mixture over partially baked crust.

5 Bake 12 to 15 minutes or until thoroughly heated and crust is golden brown.

6 Set oven control to broil. Broil with top of pan 6 inches from heat 2 to 3 minutes or until filling is golden brown. Cool 10 minutes. Cut into 8 rows by 6 rows.

Nutritional Info: 1 Appetizer: Calories 120; Total Fat 9g (Saturated Fat 2g); Sodium 240mg; Total Carbohydrate 7g (Dietary Fiber 1g); Protein 3g. Exchanges: 1/2 Starch, 1-1/2 Fat. Carbohydrate Choices: 1/2.

Betty's Kitchen Tip

This recipe is all inclusive—no dippers needed. The dip is baked right into the crust!

red pepper-filled appetizer hearts

Prep Time: 15 Minutes
Start to Finish: 50 Minutes
Servings: 24

1-1/2	cups Original Bisquick® Mix
2	teaspoons dried oregano leaves
1/3	cup water
1/4	cup garlic-and-herbs spreadable cheese (from 6.5-oz container)
1/2	cup finely chopped red bell pepper
2	tablespoons butter, melted

1 In a medium bowl, stir Bisquick mix, oregano and water until mixture comes together. On work surface sprinkled with additional Bisquick mix, knead dough 5 times. Roll dough into 13x10-inch rectangle, about 1/8 inch thick.

2 In small bowl, mix cheese and bell pepper. Spread mixture evenly over the dough. Carefully roll long edges of dough to meet in the center. Place on cookie sheet lined with cooking parchment paper. Freeze 10 to 15 minutes or until firm.

3 Meanwhile, heat oven to 400°F. Spray a large cookie sheet with cooking spray.

4 Transfer dough to a cutting board. With a sharp knife, cut dough into 1/2-inch slices. Place slices, cut sides down, on sprayed cookie sheet. Slightly pinch base of heart into a point. Brush butter over hearts.

5 Bake 7 to 9 minutes or until tops are lightly golden. Cool hearts 10 minutes before serving.

Nutritional Info: 1 Appetizer: Calories 45; Total Fat 2g (Saturated Fat 1g); Sodium 95mg; Total Carbohydrate 5g (Dietary Fiber 0g); Protein 0g. Exchanges: 1/2 Other Carbohydrate, 1/2 Fat. Carbohydrate Choices: 1/2.

EASY LOW FAT

Betty's Kitchen Tip

These heart-shaped appetizers are the perfect starter to a romantic Valentine's Day dinner or any party celebrating love. Serve these flavorful little biscuits alongside a Greek salad.

roasted tomatillo-poblano salsa

Prep Time: 20 Minutes
Start to Finish: 50 Minutes
Servings: 12 (1/4 cup each)

LOW FAT

- 1 lb tomatillos, husks removed, rinsed and cut in half
- 2 medium poblano chiles
- 1 small red onion, cut into wedges
- 2 tablespoons canola oil
- 1 jalapeño chile, seeded and chopped

- 1/4 cup fresh cilantro leaves
- 1/4 cup frozen (thawed) limeade concentrate (from 6-oz can)
- 1 teaspoon roasted ground cumin or ground cumin
- 1/2 teaspoon salt

1 Heat oven to 475°F. Line 15x10x1-inch pan with foil. Arrange tomatillos in a single layer on one end of pan; place poblano chiles and onion on the other end. Drizzle oil over vegetables.

2 Roast uncovered 15 minutes or until vegetables are browned and tender.

3 Place poblano chiles in a resealable food-storage plastic bag; seal bag. Let stand 15 minutes. Peel poblano chiles; discard seeds and membranes.

4 In a food processor, place the poblano chiles, tomatillos, onion and remaining ingredients. Cover; process until smooth. Spoon into a serving bowl. Store tightly covered in refrigerator.

Nutritional Info: 1 Serving: Calories 54; Total Fat 3g (Saturated Fat 0g); Sodium 100mg; Total Carbohydrate 7g (Dietary Fiber 1g); Protein 1g. Exchanges: 1 Vegetable, 1/2 Fat. Carbohydrate Choices: 1/2.

Betty's Kitchen Tip

Serve this salsa the traditional way with tortilla chips or use it to top grilled chicken or fish. It also makes a zesty topping for fajitas or tacos.

roasted red pepper dip

Prep Time: 10 Minutes
Start to Finish: 1 Hour 10 Minutes
Servings: 8 (2 tablespoons each)

EASY

- 1 jar (7 or 7.25 oz) roasted red bell peppers, well drained
- 1 tablespoon chopped fresh basil leaves
- 1 small clove garlic
- 1/2 cup reduced-fat cream cheese (from 8-oz container)
- 1 tablespoon sliced almonds, if desired

Cut-up fresh vegetables for dipping, if desired

1. In a food processor, place the roasted peppers, basil and garlic. Cover; process until finely chopped. Add cream cheese. Cover; process until smooth.

2. Spoon the dip into a serving bowl. Cover; refrigerate 1 hour.

3. Just before serving, sprinkle with the sliced almonds. Serve with fresh vegetables for dipping.

Nutritional Info: 1 Serving: Calories 45; Total Fat 4g (Saturated Fat 2g); Sodium 60mg; Total Carbohydrate 2g (Dietary Fiber 0g); Protein 2g. Exchanges: 1 Fat. Carbohydrate Choices: 0.

Betty's Kitchen Tip

Add some extra bite to Roasted Red Pepper Dip by sprinkling crushed red pepper flakes on top. Serving a bigger crowd? The recipe can be doubled with no trouble at all.

herbed popcorn mix

Prep Time: 10 Minutes
Total: 40 Minutes
Servings: 8 (1 cup each)

EASY

- 6 cups hot-air-popped popcorn
- 2 cups fat-free pretzel sticks
- 1 cup tiny fish-shaped crackers
- 2 tablespoons butter or margarine, melted
- 1/2 teaspoon garlic powder
- 1/2 teaspoon onion powder
- 1/2 teaspoon dried basil leaves
- 1/2 teaspoon dried oregano leaves
- 1/8 teaspoon red pepper sauce

1 Heat oven to 300°F. In an ungreased 13x9-inch pan, mix the popcorn, pretzels and crackers.

2 In a small bowl, combine the remaining ingredients. Drizzle over popcorn mixture; toss until evenly coated.

3 Bake uncovered about 30 minutes, stirring every 10 minutes, until toasted. Serve warm or cool. Store tightly covered at room temperature.

Nutritional Info: 1 Serving: Calories 120; Total Fat 5g (Saturated Fat 1g); Sodium 300mg; Total Carbohydrate 19g (Dietary Fiber 2g); Protein 2g. Exchanges: 1 Starch, 1 Fat. Carbohydrate Choices: 1.

Betty's Kitchen Tip

If you don't have a hot-air popper or don't have time to pop popcorn, purchase popped corn from the grocery store. Just check to make sure that it is the "light" variety.

asiago pastry straws

Prep Time: 20 Minutes
Start to Finish: 35 Minutes
Servings: 44 straws

LOW FAT

1 box refrigerated pie crusts, softened as directed on box
2 tablespoons garlic and herb whipped cream cheese spread (from 8-oz container)
3/4 teaspoon dried rosemary leaves, crushed
1/4 cup shredded Asiago cheese (1 oz)

1 Heat oven to 425°F. Remove pie crusts from pouches. Unroll 1 crust on work surface.

2 Evenly spread cream cheese over the crust; sprinkle with rosemary and Asiago cheese.

3 Unroll the remaining crust over filling; press firmly over entire crust.

4 Cut into 24 (1/2-inch) strips. Cut strips in half; twist each strip 4 to 5 times. On ungreased cookie sheets, place strips 1 inch apart, pressing ends to secure.

5 Bake 9 to 11 minutes or until golden brown. Serve warm or cool.

Nutritional Info: 1 Straw: Calories 45; Total Fat 3g (Saturated Fat 1g); Sodium 60mg; Total Carbohydrate 4g (Dietary Fiber 0g); Protein 0g. Exchanges: 1/2 Starch. Carbohydrate Choices: 1/2.

Betty's Kitchen Tip

For a festive presentation, use fresh chives to tie a few pastry straws into a bundle, and garnish with fresh rosemary and currants.

pop art cookies

Prep Time: 25 Minutes
Start to Finish: 1 Hour 5 Minutes
Servings: 12

- 1 pouch (1 lb 1.5 oz) Betty Crocker® sugar cookie mix
- 1/3 cup butter or margarine, melted
- 2 tablespoons Gold Medal® all-purpose flour
- 1 egg
- 12 wooden sticks with rounded ends
- 1 container (1 lb) Betty Crocker® Rich & Creamy frosting (any white variety)

Food colors in desired colors
Assorted candy decorations

1 Heat oven to 375°F. In a medium bowl, stir the cookie mix, butter, flour and egg until soft dough forms.

2 On a floured surface, roll the dough until it is about 1/4-inch thick. Cut with a 3-inch round cookie cutter. On an ungreased cookie sheet, place shapes 2 inches apart. Carefully insert a wooden stick into the side of each cookie.

3 Bake 9 to 11 minutes or until edges are light golden brown. Cool 1 minute before removing from cookie sheet to cooling rack. Cool completely, about 30 minutes.

4 In 4 small bowls, divide frosting. Tint frosting in 3 of the bowls with different food colors. Reserve some of the tinted frostings for piping on designs. Frost cookies with remaining white and tinted frostings. For piping, place each tinted frosting in a small resealable food-storage plastic bag; cut off a tiny corner of the bag. Pipe frostings on cookies in desired designs. Decorate with candy decorations.

Nutritional Info: 1 Serving: Calories 370; Total Fat 15g (Saturated Fat 5g); Sodium 240mg; Total Carbohydrate 57g (Dietary Fiber 0g); Protein 2g. Exchanges: 1 Starch, 3 Other Carbohydrate, 3 Fat. Carbohydrate Choices: 4.

Betty's Kitchen Tip

Serve cookie pops from glasses in coordinating colors. Fill the glasses with jelly beans or other small candies to hold the pops upright.

mint-swirl lollipop cookies

Prep Time: 35 Minutes
Start to Finish: 1 Hour 55 Minutes
Servings: 20

∙∙∙

- 2 pouches (1 lb 1.5 oz each) Betty Crocker® sugar cookie mix
- 1/2 cup butter, softened
- 3 tablespoons Gold Medal® all-purpose flour
- 2 eggs, slightly beaten
- 1/4 teaspoon mint extract
- 1/4 teaspoon red or green food color gel or paste

Coarse white sparkling sugar
- 20 paper lollipop sticks

∙∙∙

1 Heat oven to 375°F. In a large bowl, stir cookie mix, butter, flour, eggs and mint extract with a spoon until soft dough forms. Divide dough in half. Roll one portion between 2 sheets of waxed paper into 13x10-1/2-inch rectangle. Remove top sheet of waxed paper.

2 To remaining half of dough, add food color; mix until uniform in color. Shape into a ball. Roll between 2 sheets of waxed paper into a 13x10-1/2-inch rectangle. Remove top sheet of waxed paper; invert colored dough onto plain dough. Peel off top sheet of waxed paper. Trim dough to a 11x9-inch rectangle. Tightly roll into a log, starting at the long side and using bottom sheet of waxed paper as a guide.

3 Roll cookie log in coarse sugar; cut into 1/2-inch slices. On an ungreased cookie sheet, place slices 2 inches apart.

4 Bake 8 to 10 minutes or until edges are lightly browned. Immediately insert 1 lollipop stick halfway into each cookie. With a spatula, carefully remove cookies from cookie sheet to a cooling rack. Cool completely, about 20 minutes.

Nutritional Info: 1 Serving: Calories 270; Total Fat 10g (Saturated Fat 4g); Sodium 163mg; Total Carbohydrate 41g (Dietary Fiber 0g); Protein 3g. Exchanges: 1 Starch, 1-1/2 Other Carbohydrate, 2 Fat. Carbohydrate Choices: 2-1/2.

Betty's Kitchen Tip

Showcase a batch of Mint-Swirl Lollipop Cookies in your party buffet, but consider baking extras to pack in cellophane bags. You can send guests home with a fun parting gift.

parmesan-tomato rounds

Prep Time: 40 Minutes
Start to Finish: 2 Hours 40 Minutes
Servings: 90

LOW FAT

3 cups shredded Parmesan cheese (12 oz)	1 teaspoon dried basil leaves
1/2 cup butter, softened	1/4 teaspoon salt
1/4 cup tomato paste	1/8 teaspoon ground red pepper (cayenne)
1-1/2 cups Gold Medal® all-purpose flour	

1 In food processor, place cheese, butter and tomato paste. Cover; process 2 to 3 minutes or until well mixed. Add flour, basil, salt and red pepper. Cover; process until well combined. (Dough should be firm but not dry.) If dry, add water, 1 tablespoon at a time and pulse 30 seconds after each addition, until dough holds together and a soft, clay-like dough is formed.

2 Rub a wet paper towel over work surface; place 12-inch piece of plastic wrap on dampened surface. Scoop half of dough onto plastic wrap and form into a rough log shape (about 12 inches long and 1-1/4 inches in diameter). Roll log in plastic wrap and seal ends. Repeat with remaining half of dough. Refrigerate at least 2 hours or until firm. (Dough can be made ahead and refrigerated up to 3 days.) Heat oven to 400°F. Line 2 large cookie sheets with cooking parchment paper. Remove logs from refrigerator and unwrap. With a serrated knife, cut into 1/4-inch slices. On cookie sheets, place slices about 1/2 inch apart.

3 Bake 10 to 12 minutes or until lightly browned around edges. Cool 2 minutes. Remove rounds from cookie sheets to cooling racks. Serve warm or at room temperature. Store tightly covered.

Nutritional Info: 1 Serving: Calories 35; Total Fat 2g (Saturated Fat 1g); Sodium 90mg; Total Carbohydrate 2g (Dietary Fiber 0g); Protein 2g. Exchanges: 1/2 Fat. Carbohydrate Choices: 0.

Betty's Kitchen Tip

Enjoy these homemade crackers on their own, or paired with a wide variety of toppings, from cream cheese and lox to guacamole and bacon.

creamy fruit dip

Prep Time: 10 Minutes
Start to Finish: 10 Minutes
Servings: 80 (1 tablespoon each)

2	packages (8 oz each) cream cheese, softened
1-1/2	cups Yoplait® Original 99% Fat Free vanilla yogurt (from 2-lb container)
1/4	cup packed brown sugar
2	tablespoons honey
1	teaspoon ground cinnamon
1	cup whipping cream

1 In a large bowl, beat cream cheese with an electric mixer on low speed until smooth. Add yogurt, brown sugar, honey and cinnamon; beat on low speed 30 to 60 seconds until blended and smooth.

2 In a chilled medium bowl, beat whipping cream with an electric mixer on high speed until soft peaks form. (Do not overbeat.) Fold whipped cream into cream cheese mixture. Serve immediately or cover and refrigerate until serving time.

Nutritional Info: 1 Serving: Calories 38; Total Fat 3g (Saturated Fat 2g); Sodium 21mg; Total Carbohydrate 2g (Dietary Fiber 0g); Protein 1g. Exchanges: 1/2 Fat. Carbohydrate Choices: 0.

EASY QUICK LOW FAT

Betty's Kitchen Tip

Fresh fruit pairs nicely with this fluffy dip. We also recommend serving it with cinnamon-flavored pita chips, waffles or French toast for a winning snack or brunch item.

chicken spring rolls with hoisin sauce

Prep Time: 1 Hour
Start to Finish: 1 Hour
Servings: 4 (2 spring rolls each)

1/2　cup uncooked short-grain Arborio rice
1　cup water
1/3　cup hoisin sauce
1　tablespoon low-sodium soy sauce
1　tablespoon sesame oil
1　tablespoon rice vinegar
1　clove garlic, finely chopped
1　teaspoon grated gingerroot

2　cups diced or shredded deli rotisserie chicken (from 2-lb chicken)
1　cup sweet-and-sour or Asian coleslaw (from deli), drained
1/4　cup shredded carrots (from 10-oz bag)
2　medium green onions, chopped (2 tablespoons)
8　spring roll wrappers (8 inch)
8　fresh cilantro leaves

1　Cook rice in water as directed on package. In a small bowl, mix hoisin sauce, soy sauce, oil, vinegar, garlic and gingerroot. In a medium bowl, mix chicken, coleslaw, carrots and onions; set aside.

2　Fill a pie plate with water. Place 1 spring roll wrapper in water 45 to 60 seconds or until pliable but not completely softened. Gently remove the wrapper from water, shaking to drain excess water; place on a damp paper towel. Place 1 cilantro leaf in the center of wrapper. Spoon about 2 tablespoons cooked rice in a line about 4 inches long over the cilantro leaf. Spoon about 1/3 cup chicken mixture on rice; press into log shape. Pull wrapper over filling; bring up the 2 ends and roll up, tucking in loose ends. Repeat.

3　Serve spring rolls immediately, accompanied by hoisin sauce mixture.

Nutritional Info: 1 Serving: Calories 440; Total Fat 13g (Saturated Fat 2.5g); Sodium 750mg; Total Carbohydrate 54g (Dietary Fiber 3g); Protein 24g. Exchanges: 2-1/2 Starch, 1/2 Other Carbohydrate, 1-1/2 Vegetable, 2 Lean Meat, 1 Fat. Carbohydrate Choices: 3-1/2.

Betty's Kitchen Tip

For zestier flavor, add additional rice vinegar to the chicken mixture before rolling. If rice vinegar is not available, use cider vinegar.

baked artichoke squares

Prep Time: 20 Minutes
Start to Finish: 45 Minutes
Servings: 60

- 1 box (9 oz) Green Giant® frozen chopped spinach
- 2 cans (8 oz each) Pillsbury® refrigerated crescent dinner rolls or 2 cans (8 oz each) refrigerated seamless dough sheet
- 1 can (14 oz) Progresso® artichoke hearts, drained, chopped
- 3/4 cup grated Parmesan cheese
- 2/3 cup mayonnaise or salad dressing
- 2/3 cup sour cream
- 1/8 teaspoon garlic powder

Lemon peel strips, if desired

1 Heat oven to 375°F. Cook the spinach in microwave as directed on box. Drain spinach in a strainer; cool 5 minutes. Carefully squeeze spinach with a paper towel to drain well.

2 Unroll both cans of dough on a work surface. If using crescent rolls, separate into 4 long rectangles. If using dough sheets, cut into 4 long rectangles. Place crosswise in ungreased 15x10x1-inch pan; press dough over bottom and 1 inch up sides to form crust. Firmly press perforations to seal.

3 Bake 10 to 12 minutes or until light golden brown. Meanwhile, in medium bowl, mix spinach, artichokes, cheese, mayonnaise, sour cream and garlic powder. Spread mixture evenly over partially baked crust.

4 Bake 8 to 10 minutes longer or until topping is hot. Cut into 1-1/2-inch squares. Serve warm.

Nutritional Info: 1 Serving: Calories 60; Total Fat 5g (Saturated Fat 2g); Sodium 115mg; Total Carbohydrate 4g (Dietary Fiber 0g); Protein 1g. Exchanges: 1/2 Starch, 1/2 Fat. Carbohydrate Choices: 1/2.

Betty's Kitchen Tip

Use a pizza cutter to easily cut these warm-from-the-oven appetizers.

roasted vegetable hummus

Prep Time: 20 Minutes
Start to Finish: 1 Hour
Servings: 20 (1/4 cup each)

- -

1 bulb garlic	1/4 cup sesame tahini paste
2/3 cup olive oil	1/3 cup lemon juice
1 medium eggplant (1 lb), cut lengthwise in half	1 teaspoon salt
1 medium red bell pepper, cut in half	1/4 teaspoon smoked paprika
2 cans (19 oz each) Progresso® chick peas (garbanzo beans), drained	Cut-up fresh vegetables for dipping, if desired

- -

1 Heat oven to 450°F. Line a 15x10x1-inch pan with foil. Cut one-fourth off top of bulb of garlic; drizzle with 1 teaspoon of the oil. Wrap bulb in foil. Place eggplant and bell pepper on cookie sheet. Drizzle 2 tablespoons oil over vegetables; toss to coat. Place wrapped garlic on cookie sheet.

2 Roast uncovered 30 minutes or until vegetables are tender. Cool 10 minutes. Remove peel from eggplant and red pepper. Cut peeled vegetables into small pieces.

3 In a food processor with a metal blade, place chick peas. Cover; process until smooth. Squeeze pulp from garlic bulb into food processor. Add roasted vegetables, tahini paste, lemon juice, salt and paprika. Cover; process until blended. With food processor running, gradually pour the remaining oil through feed tube; process until smooth, stopping twice to scrape down sides. Spoon into serving bowl. Serve immediately with vegetables or refrigerate until serving time.

Nutritional Info: 1 Serving: Calories 121; Total Fat 10g (Saturated Fat 1g); Sodium 200mg; Total Carbohydrate 7g (Dietary Fiber 2g); Protein 3g. Exchanges: 1/2 Starch, 2 Fat. Carbohydrate Choices: 1/2.

Betty's Kitchen Tip

For an authentic Middle Eastern look, drizzle additional olive oil over the hummus so it forms shallow pools. Finish with a sprinkling of toasted pine nuts across the top.

moroccan olives

Prep Time: 10 Minutes
Start to Finish: 4 Hours 10 Minutes
Servings: 6 (1/4 cup each)

2	tablespoons extra-virgin olive oil
1	teaspoon fennel seed
1	teaspoon coriander seed
1/2	teaspoon cumin seed
1/2	teaspoon crushed red pepper flakes
1	large clove garlic, finely chopped
1-1/2	cups good-quality imported green and ripe assorted olives
1	tablespoon grated orange peel
3/4	cup extra-virgin olive oil

1 In an 8-inch nonstick skillet, heat 2 tablespoons oil 1 minute. Add fennel seed, coriander seed, cumin seed, pepper flakes and garlic; cook and stir over medium heat 1 minute or until fragrant. Remove from heat. Add olives and orange peel; stir until olives are coated.

2 Divide mixture between 2 small jars or containers with tight-fitting lids. Pour 3/4 cup oil over mixture in jars. Cover; refrigerate at least 4 hours before serving. Serve at room temperature. Store in the refrigerator up to 1 week.

Nutritional Info: 1 Serving: Calories 308; Total Fat 34g (Saturated Fat 5g); Sodium 205mg; Total Carbohydrate 2g (Dietary Fiber 1g); Protein 0g. Exchanges: 7 Fat. Carbohydrate Choices: 0.

Betty's Kitchen Tip

The longer the olives marinate, the more flavorful they become. Olives should be stored in the refrigerator, but they are best enjoyed at room temperature as an appetizer, condiment with meats or as a salad topper.

asian snack mix

Prep Time: 15 Minutes
Start to Finish: 45 Minutes
Servings: 16 (1/2 cup each)

EASY

- 8 cups unsalted unbuttered popped popcorn
- 2 cups sesame sticks
- 1 cup cashew halves or slivered almonds
- 3 tablespoons butter or margarine, melted
- 1 tablespoon soy sauce
- 1 tablespoon fresh lime juice
- 1/2 teaspoon sesame oil
- 1 teaspoon grated gingerroot
- 1 cup wasabi dried green peas

1 Heat oven to 250°F. In a broiler pan, mix popcorn, sesame sticks and nuts.

2 In a small bowl, mix butter, soy sauce, lime juice, oil and gingerroot. Pour over popcorn mixture; toss to coat.

3 Bake uncovered 30 minutes, stirring every 10 minutes, until mixture is dry and crisp. Spread on paper towels to cool. Add green peas. Store tightly covered at room temperature.

Nutritional Info: 1 Serving: Calories 163; Total Fat 9g (Saturated Fat 3g); Sodium 280mg; Total Carbohydrate 17g (Dietary Fiber 1g); Protein 4g. Exchanges: 1 Starch, 2 Fat. Carbohydrate Choices: 1.

Betty's Kitchen Tip

Wasabi is the Japanese version of horseradish and has a sharp, pungent flavor. Wasabi-coated peas add a fiery sweet flavor to the snack mix. If you choose not to use them in this recipe, substitute 1 cup sesame sticks.

rosemary snack mix

Prep Time: 10 Minutes
Start to Finish: 10 Minutes
Servings: 16 (1/2 cup each)

EASY QUICK

- 1/4 cup butter or margarine
- 4-1/2 teaspoons chopped fresh rosemary leaves
- 1 teaspoon garlic salt
- 2 cups Corn Chex® cereal
- 2 cups Rice Chex® cereal
- 2 cups Wheat Chex® cereal
- 1 cup unblanched whole almonds, toasted
- 1 cup bite-size Parmesan-and-Cheddar-flavored cheese crackers

1 In a large microwavable bowl, microwave butter on High about 45 seconds or until melted. Stir in the rosemary and garlic salt. Add cereals, almonds and crackers; mix well.

2 Microwave uncovered on High 3 to 4 minutes, stirring once. Spread on a cookie sheet to cool. Store snack mix tightly covered at room temperature.

Nutritional Info: 1 Serving: Calories 159; Total Fat 9g (Saturated Fat 3g); Sodium 243mg; Total Carbohydrate 18g (Dietary Fiber 2g); Protein 4g. Exchanges: 1 Starch, 1-1/2 Fat. Carbohydrate Choices: 1.

Betty's Kitchen Tip

The aroma and flavor of rosemary make this snack mix special. Kids may like the mix just as well without the herb.

italian chicken fingers

Prep Time: 20 Minutes
Start to Finish: 40 Minutes
Servings: 4

1-1/4 cups Original Bisquick® mix
1 teaspoon Italian seasoning
1 package (14 oz) uncooked chicken breast tenders (not breaded)

1 egg, beaten
3 tablespoons butter or margarine, melted
1 cup tomato pasta sauce, heated

1 Heat oven to 450°F. Spray 15x10x1-inch pan with cooking spray.

2 In a resealable food-storage plastic bag, shake Bisquick mix and Italian seasoning. In a medium bowl, toss chicken and egg. Add chicken to bag; seal and shake to coat. Place chicken in a single layer in pan. Drizzle with butter.

3 Bake 14 to 16 minutes, turning chicken after 6 minutes, until chicken is brown and crisp on the outside and no longer pink in center. Serve with warm pasta sauce for dipping.

Nutritional Info: 1 Serving: Calories 450; Total Fat 18g (Saturated Fat 8g); Sodium 1000mg; Total Carbohydrate 36g (Dietary Fiber 2g); Protein 35g. Exchanges: 2 Starch, 1/2 Other Carbohydrate, 2 Very Lean Meat, 2 Lean Meat, 2 Fat. Carbohydrate Choices: 2-1/2.

Betty's Kitchen Tip

For a complete meal, serve with carrot and celery sticks and French fries. Try boneless skinless turkey breast or tenderloin instead of packaged chicken tenders.

ENTICING ENTREES

p.42

50

72

51

spinach-topped buffalo chicken

Prep Time: 25 Minutes
Start to Finish: 25 Minutes
Servings: 4

QUICK

4 boneless skinless chicken breasts (1-1/4 lb)	2 teaspoons Italian seasoning
1 egg	2 tablespoons vegetable oil
1/3 cup Buffalo wing sauce	2 tablespoons French dressing
1/2 cup Bisquick Heart Smart® mix	1 cup packed fresh baby spinach
2 tablespoons cornmeal	1/4 cup crumbled blue cheese (1 oz)

1 Between pieces of plastic wrap or waxed paper, place each chicken breast smooth side down; gently pound with flat side of meat mallet or rolling pin until about 1/4 inch thick.

2 In a shallow dish, beat the egg and 2 tablespoons of the Buffalo wing sauce with a whisk. In another shallow dish, stir Bisquick mix, cornmeal and Italian seasoning. Dip chicken in egg mixture, then coat with Bisquick mixture.

3 In a 12-inch skillet, heat the oil over medium-high heat. Cook the chicken in oil 6 to 10 minutes, turning once, or until golden brown on the outside and no longer pink in the center.

4 Meanwhile, in a small bowl, mix the remaining Buffalo wing sauce and the French dressing. Top each chicken breast with 1/4 cup spinach and 1 tablespoon cheese. Drizzle each with 2 tablespoons dressing mixture.

Nutritional Info: 1 Serving: Calories 410; Total Fat 21g (Saturated Fat 5g); Sodium 1150mg; Total Carbohydrate 17g (Dietary Fiber 0g); Protein 37g. Exchanges: 1 Other Carbohydrate, 5-1/2 Lean Meat, 1 Fat. Carbohydrate Choices: 1.

Betty's Kitchen Tip

If someone in your family doesn't care for blue cheese, substitute crumbled feta cheese, which is milder in flavor.

barbecue crispy chicken melts

Prep Time: 10 Minutes
Start to Finish: 40 Minutes
Servings: 4

EASY

3	tablespoons butter or margarine
1/2	cup Original Bisquick® mix
1/4	teaspoon pepper
1/4	cup milk
4	boneless skinless chicken breasts (about 1-1/4 lb)
1/4	cup barbecue sauce
1/2	cup shredded Cheddar cheese (2 oz)

1 Heat oven to 425°F. In a 13x9-inch pan, melt butter in the oven.

2 In a shallow dish, combine the Bisquick mix and pepper. Pour the milk into a small bowl. Coat chicken with Bisquick mixture; dip coated chicken into the milk, then coat again with the Bisquick mixture. Place in the heated pan.

3 Bake uncovered about 30 minutes or until juice of chicken is clear when center of the thickest part is cut (or a thermometer registers 165°F).

4 In a small microwavable bowl, microwave barbecue sauce uncovered on High about 30 seconds or until warm. Spoon sauce evenly over the chicken; top with cheese.

Nutritional Info: 1 Serving: Calories 400; Total Fat 20g (Saturated Fat 11g); Sodium 590mg; Total Carbohydrate 17g (Dietary Fiber 0g); Protein 37g. Exchanges: 1/2 Starch, 1/2 Other Carbohydrate, 4 Very Lean Meat, 1 High-Fat Meat, 2 Fat. Carbohydrate Choices: 1.

Betty's Kitchen Tip

Experiment with different flavors of barbecue sauce—sweet, spicy and tangy—to find your favorite combination in this recipe. Serve in toasted buns for a meal on the go.

chicken milanese

Prep Time: 30 Minutes
Start to Finish: 30 Minutes
Servings: 4

QUICK

6-1/2 teaspoons olive oil

2 cups grape tomatoes cut lengthwise in half

1 large shallot, chopped

1/4 teaspoon salt

1/4 teaspoon freshly ground pepper

1/4 cup dry red wine

1/2 cup chopped fresh basil leaves

1/2 cup Progresso® Italian-style panko crispy bread crumbs

1/4 cup grated fresh Parmesan cheese

4 boneless skinless chicken breasts (1-1/2 lb)

Cooking spray

1 In a 12-inch nonstick skillet, heat 2 teaspoons of the olive oil over medium-high heat. Cook tomatoes, shallot, salt and pepper in oil 4 minutes, stirring frequently, until shallots are tender. Stir in wine; cook 30 seconds longer. Remove from heat; transfer to medium bowl. Stir in basil; cover to keep warm.

2 In a shallow bowl, mix the bread crumbs and cheese. In the same skillet, heat remaining 4-1/2 teaspoons of olive oil over medium heat. Spray both sides of chicken with cooking spray; coat with the bread crumb mixture. Cook the chicken in oil 12 to 15 minutes, turning once, until juice of chicken is clear when center of thickest part is cut (and a thermometer registers at least 165°F).

3 On each of 4 plates, place 1 chicken breast; spoon tomato mixture evenly over chicken.

Nutritional Info: 1 Serving: Calories 346; Total Fat 14g (Saturated Fat 3g); Sodium 427mg; Total Carbohydrate 12g (Dietary Fiber 2g); Protein 39g. Exchanges: 4-1/2 Lean Meat, 2 Fat. Carbohydrate Choices: 1.

Betty's Kitchen Tip

A green salad tossed with grated Parmesan cheese will tie this meal together and make it feel like summer any time of year!

skillet fish and veggies

Prep Time: 25 Minutes
Start to Finish: 25 Minutes
Servings: 4

- 2 tablespoons butter or margarine
- 1 cup sliced leeks
- 1 cup shredded carrots (from 10-oz bag)
- 1 lb cod fillets, cut into 4 serving pieces
- 1 can (11 oz) Green Giant® Mexicorn® whole kernel corn with red and green peppers, drained

Lemon wedges, if desired

1 In a 10-inch skillet, melt the butter over medium-high heat. Cook leeks and carrots in butter 3 minutes, stirring frequently, until softened.

2 Mound the vegetable mixture into 4 sections in the skillet. Place 1 piece of fish on each mound. Pour corn over fish. Reduce heat to medium-low. Cover; cook 10 minutes or until fish flakes easily with a fork. Serve with lemon wedges.

Nutritional Info: 1 Serving. Calories 200, Total Fat 7g (Saturated Fat 4g); Sodium 550mg; Total Carbohydrate 10g (Dietary Fiber 2g); Protein 23g. Exchanges: 1/2 Starch, 3 Very Lean Meat, 1 Fat. Carbohydrate Choices: 1/2.

Betty's Kitchen Tip

Snapper, grouper or any other fish with mild flavor and medium-firm to firm texture can be used instead of cod. For an extra zesty flavor, add your favorite variety of salsa to the corn before you dress the fish fillets.

chicken in mustard cream sauce

Prep Time: 40 Minutes
Start to Finish: 40 Minutes
Servings: 4

2 slices bacon, cut into 1/4-inch pieces
2 cloves garlic, finely chopped
4 boneless chicken thighs
2 tablespoons Progresso® chicken broth
(from 32-oz carton)

2 tablespoons whipping cream
2 oz cream cheese, softened, cut into cubes
1 teaspoon Dijon mustard
1 teaspoon chopped fresh thyme leaves
Fresh thyme sprigs, if desired

1 In a 10-inch nonstick skillet, cook bacon over medium-high heat 3 minutes, stirring occasionally. Add garlic and chicken. Reduce heat to medium. Cover; cook 10 to 15 minutes, turning once, until juice of chicken is clear when center of thickest part is cut (at least 165°F). Remove chicken to plate; cover to keep warm.

2 Drain drippings, reserving bacon and garlic in skillet. Reduce heat to medium-low. Carefully stir in the broth and whipping cream; cook and stir until hot. Using a whisk, slowly stir in cream cheese and mustard until cheese is melted and sauce is smooth. Stir in chopped thyme. Cook about 3 minutes longer, stirring occasionally, until sauce just starts to boil and is thickened.

3 Serve sauce with chicken. Garnish with thyme sprigs.

Nutritional Info: 1 Serving: Calories 230; Total Fat 17g (Saturated Fat 8g); Sodium 340mg; Total Carbohydrate 2g (Dietary Fiber 0g); Protein 18g. Exchanges: 2-1/2 Lean Meat, 2 Fat. Carbohydrate Choices: 0.

Betty's Kitchen Tip

Cream cheese can curdle or scorch if it's cooked too quickly or if the heat is too high. For a creamy, smooth sauce, cook cream cheese over low heat and slowly incorporate the broth, adding a tablespoon at a time.

sweet orange baked chicken

Prep Time: 25 Minutes
Start to Finish: 1 Hour 5 Minutes
Servings: 8

- 1 box (6.2 oz) fast-cooking long-grain and wild rice mix (with seasoning packet)
- 1/2 cup sliced almonds, toasted
- 2 tablespoons butter or margarine
- 8 boneless skinless chicken breasts (3 lb)
- 1/2 teaspoon salt
- 1 cup orange marmalade
- 1/4 cup honey
- 2 tablespoons Dijon mustard
- 2 teaspoons chopped fresh thyme leaves

1 Heat oven to 425°F. Cook rice as directed on package, omitting butter. Stir in almonds and butter.

2 Coat a 15x10x1-inch pan with cooking spray. Cut a slit in each chicken breast to form a pocket. Spoon about 1/4 cup rice mixture into each pocket. Place chicken in the pan; sprinkle evenly with salt.

3 In a small bowl, mix the marmalade, honey, mustard and thyme until blended. Reserve 1/2 cup of the mixture for serving. Brush the remaining marmalade mixture over chicken.

4 Bake 35 to 40 minutes or until juice of chicken is clear when center of thickest part is cut (and a thermometer reads at least 165°F).

5 Heat the reserved marmalade mixture over medium heat and pour evenly over each chicken breast.

Nutritional Info: 1 Serving: Calories 551; Total Fat 12g (Saturated Fat 4g); Sodium 696mg; Total Carbohydrate 53g (Dietary Fiber 1g); Protein 57g. Exchanges: 1-1/2 Starch, 2 Other Carbohydrate, 6 Very Lean Meat, 1-1/2 Fat. Carbohydrate Choices: 3-1/2.

Betty's Kitchen Tip

The marmalade basting sauce for Sweet Orange Baked Chicken delivers a bright citrus flavor without adding any fat. It would complement many pork tenderloin dishes, as well.

summer garden chicken stir-fry

Prep Time: 30 Minutes
Start to Finish: 30 Minutes
Servings: 4

QUICK LOW FAT

1 lb boneless skinless chicken breasts, cut into 1-inch pieces
2 cloves garlic, finely chopped
2 teaspoons finely chopped gingerroot
1 medium onion, cut into thin wedges
1 cup ready-to-eat baby-cut carrots, cut lengthwise in half
1 cup fat-free chicken broth

3 tablespoons reduced-sodium soy sauce
2 to 3 teaspoons sugar
2 cups fresh broccoli florets
1 cup sliced fresh mushrooms (3 oz)
1/2 cup chopped bell pepper (any color)
2 teaspoons cornstarch
Hot cooked brown rice, if desired

1 Heat a 12-inch nonstick skillet or wok over medium-high heat. Add chicken, garlic and gingerroot; cook and stir 2 to 3 minutes or until chicken is brown.

2 Stir in the onion, carrots, 3/4 cup of the broth, soy sauce and sugar. Reduce heat to medium. Cover; cook 5 minutes, stirring occasionally.

3 Stir in the broccoli, mushrooms and bell pepper. Cover; cook about 5 minutes, stirring occasionally, until the vegetables are crisp-tender and chicken is no longer pink in the center.

4 In a small bowl, mix the cornstarch and remaining 1/4 cup broth; stir into the chicken mixture. Cook and stir until the sauce is thickened. Serve over rice.

Nutritional Info: 1 Serving: Calories 220; Total Fat 4g (Saturated Fat 1g); Sodium 710mg; Total Carbohydrate 16g (Dietary Fiber 3g); Protein 29g. Exchanges: 1/2 Other Carbohydrate, 1-1/2 Vegetable, 3-1/2 Very Lean Meat, 1/2 Fat. Carbohydrate Choices: 1.

Betty's Kitchen Tip

To lower the carb count, use sugar substitute instead of the regular table sugar called for in this recipe. One packet of NutraSweet® sweetener is equal to 1 teaspoon of sugar, whereas one packet of Splenda® sweetener is equal to 2 teaspoons of sugar.

spicy chicken enchiladas

Prep Time: 20 Minutes
Start to Finish: 40 Minutes
Servings: 8

1-1/2   cups sour cream
1   can (14.5 oz) Muir Glen® organic fire roasted diced tomatoes, drained
2-1/2   cups shredded pepper Jack cheese (10 oz)
1   teaspoon salt-free Southwest chipotle seasoning blend

3   cups shredded cooked chicken
1-1/2   cups Old El Paso® mild salsa
1   package (11.5 oz) Old El Paso® flour tortillas for burritos (8 tortillas; 8 inch)
Sliced green onions, if desired

1 Heat oven to 350°F. Spray a 13x9-inch (3-quart) glass baking dish with cooking spray. In a large bowl, mix the sour cream, tomatoes, 1 cup of the cheese and the seasoning blend. Stir in the chicken.

2 Spread 1/2 cup of the salsa in the baking dish. Spoon 1/2 cup chicken mixture down the center of each tortilla; roll up. Place enchiladas, seam side down, over salsa in baking dish. Spoon remaining 1 cup salsa over filled enchiladas; top with remaining 1-1/2 cups cheese.

3 Bake uncovered 20 minutes or until cheese is melted and enchiladas are thoroughly heated. Garnish with green onions.

Nutritional Info: 1 Serving: Calories 444; Total Fat 24g (Saturated Fat 13g); Sodium 835mg; Total Carbohydrate 29g (Dietary Fiber 0g); Protein 25g. Exchanges: 1-1/2 Starch, 1 Vegetable, 1-1/2 Very Lean Meat, 1 High-Fat Meat, 2-1/2 Fat. Carbohydrate Choices: 2.

Betty's Kitchen Tip

If you really want to kick up the heat in these enchiladas, use your favorite hot salsa.

lip-smackin' bar-b-q chicken bake

Prep Time: 20 Minutes
Start to Finish: 50 Minutes
Servings: 6

LOW FAT

- 2/3 cup Reduced Fat Bisquick® mix
- 2 tablespoons water
- 1 egg
- 1-1/2 cups shredded reduced-fat Cheddar cheese (6 oz)
- 2 teaspoons vegetable oil
- 3 boneless skinless chicken breasts (about 1 lb), cut into 1/2-inch pieces
- 3/4 cup barbecue sauce

1 Heat oven to 400°F. Coat a 9-inch glass pie plate or 9-inch square baking dish with cooking spray.

2 In a small bowl, stir Bisquick mix, water and egg. Spread in the bottom of pie plate. Sprinkle with 1-1/4 cups of the cheese.

3 In a 10-inch skillet, heat oil over medium-high heat. Cook chicken in oil, stirring occasionally, until no longer pink in the center; drain. Stir in barbecue sauce; heat just until hot. Spoon over batter to within 1/2 inch of edge.

4 Bake 22 to 25 minutes or until the edge is dark golden brown. Sprinkle with remaining 1/4 cup cheese. Bake 1 to 3 minutes longer or until cheese is melted; loosen from side of plate.

Nutritional Info: 1 Serving: Calories 240; Total Fat 7g (Saturated Fat 2.5g); Sodium 770mg; Total Carbohydrate 20g (Dietary Fiber 0g); Protein 22g. Exchanges: 1 Starch, 1/2 Other Carbohydrate, 2 1/2 Very Lean Meat, 1 Fat. Carbohydrate Choices: 1.

Betty's Kitchen Tip

For an even lower-fat version, decrease the cheese to a total of 1 cup—sprinkle 3/4 cup over the batter and 1/4 cup onto the bake.

cranberry-orange glazed turkey

Prep Time: 25 Minutes
Start to Finish: 3 Hours 40 Minutes
Servings: 12

1/3 cup packed brown sugar
2 tablespoons grated orange peel
2/3 cup orange juice
1 can (14 oz) whole berry cranberry sauce
1 whole turkey (12 to 14 lb), thawed if frozen

2 tablespoons butter or margarine, melted
2 teaspoons kosher (coarse) salt
2 teaspoons freshly ground pepper
Fresh thyme and rosemary sprigs, fresh cranberries and kumquats, if desired

1 Heat oven to 350°F. In a 1-quart saucepan, heat the brown sugar, orange peel, orange juice and cranberry sauce to boiling. Reduce heat to low; simmer 10 minutes, stirring occasionally, until thickened. Cool completely. Set aside 1/2 cup of cranberry mixture for basting; refrigerate remaining cranberry mixture for serving.

2 Fold the wings across the back of the turkey so tips are touching. Tie legs together with heavy string. On a rack in a shallow roasting pan, place the turkey, breast side up. Brush butter over the turkey. Sprinkle with salt and pepper. Insert an ovenproof meat thermometer so the tip is in thickest part of the inside thigh and does not touch bone.

3 Roast uncovered 2 hours 30 minutes to 3 hours, basting with 1/2 cup cranberry mixture after 2 hours. Turkey is done when thermometer reads at least 165°F and legs move easily when lifted or twisted. Place turkey on a warm platter; cover with foil. Let stand 15 minutes before carving. Serve with reserved cranberry mixture. Garnish with herbs, cranberries and kumquats.

Nutritional Info: 1 Serving: Calories 633; Total Fat 27g (Saturated Fat 9g); Sodium 522mg; Total Carbohydrate 20g (Dietary Fiber 1g); Protein 73g. Exchanges: 1/2 Fruit, 1 Other Carbohydrate, 10 Very Lean Meat, 3-1/2 Fat. Carbohydrate Choices: 1-1/2.

Betty's Kitchen Tip

For a divine after-dinner treat, drizzle leftover cranberry-orange glaze over vanilla ice cream.

pork with apricot glaze

Prep Time: 10 Minutes
Start to Finish: 1 Hour 45 Minutes
Servings: 10

EASY

1	boneless pork loin roast (3 lb)
1	teaspoon salt
1/4	teaspoon pepper
1	cup apricot preserves
1/4	cup dry sherry, cooking sherry or apple juice
2	teaspoons dried rosemary leaves, crumbled
2	cloves garlic, finely chopped

Apricot halves, if desired

Fresh rosemary sprigs, if desired

1. Heat oven to 350°F. Place pork in a 13x9-inch (3-quart) glass baking dish. Sprinkle with salt and pepper.

2. In a 1-quart saucepan, heat the preserves, sherry, dried rosemary and garlic over medium heat, stirring frequently, until thickened. If necessary, mash apricot pieces into small pieces using a fork. Spoon 1/4 cup of the apricot mixture onto the pork; reserve the remaining mixture for serving.

3. Bake pork uncovered 1 hour 15 minutes to 1 hour 30 minutes or until a meat thermometer inserted into the center of the pork reads 145°F. Cover pork with foil; let stand 3 minutes before slicing. Heat reserved apricot mixture; serve with sliced pork. Garnish with apricot halves and fresh rosemary.

Nutritional Info: 1 Serving: Calories 310; Total Fat 11g (Saturated Fat 3.5g); Sodium 300mg; Total Carbohydrate 22g (Dietary Fiber 0g); Protein 30g. Exchanges: 1-1/2 Other Carbohydrate, 4 Lean Meat. Carbohydrate Choices: 1-1/2.

Betty's Kitchen Tip

If you have fresh rosemary, chop 1 tablespoon of the leaves to add to the sauce. For a pretty presentation, arrange some of the rosemary sprigs, along with fresh or dried apricots, around the roast on the serving dish.

"healthified" lasagna

Prep Time: 30 Minutes
Start to Finish: 1 Hour 40 Minutes
Servings: 12

LOW FAT

9	uncooked lasagna noodles
1	lb extra-lean (at least 90%) ground beef
2	cloves garlic, finely chopped
1	jar (25.5 oz) Muir Glen® organic Italian herb pasta sauce
1/8	teaspoon ground red pepper (cayenne)
1-1/2	teaspoons dried basil leaves

1	egg
1	container (15 oz) reduced-fat ricotta cheese
2	cups shredded reduced-fat mozzarella cheese (8 oz)
1/3	cup shredded Parmesan cheese

Fresh basil, if desired

1 Spray a 13x9-inch (3-quart) glass baking dish with cooking spray. Cook and drain noodles as directed on package. Place in cold water.

2 Meanwhile, in 12-inch skillet, cook beef and garlic over medium-high heat 5 to 7 minutes, stirring frequently, until beef is thoroughly cooked; drain. Stir in pasta sauce, red pepper and 1 teaspoon of the basil. Heat to boiling, stirring occasionally. Remove from heat.

3 Heat oven to 350°F. In a medium bowl, beat egg slightly. Stir in ricotta cheese and remaining 1/2 teaspoon basil until blended. Drain noodles. Spread about 1/2 cup sauce mixture over the bottom of the baking dish. Top with 3 noodles, 1-1/2 cups of the sauce mixture, half of the ricotta mixture and 3/4 cup of the mozzarella cheese. Repeat layers once. Top with remaining noodles, sauce and mozzarella cheese; sprinkle with Parmesan cheese.

4 Spray 15-inch piece of foil with cooking spray; cover lasagna with foil. Bake 45 minutes. Uncover; bake 10 to 15 minutes longer or until bubbly. Let stand 10 minutes before serving.

Nutritional Info: 1 Serving: Calories 240; Total Fat 9g (Saturated Fat 4.5g); Sodium 400mg; Total Carbohydrate 21g (Dietary Fiber 2g); Protein 20g. Exchanges: 1 Starch, 1/2 Other Carbohydrate, 2-1/2 Lean Meat. Carbohydrate Choices: 1-1/2.

Betty's Kitchen Tip

To reduce the fat, we used extra-lean ground beef, light cheeses and only 1 egg instead of 2. Basil and a touch of ground red pepper enhance the flavor. Pair this crowd pleaser with a green salad tossed with reduced-fat salad dressing.

spiced chicken thighs

Prep Time: 20 Minutes
Start to Finish: 20 Minutes
Servings: 4

QUICK

- 1/2 teaspoon ground cumin
- 1/2 teaspoon dried thyme leaves
- 1/2 teaspoon smoked paprika
- 1/4 teaspoon salt
- 8 boneless skinless chicken thighs (1-1/2 lb)
- 1 can (14.5 oz) fire-roasted diced tomatoes with garlic, undrained

1 In a small bowl, mix cumin, thyme, paprika and salt. Rub mixture over the chicken.

2 Coat a 12-inch skillet with cooking spray; heat over medium-high heat. Add the chicken; cook 2 minutes. Turn the chicken over; stir in the tomatoes. Heat to boiling; reduce heat. Cover; simmer 10 minutes or until the juice of chicken is clear when center of thickest part is cut (or a thermometer reads at least 165°F). Uncover; cook 1 minute longer or until the liquid is reduced by half.

Nutritional Info: 1 Serving: Calories 383; Total Fat 18.6g (Saturated Fat 5.2g); Sodium 579mg; Total Carbohydrate 5.4g (Dietary Fiber 1.2g); Protein 31g. Exchanges: 1 Vegetable, 4 Lean Meat, 1 Fat. Carbohydrate Choices: 0.

Betty's Kitchen Tip

Couscous is a great complement to this chicken dish, and it's ready in minutes. Try one of the several seasoned varieties available in the rice aisle of the supermarket.

pecan chicken and gravy

Prep Time: 35 Minutes
Start to Finish: 35 Minutes
Servings: 4

1 cup soft bread crumbs
1 cup pecan halves, finely chopped
3/4 cup Gold Medal® all-purpose flour
3/4 teaspoon freshly ground pepper
4 boneless skinless chicken breasts (1 lb), flattened to 1/8 inch thick

1 teaspoon salt
2 eggs, beaten
6 tablespoons butter
3 cups milk

1 In a shallow dish, mix the bread crumbs and pecans. In another shallow dish, mix 1/2 cup of the flour and 1/4 teaspoon of the pepper. Sprinkle chicken with 1/2 teaspoon salt. Coat the chicken in the flour mixture, then dip into the eggs and then coat with the pecan mixture.

2 In a 10-inch nonstick skillet, melt 2 tablespoons of the butter over medium heat. Cook 2 chicken breasts 6 to 8 minutes, turning once, until no longer pink in center. Remove from skillet; cover to keep warm. Repeat with 2 tablespoons butter and remaining chicken.

3 In the same skillet, melt the remaining 2 tablespoons butter over medium heat. Add the remaining 1/4 cup flour; stir until blended. Gradually add the milk; cook 8 to 10 minutes, stirring frequently, until thickened. Stir in the remaining 1/2 teaspoon salt and 1/2 teaspoon pepper. Serve gravy with chicken.

Nutritional Info: 1 Serving: Calories 790; Total Fat 46g (Saturated Fat 17g); Sodium 1117mg; Total Carbohydrate 51g (Dietary Fiber 4g); Protein 45g. Exchanges: 2-1/2 Starch, 1 Low-Fat Milk, 4 Very Lean Meat, 7 Fat. Carbohydrate Choices: 3-1/2.

Betty's Kitchen Tip

Partner this dish with lemon-dressed arugula and smashed red-skinned potatoes for a hearty down-home meal.

buffalo chicken pie

Prep Time: 15 Minutes
Start to Finish: 45 Minutes
Servings: 6

Jamie Jones
Madison, GA
Better with Bisquick® Recipe Contest

EASY

2	cups cooked chicken strips
1/2	cup Buffalo wing sauce
1	cup shredded Cheddar cheese (4 oz)
1/2	cup crumbled blue cheese (2 oz)
1	cup chopped celery (about 2-1/2 stalks)
1	cup Original Bisquick® mix
1/2	cup cornmeal
1/2	cup milk
1	egg
2/3	cup blue cheese dressing

1 Heat oven to 400°F. In a large bowl, toss chicken and Buffalo wing sauce until well coated. Stir in cheeses and celery. Pour into an ungreased 9-inch glass pie plate.

2 In a medium bowl, combine Bisquick mix, cornmeal, milk and egg. Pour over chicken mixture; spread to cover.

3 Bake 25 to 30 minutes or until topping is golden brown. Cut into wedges; drizzle with blue cheese dressing.

Nutritional Info: 1 Serving: Calories 600; Total Fat 40g (Saturated Fat 11g); Sodium 1730mg; Total Carbohydrate 38g (Dietary Fiber 2g); Protein 21g. Exchanges: 2-1/2 Starch, 1-1/2 Medium-Fat Meat, 1/2 High-Fat Meat, 5-1/2 Fat. Carbohydrate Choices: 2-1/2.

Betty's Kitchen Tip

Use refrigerated cooked chicken strips (from two 6-oz packages) or any cooked chicken for this recipe. Look for bottled Buffalo wing sauce in the condiment aisle of the grocery store.

pumpkin and sausage manicotti

Prep Time: 30 Minutes
Start to Finish: 1 Hour 15 Minutes
Servings: 8

16	uncooked manicotti pasta shells
1	lb bulk Italian pork sausage
2	large cloves garlic, finely chopped
2	tablespoons finely chopped fresh sage leaves
1	egg
1	container (15 oz) part-skim ricotta cheese

1	cup canned pumpkin (not pumpkin pie mix)
1/2	cup shredded Parmesan cheese
1/2	teaspoon freshly ground pepper
2	cups shredded Italian cheese blend or mozzarella cheese (8 oz)
3	cups Alfredo pasta sauce (from two 16-oz jars)

Fresh sage leaves, if desired

1 Heat oven to 350°F. Cook and drain pasta shells as directed on package, using minimum cook time. Meanwhile, in a 12-inch skillet, cook the sausage, garlic and 1 tablespoon of the chopped sage over medium heat 8 to 10 minutes, stirring occasionally, until the sausage is no longer pink; drain.

2 In a medium bowl, beat the egg. Stir in ricotta cheese, pumpkin, Parmesan cheese, pepper, 1 cup of the Italian cheese, the remaining 1 tablespoon chopped sage and the sausage.

3 Spread 1 cup of the Alfredo sauce in an ungreased 13x9-inch (3-quart) glass baking dish. Fill pasta shells with sausage mixture. Arrange stuffed shells over sauce in dish. Pour remaining 2 cups of the Alfredo sauce evenly over the shells.

4 Cover; bake 30 to 35 minutes or until hot. Uncover; top with remaining 1 cup Italian cheese. Bake 5 to 10 minutes longer or until cheese is melted. Garnish with sage leaves.

Nutritional Info: 1 Serving: Calories 561; Total Fat 35g (Saturated Fat 18g); Sodium 1641mg; Total Carbohydrate 35g (Dietary Fiber 2g); Protein 28g. Exchanges: 2-1/2 Starch, 3 High-Fat Meat, 1 Fat. Carbohydrate Choices: 2-1/2.

Betty's Kitchen Tip

Don't be overwhelmed by the longer start-to-finish time of this recipe. You'll love how simple Pumpkin and Sausage Manicotti is to assemble, making it a tasty choice any night of the week.

tilapia tacos

Prep Time: 20 Minutes
Start to Finish: 20 Minutes
Servings: 5 (2 tacos each)

QUICK

1	box (8.8 oz) Old El Paso® Stand 'N Stuff® taco dinner kit
1	lb tilapia fillets, cut into 1-inch pieces
2-1/2	cups coleslaw mix (from 16-oz bag)
1/4	cup coleslaw dressing
1	avocado, pitted, peeled and diced

Lime wedges, if desired

1 Heat oven to 375°F. Spray a large cookie sheet with cooking spray.

2 In a large resealable food-storage plastic bag, place seasoning mix (from dinner kit) and fish pieces. Seal bag; shake to coat fish with seasoning. Place fish on one side of the cookie sheet. Bake 8 to 10 minutes or until fish flakes easily with fork. Place taco shells (from dinner kit) on the other side of cookie sheet last 4 minutes of baking time.

3 Meanwhile, in medium bowl, toss coleslaw and dressing.

4 Divide the coleslaw evenly among warmed taco shells. Top each with fish, diced avocado and 2 teaspoons taco sauce (from dinner kit). Serve with lime wedges.

Nutritional Info: 1 Serving: Calories 220; Total Fat 11g (Saturated Fat 2g); Sodium 350mg; Total Carbohydrate 11g (Dietary Fiber 3g); Protein 18g. Exchanges: 1/2 Starch, 2-1/2 Very Lean Meat, 2 Fat. Carbohydrate Choices: 1.

Betty's Kitchen Tip

Tilapia is a mild white fish that is available any time of year. Other whitefish, such as cod, pollack or halibut, would be a good substitute. Warming the taco shells helps bring out the corn flavor and crisps them up, too!

chicken, provolone and ham bundles

Prep Time: 15 Minutes
Start to Finish: 50 Minutes
Servings: 4

EASY

- 2 cups Original Bisquick® mix
- 1/2 teaspoon garlic powder
- 1/2 cup boiling water
- 4 slices (3/4 oz each) provolone cheese
- 4 thin slices (about 1 oz each) cooked ham

- 4 large (about 2 oz each) uncooked chicken breast tenders (not breaded)
- 1 tablespoon butter or margarine, melted
- 4 teaspoons grated Parmesan cheese
- 1/2 cup tomato pasta sauce, heated

1 Heat oven to 375°F (350°F for a dark or nonstick pan). In a medium bowl, stir Bisquick mix, garlic powder and boiling water until dough forms.

2 Divide the dough into fourths. Place pieces on a surface sprinkled with Bisquick mix and roll to coat. Press or roll each piece into a 7x5-inch rectangle, 1/4 inch thick.

3 On each rectangle, center 1 ham slice and 1 provolone cheese slice, folding to fit if needed. Top each with 1 chicken tender. Starting on the long side, roll up each bundle. Press ends and seam to seal. Tuck ends under. On an ungreased cookie sheet, place bundles, seam side down. Brush with butter; sprinkle with Parmesan cheese.

4 Bake 25 to 33 minutes or until golden brown and meat thermometer inserted in center of chicken reads 165°F. Serve topped with pasta sauce.

Nutritional Info: 1 Serving: Calories 490; Total Fat 21g (Saturated Fat 9g); Sodium 1620mg; Total Carbohydrate 46g (Dietary Fiber 2g); Protein 30g. Exchanges: 3 Starch, 3 Very Lean Meat, 3-1/2 Fat. Carbohydrate Choices: 3.

Betty's Kitchen Tip

Instead of the pasta sauce, dare to try some other sauces. Need ideas? Consider Alfredo sauce, ranch dressing or warmed cheese sauce. If you're looking for a healthy twist, skip the pasta sauce and serve these tasty bundles on a bed of greens drizzled with a low-fat creamy dressing. All you need to make the meal complete is a quick veggie side dish. A bowl of ice cream topped with a little chocolate or caramel sauce is an easy dessert treat.

spiced tilapia with honeyed mango-lime sauce

Prep Time: 30 Minutes
Start to Finish: 30 Minutes
Servings: 4

QUICK

Veronica Callaghan
Glastonbury, CT
Better with Bisquick® Recipe Contest

Sauce

- 1 ripe mango, seed removed, peeled and diced
- Grated peel and juice of 1 medium lime
- 2 green onions, coarsely chopped (2 tablespoons)
- 1 tablespoon honey
- 1/2 teaspoon kosher (coarse) salt

Fish

- 1 egg
- 2 tablespoons milk
- 1 cup Original Bisquick® mix
- 1/2 teaspoon kosher (coarse) salt
- 1/4 teaspoon freshly ground pepper
- 4 tilapia fillets (1 lb)
- 1/4 cup vegetable or canola oil
- 1 teaspoon chili paste
- 1 tablespoon chopped fresh cilantro

1 In a food processor, place all sauce ingredients. Cover; process until smooth. Set aside until serving time.

2 In shallow dish, beat egg and milk with fork. In another shallow dish, mix Bisquick mix, salt and pepper. Dip fillets in egg mixture; coat with Bisquick mixture.

3 In a 12-inch skillet, heat oil and chili paste over medium heat; stir to combine. Cook fillets in oil 4 to 6 minutes, turning once, until golden brown and fish flakes easily with fork.

4 To serve, place fish on serving platter or individual plates. Drizzle evenly with sauce; sprinkle with cilantro.

Nutritional Info: 1 Serving: Calories 420; Total Fat 20g (Saturated Fat 4g); Sodium 800mg; Total Carbohydrate 34g (Dietary Fiber 2g); Protein 26g. Exchanges: 1 Starch, 1/2 Fruit, 1 Other Carbohydrate, 3 Very Lean Meat, 3-1/2 Fat. Carbohydrate Choices: 2.

Betty's Kitchen Tip

To peel the mango, use a sharp knife to cut through one side of the fruit next to the seed. Repeat on the other side of the seed, making 2 large pieces. Make crosshatch cuts through the flesh just to the peel; bend peel back and carefully slide knife between peel and flesh to separate. Discard the peel; dice the flesh.

cheesy chicken and rice casserole

Prep Time: 5 Minutes
Start to Finish: 45 Minutes
Servings: 4

EASY

- 1   can (18.5 oz) Progresso® chicken enchilada soup
- 3/4 cup water
- 3/4 cup uncooked regular long-grain white rice
- 1/2 teaspoon ground cumin
- 1/4 teaspoon ground black pepper
- 1   can (15 oz) Progresso® black beans, drained, rinsed
- 1   box (9 oz) Green Giant® Niblets® frozen corn
- 4   boneless skinless chicken breasts (1 lb)
- 1   cup shredded Colby-Monterey Jack cheese blend (4 oz)

1   Heat oven to 375°F. In an ungreased 11x7-inch (2-quart) glass baking dish, mix soup, water, rice, cumin, pepper, beans and corn. Top with chicken.

2   Cover and bake about 30 minutes or until juice of chicken is clear when center of thickest part is cut (and a thermometer registers at least 165°F) and rice is tender. Stir rice around chicken. Top with cheese. Bake uncovered 5 to 10 minutes or until cheese is melted.

Nutritional Info: 1 Serving: Calories 610; Total Fat 20g (Saturated Fat 9g); Sodium 1120mg; Total Carbohydrate 62g (Dietary Fiber 7g); Protein 46g. Exchanges: 4 Starch, 1 Very Lean Meat, 4 Lean Meat, 1 Fat. Carbohydrate Choices: 4.

Betty's Kitchen Tip

Instead of long-grain white rice, swap in brown rice for a more healthful spin on Cheesy Chicken and Rice Casserole. Plan on a little extra time, as brown rice takes longer to cook.

blue cheese pork chops with apples

Prep Time: 25 Minutes
Start to Finish: 1 Hour 30 Minutes
Servings: 4

- 1/3 cup chopped walnuts, toasted
- 1/2 cup butter, softened
- 1/2 cup crumbled blue cheese (2 oz)
- 1/4 teaspoon freshly ground pepper
- 1/4 cup Progresso® panko crispy bread crumbs
- 3 Gala apples, each cut into 8 wedges

- 1 tablespoon butter or margarine
- 4 bone-in pork loin chops, 1 inch thick (about 2 lb)
- 2 teaspoons balsamic glaze

Fresh sage leaves, if desired

1 In a food processor, place walnuts. Cover; process, using quick pulses, until it is the consistency of coarse meal. Add 1/2 cup butter, the blue cheese and pepper; process until combined. Add bread crumbs to the mixture; process until combined, stopping to scrape down sides as needed. Divide butter mixture evenly among 4 sheets of plastic wrap or waxed paper; flatten each to match width and shape of pork chops, forming 4 disks. Wrap tightly; freeze at least 20 minutes.

2 Heat oven to 450°F. In a 15x10x1-inch pan, arrange apple wedges. Bake 30 to 35 minutes or just until tender. In large bowl, toss apples with 1 tablespoon butter; cover to keep warm.

3 Spray a 12-inch cast-iron or other ovenproof skillet with cooking spray; heat over medium-high heat. Add pork chops; cook 6 to 8 minutes, turning once, until browned. Remove from heat; top each chop with 1 butter disk.

4 Set oven control to broil. Broil chops in skillet 3 to 4 inches from heat 2 to 3 minutes or until butter begins to bubble and turns golden brown. Place chops on serving plates. Spoon apples evenly over chops; drizzle with balsamic glaze and garnish with chopped fresh sage leaves.

Nutritional Info: 1 Serving: Calories 614; Total Fat 45g (Saturated Fat 22g); Sodium 460mg; Total Carbohydrate 19g (Dietary Fiber 2g); Protein 36g. Exchanges: 1/2 Starch, 1 Fruit, 4-1/2 Very Lean Meat, 1/2 High-Fat Meat, 5-1/2 Fat. Carbohydrate Choices: 1.

Betty's Kitchen Tip

Aromatic sage can be pungent, especially when it's fresh. Start with a small amount and adjust according to your taste. Or, try fresh chopped thyme or marjoram leaves in its place.

chicken topped with mango salsa

Prep Time: 25 Minutes
Start to Finish: 25 Minutes
Servings: 4

- 1 cup chopped peeled mango
- 2 teaspoons finely chopped fresh mint leaves
- 1 teaspoon grated lime peel
- 2 teaspoons lime juice
- 1 teaspoon finely chopped jalapeño chile
- 4 boneless skinless chicken breasts (1-1/4 lb)
- 1 teaspoon ground cumin
- 1/2 teaspoon salt
- 1 tablespoon canola oil

Fresh mint leaves, if desired

1 In a small bowl, mix mango, chopped mint, lime peel, lime juice and chile. Refrigerate until serving time.

2 Between pieces of plastic wrap or waxed paper, place each chicken breast smooth side down; gently pound with flat side of a meat mallet or rolling pin until about 1/2 inch thick. In a small bowl, mix cumin and salt; rub the mixture evenly over chicken.

3 In a 10-inch nonstick skillet, heat oil over medium-high heat. Cook chicken in oil 8 to 10 minutes, turning once, until no longer pink in the center.

4 Serve the chicken with mango salsa. Garnish with mint leaves.

Nutritional Info: 1 Serving: Calories 230; Total Fat 8g (Saturated Fat 1.5g); Sodium 380mg; Total Carbohydrate 8g (Dietary Fiber 1g); Protein 32g. Exchanges: 1/2 Fruit, 4-1/2 Very Lean Meat, 1 Fat. Carbohydrate Choices: 1/2.

Betty's Kitchen Tip

Want your salsa even spicier? Bump up the jalapeño and include the seeds and membranes.

coffee-crusted pork loin

Prep Time: 10 Minutes
Start to Finish: 1 Hour 15 Minutes
Servings: 8

EASY

2   tablespoons freshly ground coffee or
    instant espresso powder
2   tablespoons packed light brown
    sugar
3   teaspoons kosher (coarse) salt
2   teaspoons coarse ground pepper
1   teaspoon garlic powder

1   boneless pork loin roast (3 to 3-1/2 lb)
8   large carrots, cut into 3-inch pieces
6   large cloves garlic, peeled
1   large red onion, cut into 8 wedges
2   tablespoons olive oil
2   tablespoons adobo sauce (from can
    of chipotle chiles)

1   Heat oven to 425°F. In a small bowl, mix coffee, brown sugar, 2 teaspoons of the salt, the pepper and garlic powder. Rub coffee mixture on all sides of the pork, coating completely. Wrap tightly in plastic wrap; let stand at least 10 minutes or refrigerate up to 2 hours to absorb flavors.

2   Coat a shallow roasting pan or broiler pan with cooking spray. Place pork, fat side up, in pan. In a medium bowl, toss carrots, garlic and onion with oil. Sprinkle with remaining 1 teaspoon salt. Arrange vegetables around pork in pan.

3   Roast 40 to 50 minutes or until a meat thermometer inserted into center of pork reads 145°F. Place pork on a serving platter. Cover with foil and let stand 3 minutes before slicing. Stir adobo sauce into pan drippings, tossing with roasted vegetables. Spoon vegetables and sauce onto the platter around pork.

Nutritional Info: 1 Serving: Calories 341; Total Fat 12g (Saturated Fat 3g); Sodium 891mg; Total Carbohydrate 13g (Dietary Fiber 3g); Protein 43g. Exchanges: 1-1/2 Starch, 1 Vegetable, 5-1/2 Lean Meat. Carbohydrate Choices: 1.

Betty's Kitchen Tip

Save yourself a little preparation time and substitute an equal amount of baby carrots for those you'd need to peel and chop. Here, it's about a pound.

tuscan chicken and white beans

Prep Time: 30 Minutes
Start to Finish: 30 Minutes
Servings: 4

QUICK

1/3 cup Italian dressing

4 boneless skinless chicken breasts (about 1-1/4 lb)

1/4 cup water

2 medium carrots, sliced (1 cup)

2 medium stalks celery, sliced (1 cup)

1/4 cup coarsely chopped drained sun-dried tomatoes in oil

1 teaspoon dried rosemary leaves, crushed

1 can (19 oz) Progresso® cannellini beans, drained, rinsed

1 In 12-inch skillet, heat dressing over medium-high heat. Cook chicken in dressing 4 to 6 minutes, turning once, until lightly browned.

2 Reduce heat to medium-low. Add water, carrots, celery, tomatoes and rosemary to the skillet. Cover; simmer about 10 minutes or until carrots are crisp-tender and juice of chicken is clear when center of thickest part is cut (and a thermometer reads at least 165°F).

3 Stir in the beans. Cover; cook 5 to 6 minutes longer or until the beans are thoroughly heated.

Nutritional Info: 1 Serving: Calories 410; Total Fat 12g (Saturated Fat 2g); Sodium 800mg; Total Carbohydrate 33g (Dietary Fiber 8g); Protein 42g. Exchanges: 1 Starch, 1/2 Other Carbohydrate, 2 Vegetable, 5 Very Lean Meat, 2 Fat. Carbohydrate Choices: 2.

Betty's Kitchen Tip

For a change of pace, substitute 8 boneless skinless chicken thighs for the chicken breasts.

southwestern chicken scaloppine

Prep Time: 30 Minutes
Start to Finish: 30 Minutes
Servings: 4

QUICK LOW FAT

- 4 boneless skinless chicken breasts (about 1-1/4 lb)
- 1/4 cup Gold Medal® all-purpose flour
- 1 teaspoon ground cumin
- 1/2 teaspoon salt
- 4-1/2 teaspoons canola oil
- 1/2 cup Progresso® chicken broth (from 32-oz carton)
- 1/4 teaspoon red pepper sauce, if desired
- 2 tablespoons lime juice
- 2 tablespoons chopped fresh cilantro
- 1 can (15 oz) Progresso® black beans, drained, rinsed, if desired

Hot cooked Spanish rice, if desired

1 Between pieces of plastic wrap or waxed paper, place each chicken breast smooth side down; gently pound with the flat side of a meat mallet or rolling pin until about 1/4 inch thick. Cut chicken into smaller pieces, if desired.

2 In shallow dish, mix flour, cumin and salt. Reserve 1 teaspoon flour mixture. Coat chicken with remaining flour mixture.

3 In a 12-inch nonstick skillet, heat canola oil over medium heat. Cook the chicken in oil 6 to 10 minutes, turning once, until golden brown and no longer pink in the center. Remove the chicken from the skillet; cover to keep warm.

4 In a small bowl, stir reserved 1 teaspoon of the flour mixture into the broth. Gradually stir the broth mixture and pepper sauce into the skillet. Heat to boiling; stir in lime juice and cilantro. Serve sauce over the chicken. Sprinkle with cilantro. Stir beans into rice; serve with chicken.

Nutritional Info: 1 Serving: Calories 250; Total Fat 10g (Saturated Fat 1.5g); Sodium 480mg; Total Carbohydrate 7g (Dietary Fiber 0g); Protein 33g. Exchanges: 1/2 Starch, 2-1/2 Very Lean Meat, 2 Lean Meat, 1/2 Fat. Carbohydrate Choices: 1/2.

Betty's Kitchen Tip

For a variation, use 1 pound of pork tenderloin in place of the chicken. Cut pork into 4 pieces and flatten as directed. Serve with cornbread, steamed green beans or broccoli and fresh fruit for a scrumptious dinner.

caribbean chicken fried rice

Prep Time: 30 Minutes
Start to Finish: 30 Minutes
Servings: 4

QUICK LOW FAT

- 1 box (4.8 oz) Betty Crocker® Asian Helper® chicken fried rice
- 1-3/4 cups Progresso® reduced-sodium chicken broth (from 32-oz carton)
- 6 medium green onions
- 1 tablespoon Gold Medal® all-purpose flour
- 3/4 teaspoon ground allspice
- 1/2 teaspoon garlic powder
- 1 package (14 oz) chicken breast tenders (not breaded), cut in half crosswise
- 1 tablespoon canola oil
- 1 can (8 oz) pineapple tidbits, drained
- 1 cup Green Giant® Valley Fresh Steamers® frozen sweet peas (from 12-oz bag), thawed

1 In a 2-quart saucepan, place uncooked rice and seasoning mix (from Asian Helper box); stir in broth. Heat to boiling; reduce heat to medium-low. Cover; cook 15 to 18 minutes, stirring once, until rice is tender.

2 Meanwhile, reserve tops of 2 of the green onions; slice remaining onions. In a large resealable food-storage plastic bag, mix flour, allspice and garlic powder. Add chicken to bag; seal and shake to coat chicken with spices.

3 In a 10-inch nonstick skillet, heat oil over medium-high heat. Cook the chicken and sliced onions in oil 3 to 4 minutes, turning chicken once, until it is no longer pink in the center. Add pineapple, peas and cooked rice to skillet with chicken. Cook and stir 1 minute or until heated through.

4 Slice reserved green onion tops diagonally into 1-inch pieces; sprinkle them over the chicken mixture.

Nutritional Info: 1 Serving: Calories 280; Total Fat 4g (Saturated Fat 0g); Sodium 750mg; Total Carbohydrate 36g (Dietary Fiber 2g); Protein 25g. Exchanges: 1 Starch, 1/2 Fruit, 1/2 Other Carbohydrate, 1/2 Vegetable, 3 Very Lean Meat, 1/2 Fat. Carbohydrate Choices: 2-1/2.

Betty's Kitchen Tip

Infuse more Caribbean flavor by increasing the allspice. Native to the West Indies and South America, most is from Jamaica. It tastes similar to cinnamon, nutmeg and cloves.

caprese chicken

Prep Time: 25 Minutes
Start to Finish: 25 Minutes
Servings: 4

QUICK

4   boneless skinless chicken breasts (1-1/4 lb)
1   teaspoon Italian seasoning
1/2 teaspoon salt
1/2 teaspoon grated lemon peel
1   tablespoon olive oil
1   teaspoon balsamic vinegar

1   large plum (Roma) tomato, cut into 8 thin slices
1/2 cup shredded mozzarella cheese (2 oz)
1/4 cup chopped fresh basil leaves
Hot cooked linguine, if desired

1 Between 2 pieces of plastic wrap or waxed paper, place each chicken breast smooth side down; gently pound it with the flat side of a meat mallet or rolling pin until about 1/2 inch thick. In a small bowl, mix the Italian seasoning, salt and lemon peel; rub the mixture evenly over smooth side of the chicken.

2 In a 10-inch nonstick skillet, heat the olive oil and vinegar over medium-high heat. Add the chicken, seasoned side down; cook 8 to 10 minutes, turning once, until no longer pink in the center.

3 Reduce heat to low. Top each chicken breast with 2 tomato slices and 2 tablespoons cheese. Cover; cook 2 minutes or until the cheese is melted. Sprinkle with basil. Serve with linguine.

Nutritional Info: 1 Serving: Calories 250; Total Fat 11g (Saturated Fat 4g); Sodium 460mg; Total Carbohydrate 2g (Dietary Fiber 0g); Protein 36g. Exchanges: 4 Very Lean Meat, 1/2 Lean Meat, 1/2 Medium-Fat Meat, 1 Fat. Carbohydrate Choices: 0.

Betty's Kitchen Tip

Boneless skinless chicken breasts can vary greatly in thickness. Pounding the chicken breasts so they are equal in thickness results in more even cooking.

feta chicken

Prep Time: 15 Minutes
Start to Finish: 15 Minutes
Servings: 4

- 1/2 teaspoon grated lemon peel
- 2 tablespoon lemon juice
- 1 tablespoon chopped fresh mint leaves
- Dash pepper
- 8 teaspoons olive oil
- 1 package (3.5 oz) reduced-fat feta cheese
- 2/3 cup Progresso® panko crispy bread crumbs
- 2 tablespoons Italian seasoning
- 4 boneless skinless chicken breasts (1-1/2 lb)
- 1/2 teaspoon salt
- 1/4 teaspoon pepper

1 In a small bowl, mix lemon peel, lemon juice, mint, 4 teaspoons of the oil and a dash of pepper with a whisk. Add cheese; stir with whisk. Set aside.

2 In a shallow bowl, mix bread crumbs and Italian seasoning. Sprinkle both sides of chicken with salt and 1/4 teaspoon pepper; coat with bread crumb mixture.

3 In a 10–inch nonstick skillet, heat the remaining teaspoons oil over medium-high heat. Cook the chicken in oil 10 minutes, turning once, until juice of chicken is clear when center of thickest part is cut (and a thermometer reads at least 165°F).

4 On each of 4 plates, place 1 chicken breast, top with 2 1/2 tablespoons feta sauce.

Nutritional Info: 1 Serving: Calories 365; Total Fat 17g (Saturated Fat 5g); Sodium 731mg; Total Carbohydrate 11g (Dietary Fiber 2g); Protein 42g. Exchanges: 1 Starch, 4 Lean Meat, 2 Fat. Carbohydrate Choices: 1.

Betty's Kitchen Tip

Keep chicken as moist and tender as possible by not overcooking it. Check for doneness at the minimum cooking time.

tangerine chicken stir-fry

Prep Time: 20 Minutes
Start to Finish: 20 Minutes
Servings: 4 (1-1/2 cups each)

QUICK LOW FAT

1/2 cup fresh tangerine or orange juice	2 cups fresh broccoli florets
1/3 cup soy sauce	4 oz whole fresh mushrooms, cut into quarters
2 teaspoons cornstarch	1 can (8 oz) sliced water chestnuts, drained
1 tablespoon peanut or canola oil	2 tablespoons water
1-1/4 lb boneless skinless chicken breasts, cut into 1-inch pieces	1/4 cup finely chopped fresh cilantro
1 cup ready-to-eat baby-cut carrots, cut in half lengthwise in half	

1 In a small bowl, mix juice, soy sauce and cornstarch until the cornstarch is dissolved; set aside.

2 In a 12-inch wok or nonstick skillet, heat oil over medium-high heat. Cook chicken in oil 4 to 5 minutes, stirring frequently, until no longer pink in the center. Add the carrots; cook 2 to 3 minutes. Add broccoli, mushrooms, water chestnuts and water; cook 3 to 4 minutes longer, stirring frequently, until vegetables are crisp-tender.

3 Reduce heat to low. Stir juice mixture, then stir into chicken mixture. Cook and stir 1 minute or until sauce is slightly thickened. Sprinkle individual servings with 1 tablespoon cilantro.

Nutritional Info: 1 Serving: Calories 290; Total Fat 8g (Saturated Fat 2g); Sodium 1310mg; Total Carbohydrate 18g (Dietary Fiber 3g); Protein 36g. Exchanges: 1/2 Starch, 2 Vegetable, 4-1/2 Very Lean Meat, 1 Fat. Carbohydrate Choices: 1.

Betty's Kitchen Tip

The key to making a stir-fry is to cut meat and vegetables into similar sizes so they cook in about the same amount of time. Since the cooking goes quickly, always have the sauce ready before you start cooking. Stir sauce before adding to the skillet to ensure the cornstarch is completely distributed to avoid clumps.

MEALS-IN-ONE

p. 80

97

78

102

turkey-feta phyllo bake

Prep Time: 20 Minutes
Start to Finish: 45 Minutes
Servings: 12

2 tablespoons butter or margarine
1 large onion, finely chopped (1 cup)
2 lb lean (at least 93%) ground turkey
1 box (9 oz) Green Giant® frozen chopped spinach, thawed, squeezed to drain
2 teaspoons garam masala
2 cups crumbled feta cheese (8 oz)

1/3 cup pine nuts
1/2 teaspoon salt
1 egg
5 sheets frozen phyllo (filo) pastry (14x9 inch), thawed
Cooking spray

1 Heat oven to 400°F. Coat bottom and sides of a 13x9-inch (3-quart) glass baking dish with cooking spray.

2 In a 12-inch skillet, melt the butter over medium-high heat. Cook onion in butter 5 minutes, stirring occasionally, until onion is tender. Add the turkey; cook 8 to 9 minutes or until turkey is no longer pink. Add the spinach and garam masala, stirring until blended. Cool 5 minutes.

3 Stir cheese, pine nuts, salt and egg into turkey mixture until well blended. Spoon into the baking dish.

4 Unroll the phyllo sheets; cover with plastic wrap or a towel. Place 1 phyllo sheet on top of the turkey mixture; spray with cooking spray. Repeat with the remaining 4 phyllo sheets; spray top sheet. Bake 15 to 20 minutes or until phyllo is crisp and golden brown.

Nutritional Info: 1 Serving: Calories 251; Total Fat 16g (Saturated Fat 7g); Sodium 521mg; Total Carbohydrate 8g (Dietary Fiber 1g); Protein 20g. Exchanges: 1/2 Starch, 2 Very Lean Meat, 1/2 Medium-Fat Meat, 1-1/2 Fat. Carbohydrate Choices: 1/2.

Betty's Kitchen Tip

From India, garam masala is a blend of up to 12 dry-roasted ground spices, such as coriander, dried chiles and cumin. It can be found in the spice aisle of gourmet markets.

burrito pot pies

Prep Time: 25 Minutes
Start to Finish: 45 Minutes
Servings: 6

- 1-1/4 cups Bisquick Heart Smart® mix
- 3/4 cup shredded reduced-fat Cheddar cheese (3 oz)
- 1/4 cup water
- 1 egg
- 2 cups cut-up cooked chicken
- 1 jar (16 oz) Old El Paso® Thick 'n Chunky salsa
- 1 can (15 oz) Progresso® black beans, drained, rinsed
- 1 can (11 oz) Green Giant® Niblets® whole kernel corn, drained
- 1 teaspoon ground cumin
- 1 ripe avocado, pitted, peeled and chopped

Reduced fat sour cream, if desired

Lime wedges, if desired

1 Heat oven to 400°F. Spray 6 (10-oz) ramekins or custard cups with cooking spray; place on a 15x10x1-inch pan.

2 In a medium bowl, stir the Bisquick mix, 1/2 cup of the cheese, water and egg until soft dough forms. Set aside.

3 In a 3-quart saucepan, heat chicken, salsa, beans, corn and cumin to boiling. Remove from heat; fold in avocado. Divide chicken mixture evenly among ramekins. Spoon dollop of Bisquick mixture over each (dough will not cover entire top).

4 Bake 15 to 20 minutes or until the crust is golden brown and the filling is bubbly. Sprinkle with remaining 1/4 cup cheese. Serve with sour cream and lime wedges.

Nutritional Info: 1 Serving: Calories 380; Total Fat 12g (Saturated Fat 2.5g); Sodium 1330mg; Total Carbohydrate 42g (Dietary Fiber 5g); Protein 24g. Exchanges: 2-1/2 Starch, 1/2 Vegetable, 2 Lean Meat, 1 Fat. Carbohydrate Choices: 3.

Betty's Kitchen Tip

These individual pot pies are the perfect way to help control portions. Ramekins are also ideal for making individual desserts.

cheesy macaroni with ham

Prep Time: 25 Minutes
Start to Finish: 45 Minutes
Servings: 6 (1-1/2 cups each)

1-1/2	cups uncooked elbow macaroni (8 oz)	2	cups milk
1/4	cup butter or margarine	1-1/2	cups chopped cooked ham
2	cloves garlic, finely chopped	1	can (14.5 oz) diced tomatoes, drained
1/4	cup Gold Medal® all-purpose flour	2	cups shredded sharp Cheddar cheese (8 oz)
1/2	teaspoon salt	1	cup soft bread crumbs (about 1-1/2 slices bread)
1/4	teaspoon ground mustard	2	tablespoons butter or margarine, melted
1/8	teaspoon ground red pepper (cayenne)		

1 Heat oven to 350°F. Spray a 13x9-inch (3-quart) glass baking dish with cooking spray. Cook and drain macaroni as directed on package, using minimum cook time.

2 Meanwhile, in a 3-quart saucepan, melt 1/4 cup butter over medium-high heat. Cook garlic in butter, stirring frequently, until golden. Reduce heat to medium. Stir in flour, salt, mustard and red pepper.

Cook and stir until the mixture is smooth and bubbly. Gradually add milk, stirring constantly, until the mixture boils and thickens, about 5 minutes. Gently stir in ham, tomatoes and cooked macaroni.

3 Remove from heat; stir in the cheese until melted. Spoon into the baking dish. In a small bowl, mix bread crumbs and melted butter; sprinkle over macaroni.

4 Bake uncovered 20 minutes or until browned and bubbly.

Nutritional Info: 1 Serving: Calories 525; Total Fat 29g (Saturated Fat 17g); Sodium 1063mg; Total Carbohydrate 43g (Dietary Fiber 2g); Protein 23g. Exchanges: 2-1/2 Starch, 1 Very Lean Meat, 1 High-Fat Meat, 4 Fat. Carbohydrate Choices: 3.

Betty's Kitchen Tip

Store dry pasta in a cool, dry spot at room temperature. Store in labeled, airtight containers and use within 1 year. Discard broken pieces that have marbled, lined surfaces—they're too dry.

italian sausage and orzo skillet

Prep Time: 20 Minutes
Start to Finish: 20 Minutes
Servings: 4 (1-1/2 cups each)

QUICK

- 1 cup uncooked orzo or rosamarina pasta (6.5 oz)
- 1 bag (11 oz) Green Giant® Valley Fresh Steamers™ frozen healthy colors market blend vegetables
- 1 lb Italian pork sausage links, cut into 1/2-inch slices
- 1 can (14.5 oz) Muir Glen® fire roasted diced tomatoes, undrained
- 3/4 cup crumbled feta cheese (3 oz)

Chopped fresh parsley, if desired

1 Cook and drain pasta as directed on the package. Meanwhile, cook the vegetables as directed on the package.

2 In a 10-inch nonstick skillet, cook sausage over medium-high heat 5 to 6 minutes, stirring occasionally, until no longer pink. Drain; return sausage to the skillet.

3 Stir the tomatoes, cooked pasta and vegetables into the skillet with sausage; heat until hot. Sprinkle with cheese. Garnish with chopped fresh parsley.

Nutritional Info: 1 Serving: Calories 440; Total Fat 23g (Saturated Fat 9g); Sodium 1080mg; Total Carbohydrate 38g (Dietary Fiber 4g); Protein 21g. Exchanges: 2 Starch, 1/2 Other Carbohydrate, 2 Very Lean Meat, 4 Fat. Carbohydrate Choices: 2-1/2.

Betty's Kitchen Tip

There are two kinds of Italian sausage—sweet and hot. Either one would be a good choice in the Italian Sausage and Orzo Skillet.

champagne shrimp risotto

Prep Time: 50 Minutes
Start to Finish: 50 Minutes
Servings: 6

LOW FAT

2	tablespoons butter or margarine
1	medium onion, thinly sliced
1	lb uncooked medium shrimp in shells, thawed if frozen
1/2	cup brut Champagne, dry white wine or chicken broth
1-1/2	cups uncooked Arborio or other short-grain white rice

2	cups Progresso® chicken broth (from 32-oz carton), warmed
1	cup clam juice or water, warmed
2	cups chopped arugula, watercress or spinach
1/3	cup grated Parmesan cheese
1/2	teaspoon ground pepper

Chopped fresh parsley, if desired

1 In a 12-inch skillet or 4-quart Dutch oven, melt butter over medium-high heat. Cook onion in butter, stirring frequently, until tender. Reduce heat to medium. Stir in the shrimp. Cook uncovered about 8 minutes, turning once, until the shrimp are pink. Remove shrimp from skillet; keep warm.

2 Add Champagne to onion in the skillet; cook until liquid has evaporated. Stir in the rice. Cook uncovered over medium heat about 5 minutes, stirring frequently, until the edges of the rice kernels are translucent. Combine the broth and clam juice; pour 1/2 cup of the mixture over rice. Cook uncovered, stirring occasionally, until the liquid is absorbed. Repeat with the remaining broth mixture, 1/2 cup at a time, until the rice is tender and creamy.

3 About 5 minutes before the risotto is done, stir in shrimp, arugula, cheese and pepper. Garnish with parsley.

Nutritional Info: 1 Serving: Calories 295; Total Fat 7g (Saturated Fat 4g); Sodium 730mg; Total Carbohydrate 43g (Dietary Fiber 1g); Protein 16g. Exchanges: 2-1/2 Starch, 2 Very Lean Meat, 1 Fat. Carbohydrate Choices: 2-1/2.

Betty's Kitchen Tip

Even though you may be tempted, don't rush the process! When making risotto, adding the broth a little at a time ensures that the dish will be creamy while allowing the Arborio rice grains to remain separate.

ginger pork and snow peas

Prep Time: 20 Minutes
Start to Finish: 20 Minutes
Servings: 4 (1 cup pork mixture and 1/2 cup rice each)

QUICK LOW FAT

- 1 package (8.8 oz) microwavable long-grain white rice
- 1 lb pork tenderloin, cut into 1/4-inch slices
- 1 red bell pepper, cut into 3/4-inch pieces
- 1 package (6 oz) fresh snow pea pods, strings removed
- 1 cup orange-ginger stir-fry sauce

1 Cook rice in the microwave as directed on the package.

2 Meanwhile, spray 12-inch nonstick skillet with cooking spray; heat over medium-high heat. Add the pork; cook about 8 to 10 minutes, turning occasionally, until no longer pink. Remove pork from the skillet; cover to keep warm.

3 Add 2 tablespoons water, bell pepper and pea pods to the skillet. Cook and stir over medium-high heat 2 to 3 minutes or until crisp-tender. Stir in the stir-fry sauce. Return pork to the skillet; heat until hot. Serve pork mixture over rice.

Nutritional Info: 1 Serving: Calories 320; Total Fat 6g (Saturated Fat 1.5g); Sodium 2140mg; Total Carbohydrate 42g (Dietary Fiber 2g); Protein 25g. Exchanges: 1-1/2 Starch, 1 Other Carbohydrate, 1/2 Vegetable, 2-1/2 Very Lean Meat, 1 Fat. Carbohydrate Choices: 3.

Betty's Kitchen Tip

A bunch of fresh asparagus (cut into 2-inch pieces) or broccoli (cut into florets) can be substituted for the snow peas.

bacon-pepper mac and cheese

Prep Time: 25 Minutes
Start to Finish: 50 Minutes
Servings: 4 (1-1/2 cups each)

3 cups uncooked penne pasta (10 oz)	1 teaspoon Dijon mustard
1/3 cup butter	2-1/4 cups milk
1 red bell pepper, thinly sliced	10 slices precooked bacon (from 2.1-oz package), cut into 1/2-inch pieces
4 medium green onions, sliced (1/4 cup)	1 cup shredded sharp Cheddar cheese (4 oz)
1/4 cup Gold Medal® all-purpose flour	4 oz Muenster cheese, shredded (1 cup)
1/2 teaspoon salt	2 oz Gruyère cheese, shredded (1/2 cup)
1/4 teaspoon pepper	1/4 cup Progresso® Italian style bread crumbs

1 Heat oven to 350°F. Spray a 2-quart casserole dish with cooking spray. Cook and drain pasta as directed on package, using minimum cooking time.

2 In a 3-quart saucepan, melt butter over low heat. Reserve 1 tablespoon of the butter in a small bowl. Stir the bell pepper and onions into the butter in the saucepan. Increase heat to medium; cook and stir 1 minute. Stir in flour, salt, pepper and mustard. Cook and stir until the mixture is bubbly. Increase heat to medium-high. Gradually add the milk, stirring constantly, until the mixture boils and thickens, about 5 minutes. Gently stir in the bacon and pasta. Remove from heat; stir in the cheeses until melted. Pour into the casserole. Stir bread crumbs into the melted butter in a small bowl. Sprinkle over the pasta mixture.

3 Bake uncovered 20 to 25 minutes or until the edges are bubbly.

Nutritional Info: 1 Serving: Calories 1010; Total Fat 51g (Saturated Fat 29g); Sodium 1790mg; Total Carbohydrate 91g (Dietary Fiber 5g); Protein 45g. Exchanges: 5-1/2 Starch, 1/2 Other Carbohydrate, 4 High-Fat Meat, 3 Fat. Carbohydrate Choices: 6.

Betty's Kitchen Tip

You can use elbow macaroni in place of the penne. You can also use Swiss cheese instead of the Gruyère, although Gruyère has a more pronounced nutty flavor than regular Swiss.

slow cooker shiitake beef stew

Prep Time: 20 Minutes
Start to Finish: 8 Hours 20 Minutes
Servings: 8

LOW FAT

1	lb beef stew meat
1-1/2	lb small red potatoes (about 12), quartered
1	medium onion, chopped (1/2 cup)
1	bag (8 oz) ready-to-eat baby-cut carrots
1	package (3.4 oz) fresh shiitake mushrooms, sliced
1	can (14.5 oz) Muir Glen® organic diced tomatoes, undrained
1	can (10-1/2 oz) condensed beef broth
1/2	cup Gold Medal® all-purpose flour
1	tablespoon Worcestershire sauce
1	teaspoon salt
1	teaspoon sugar
1	teaspoon dried marjoram leaves
1/4	teaspoon pepper

1 Spray a 3-1/2- to 4-quart slow cooker with cooking spray. Cut beef stew meat into 1/2-inch pieces in the slow cooker, combine the remaining ingredients. Stir into the beef.

2 Cover; cook on Low heat setting 8 to 9 hours. Stir well before serving.

Nutritional Info: 1 Serving: Calories 230; Total Fat 7g (Saturated Fat 3g); Sodium 640mg; Total Carbohydrate 29g (Dietary Fiber 3g); Protein 16g. Exchanges: 1-1/2 Starch, 1 Vegetable, 2 Lean Meat. Carbohydrate Choices: 2.

Betty's Kitchen Tip

Shiitake mushrooms add a wonderful, rich flavor to this easy beef stew. If they aren't available, you can use 2 cups sliced regular white mushrooms.

roasted vegetable lasagna with goat cheese

Prep Time: 25 Minutes
Start to Finish: 1 Hour 25 Minutes
Servings: 8

- 3 medium bell peppers, cut into 1-inch pieces
- 3 medium zucchini or yellow summer squash, cut in half lengthwise and then into 1/2-inch slices
- 1 medium onion, cut into 8 wedges, separated into pieces
- 1 package (8 oz) sliced fresh mushrooms (about 3 cups)

Cooking spray

- 1/2 teaspoon salt
- 1/4 teaspoon pepper
- 12 uncooked lasagna noodles
- 1 package (5 to 6 oz) chèvre (goat) cheese
- 1 container (7 oz) refrigerated basil pesto
- 2 cups tomato pasta sauce
- 2 cups shredded Italian cheese blend (8 oz)

1 Heat oven to 450°F. Spray a 15x10x1-inch pan with cooking spray. In pan, place bell peppers, squash, onion and mushrooms in single layer. Spray vegetables with cooking spray; sprinkle with salt and pepper. Roast uncovered 15 to 20 minutes, turning vegetables once, until crisp-tender.

2 Meanwhile, cook and drain the noodles as directed on the package, using the minimum cook time. In a medium bowl, crumble the chèvre into the pesto; stir.

3 Spray a 13x9-inch (3-quart) glass baking dish with cooking spray. Spread 1/2 cup pasta sauce into the baking dish; top with 3 noodles. Layer with half of pesto mixture and 2 cups of the roasted vegetables. Top with 3 more noodles. Top with 3/4 cup sauce and 1 cup cheese blend. Top with 2 cups vegetables, 3 noodles, remaining pesto mixture, 2 cups vegetables, 3 noodles and 3/4 cup sauce. Sprinkle remaining 1 cup cheese blend over the top.

4 Reduce oven temperature to 375°F. Bake lasagna uncovered 20 to 30 minutes or until hot. Let stand 10 minutes before cutting the lasagna.

Nutritional Info: 1 Serving: Calories 520; Total Fat 26g (Saturated Fat 10g); Sodium 990mg; Total Carbohydrate 47g (Dietary Fiber 5g); Protein 22g. Exchanges: 1-1/2 Starch, 1 Other Carbohydrate, 2 Vegetable, 2 High-Fat Meat, 2 Fat. Carbohydrate Choices: 3.

Betty's Kitchen Tip

Not a fan of squash? Use a second package of mushrooms instead of the zucchini.

chili chicken soup with cilantro dumplings

Prep Time: 20 Minutes
Start to Finish: 45 Minutes
Servings: 5 (1 cup soup and 2 dumplings each)

Greg Fontenot
The Woodlands, TX
Better with Bisquick® Recipe Contest

Soup

1	tablespoon vegetable oil
1-1/4	lb boneless skinless chicken breasts, cut into 1-inch cubes
1	medium onion, chopped (1/2 cup)
3	teaspoons chili powder
1/2	to 1 teaspoon salt
5	cups Progresso® chicken broth (from two 32-oz cartons)

Dumplings

2	cups Original Bisquick® mix
2/3	cup milk
1/2	cup chopped fresh cilantro
1/2	teaspoon ground cumin
1	jalapeño chile, seeded and chopped, if desired

1 In a 3-quart saucepan, heat oil over medium heat. Cook chicken, onion, chili powder and salt in oil, stirring frequently, until chicken is browned. Stir in broth. Heat to boiling; reduce heat to medium. Simmer uncovered 5 minutes.

2 Meanwhile, in a medium bowl, mix the Bisquick mix and milk until a soft dough forms. Fold in the cilantro, cumin and chile. Drop dough by 10 spoonfuls onto the surface of the simmering soup. Cook uncovered 10 minutes. Cover; cook 10 minutes longer. Serve.

Nutritional Info: 1 Serving: Calories 400; Total Fat 13g (Saturated Fat 3.5g); Sodium 2000mg; Total Carbohydrate 37g (Dietary Fiber 2g); Protein 33g. Exchanges: 1-1/2 Starch, 1 Other Carbohydrate, 1 Very Lean Meat, 1-1/2 Lean Meat, 1-1/2 Medium-Fat Meat. Carbohydrate Choices: 2-1/2.

Betty's Kitchen Tip

Store fresh cilantro in a plastic bag in the refrigerator up to 1 week. Or place the bunch, stems down, in a glass of water and cover with a plastic bag. Use a rubber band to close the bag; refrigerate. Change the water every few days. Immediately before using, wash the cilantro and pat dry with paper towels.

italian sausage melt casserole

Prep Time: 20 Minutes
Start to Finish: 50 Minutes
Servings: 4 (1 cup each)

1-1/4 cups Original Bisquick® mix
  1/4 cup butter or margarine, softened
    2 tablespoons very hot water
  1/2 lb bulk spicy Italian pork sausage
    1 small green bell pepper, chopped (1/2 cup)

    1 cup Alfredo pasta sauce (from 16-oz jar)
    1 cup shredded mozzarella cheese (4 oz)
    2 tablespoons grated Parmesan cheese
  1/2 cup grape tomatoes, cut in half
    2 tablespoons fresh basil leaves, cut into strips

1 Heat oven to 400°F. Lightly spray the bottom only of an 8-inch square (2-quart) glass baking dish with cooking spray.

2 In a medium bowl, stir the Bisquick mix, butter and very hot water until dough forms. Press the dough into the bottom of a baking dish.

3 In a 10-inch skillet, cook sausage and bell pepper over medium-high heat 5 to 7 minutes, stirring occasionally, until sausage is no longer pink; drain if necessary. Spread the sausage mixture over crust; spread the Alfredo sauce over sausage. Sprinkle with cheeses.

4 Bake uncovered 25 to 30 minutes or until the casserole is bubbly around the edges and cheese is lightly browned. Sprinkle with tomatoes and basil.

Nutritional Info: 1 Serving: Calories 710; Total Fat 53g (Saturated Fat 29g); Sodium 1470mg; Total Carbohydrate 33g (Dietary Fiber 1g); Protein 24g. Exchanges: 2 Starch, 2-1/2 High-Fat Meat, 6-1/2 Fat. Carbohydrate Choices: 2.

Betty's Kitchen Tip

For a traditional pizza flavor, substitute tomato pasta sauce for the Alfredo sauce. Serve slices of this dish with a refreshing green salad and baked pears for dessert.

pizza-baked spaghetti

Prep Time: 15 Minutes
Start to Finish: 50 Minutes
Servings: 10

EASY

- 12 oz uncooked spaghetti
- 1 lb bulk Italian pork sausage
- 2 jars (14 oz each) pizza sauce
- 1 package (6 oz) diced pepperoni
- 1 cup ricotta cheese
- 1/3 cup shredded Parmesan cheese
- 2 eggs, beaten
- 2 cups shredded mozzarella cheese (8 oz)

Fresh basil, if desired

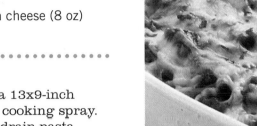

1 Heat oven to 350°F. Spray a 13x9-inch (3-quart) baking dish with cooking spray. In a Dutch oven, cook and drain pasta as directed on the package, using the minimum cook time. Return spaghetti to the Dutch oven.

2 Meanwhile, in a 10-inch skillet, cook the sausage over medium heat until it is no longer pink; drain. In the Dutch oven, toss the spaghetti, sausage, pizza sauce and pepperoni to combine.

3 In a medium bowl, mix the ricotta cheese, Parmesan cheese and eggs. Spoon half the spaghetti mixture into the baking dish. Dollop with the ricotta mixture; spread it evenly over top. Sprinkle with 1 cup of the mozzarella cheese. Top with remaining spaghetti mixture. Sprinkle with remaining 1 cup mozzarella cheese.

4 Bake uncovered 30 to 35 minutes or until bubbly. Garnish with basil.

Nutritional Info: 1 Serving: Calories 538; Total Fat 32g (Saturated Fat 13g); Sodium 1259mg; Total Carbohydrate 35g (Dietary Fiber 2g); Protein 28g. Exchanges: 2 Starch, 1 Vegetable, 2 Medium-Fat Meat, 1 High-Fat Meat, 2 Fat. Carbohydrate Choices: 2.

Betty's Kitchen Tip

Break dry spaghetti noodles in half before adding them to the boiling water to cook.

autumn gumbo

Prep Time: 45 Minutes
Start to Finish: 45 Minutes
Servings: 6 (1-1/2 cups each)

1/3	cup vegetable oil
1/3	cup Gold Medal® all-purpose flour
1	package (10 oz) frozen diced celery, onion, and red and green bell peppers, thawed, squeezed to drain
4	cloves garlic, finely chopped
2	cups cubed butternut squash
1	can (28 oz) Muir Glen® organic diced tomatoes, undrained

2	to 2-1/2 cups Progresso® chicken broth (from 32-oz carton)
1-1/2	teaspoons Creole seasoning
3	cups shredded cooked chicken
1-1/2	cups frozen cut okra, thawed
2	pouches (8.5 oz each) ready-to-serve Cajun-style rice
6	slices bacon, crisply cooked, coarsely crumbled

1 In a small microwavable bowl, stir oil and flour with a whisk. Microwave uncovered on High about 4 minutes, stirring every 45 seconds, until caramel colored.

2 Carefully pour the roux mixture into a 4-quart Dutch oven. Heat over medium heat until hot. Add bell pepper mix and garlic. Cook 2 to 3 minutes, stirring frequently. Add squash; cook 5 minutes.

3 Stir in the tomatoes, 2 cups broth and Creole seasoning. Heat to boiling; reduce heat. Cover; simmer 20 minutes, stirring occasionally and adding 1/2 cup more broth if needed. Stir in the chicken and okra; simmer 5 to 10 minutes longer.

4 Meanwhile, cook rice in the microwave as directed on the package. Serve the gumbo with rice. Sprinkle with bacon.

Nutritional Info: 1 Serving: Calories 504; Total Fat 20g (Saturated Fat 3g); Sodium 1597mg; Total Carbohydrate 48g (Dietary Fiber 5g); Protein 32g. Exchanges: 2-1/2 Starch, 2 Vegetable, 3 Very Lean Meat, 2-1/2 Fat. Carbohydrate Choices: 3.

Betty's Kitchen Tip

To achieve a richer flavor, professional chefs use concentrated soup bases instead of broth. Use 2-1/2 teaspoons concentrated chicken base mixed with 2-1/2 cups hot water in place of the chicken broth in this gumbo.

cincinnati-style chili

Prep Time: 25 Minutes
Start to Finish: 25 Minutes
Servings: 10

- 1 lb lean (at least 80%) ground beef
- 2 large onions, chopped (2 cups)
- 2 cans (14.5 oz each) Muir Glen® organic whole tomatoes, undrained
- 2 cans (15 oz each) Progresso® dark red kidney beans, undrained
- 2 cans (8 oz each) Muir Glen® organic tomato sauce
- 2 tablespoons chili powder
- 2 packages (7 oz) spaghetti
- 1-1/4 cups shredded Cheddar cheese (5 oz)

1 In a 4-quart Dutch oven, cook the ground beef and 1-1/2 cups of the onions over medium heat 8 to 10 minutes, stirring occasionally, until the beef is thoroughly cooked and the onions are tender; drain.

2 Stir in the tomatoes, beans, tomato sauce and chili powder, breaking up the tomatoes. Cook uncovered over medium heat about 10 minutes, stirring occasionally, until desired consistency. Meanwhile, cook and drain the spaghetti as directed on the package.

3 Cover and refrigerate half of chili for another meal. Serve the remaining chili over hot spaghetti; sprinkle with cheese and remaining 1/2 cup onion.

Nutritional Info: 1 Serving: Calories 380; Total Fat 11g (Saturated Fat 5g); Sodium 830mg; Total Carbohydrate 47g (Dietary Fiber 9g); Protein 23g. Exchanges: 2-1/2 Starch, 2 Vegetable, 1 Very Lean Meat, 1/2 Medium-Fat Meat, 1/2 High-Fat Meat, 1/2 Fat. Carbohydrate Choices: 3.

Betty's Kitchen Tip

Want a great way to make two meals out of one cook time? Serve one meal as suggested here. Later in the week, heat the leftover chili and serve it with corn bread or tortilla chips.

turkey and rice casserole

Prep Time: 25 Minutes
Start to Finish: 55 Minutes
Servings: 8

1 large onion, finely chopped (1 cup)
3 cups fresh broccoli florets, cut into bite-size pieces
3 cups chopped or shredded cooked turkey
1-1/2 cups shredded white Cheddar cheese (6 oz)
1 cup mayonnaise

1 can (10-3/4 oz) condensed cream of chicken soup
1 package (8.8 oz) microwavable rice
1 can (8 oz) sliced water chestnuts, drained
1 cup chopped drained roasted red bell peppers (from 7-oz jar)
3 cups coarsely crushed ridged potato chips

1 Heat oven to 350°F. Spray 3-quart casserole dish with cooking spray.

2 Heavily spray a 10-inch skillet with cooking spray; heat over medium heat. Add the onion; cook, stirring occasionally, until tender. Add the broccoli; cook 3 to 4 minutes or until crisp-tender.

3 In a large bowl, mix broccoli and onion, turkey, cheese, mayonnaise, soup, rice and water chestnuts until blended. Gently stir in roasted peppers. Spoon mixture into the casserole dish. Top with potato chips.

4 Bake uncovered 25 to 30 minutes or until bubbly and light golden brown.

Nutritional Info: 1 Serving: Calories 542; Total Fat 36g (Saturated Fat 8g); Sodium 750mg; Total Carbohydrate 24g (Dietary Fiber 3g); Protein 29g. Exchanges: 1 Starch, 1 Vegetable, 2-1/2 Very Lean Meat, 1 High-Fat Meat, 5 Fat. Carbohydrate Choices: 1-1/2.

Betty's Kitchen Tip

Turkey and Rice Casserole is a smart way to transform leftover turkey, ham or chicken. Mushroom lovers might like to add a small jar of sliced mushrooms, drained.

philly beef squares

Prep Time: 15 Minutes
Start to Finish: 1 Hour 5 Minutes
Servings: 6

EASY

- 1-1/2 teaspoons dried minced onion
- 1 lb lean (at least 80%) ground beef
- 3/4 cup cheese dip (from 8-oz jar)
- 2 cups Original Bisquick® mix
- 1 cup milk
- 1 egg
- 2 cups frozen bell pepper and onion stir-fry (from 1-lb bag), thawed, drained

1 Heat oven to 375°F. Spray 8-inch square pan or 2-quart glass baking dish with cooking spray. In a small bowl, cover the onion with hot water; set aside.

2 In a 10-inch skillet, cook the beef over medium-high heat 5 to 7 minutes, stirring frequently, until thoroughly cooked; drain. Stir in cheese dip. Cook 2 to 3 minutes or until hot.

3 In a medium bowl, mix the Bisquick mix, milk and egg with a wire whisk or fork until blended. Pour half of the batter into pan. Top with the beef mixture and bell pepper mixture. Pour the remaining batter evenly over top. Drain the onion; sprinkle over the batter.

4 Bake 40 to 45 minutes or until golden brown and the center is set. Let the dish stand 5 minutes before cutting into squares. If desired, heat the leftover cheese dip as directed on the jar and drizzle over each serving.

Nutritional Info: 1 Serving: Calories 390; Total Fat 19g (Saturated Fat 8g); Sodium 740mg; Total Carbohydrate 34g (Dietary Fiber 2g); Protein 22g. Exchanges: 1-1/2 Starch, 1/2 Other Carbohydrate, 2-1/2 High-Fat Meat. Carbohydrate Choices: 2.

Betty's Kitchen Tip

The rehydrated dried minced onion adds a toasty onion flavor to these squares.

impossibly easy beef, broccoli and mushroom pie

Prep Time: 10 Minutes
Start to Finish: 50 Minutes
Servings: 6

EASY

2   cups chopped cooked beef (about 1 lb)
4   medium green onions, chopped (1/4 cup)
1   box (9 oz) Green Giant® Simply Steam® broccoli cuts, thawed
1   jar (4.5 oz) Green Giant® sliced mushrooms, drained
1/2   cup Original Bisquick® mix

1   cup milk
1/4   cup sour cream
2   eggs
1/2   teaspoon salt
1/2   teaspoon pepper
1/2   cup shredded Swiss cheese (2 oz)
Fresh parsley, if desired

1   Heat oven to 400°F. Spray a 9-inch pie plate with cooking spray.

2   In a medium bowl, mix the beef, onions, broccoli and mushrooms; spoon into the pie plate.

3   In the same bowl, stir the Bisquick mix, milk, sour cream, eggs, salt and pepper until blended. Pour into the pie plate. Top with Swiss cheese.

4   Bake 30 to 35 minutes or until knife inserted in center comes out clean. Cool 5 minutes. Garnish with parsley, if desired.

Nutritional Info: 1 Serving: Calories 280; Total Fat 16g (Saturated Fat 7g); Sodium 390mg; Total Carbohydrate 12g; Dietary Fiber 2g); Protein 22g. Exchanges: 1/2 Starch, 1 Vegetable, 2-1/2 Medium-Fat Meat, 1/2 Fat. Carbohydrate Choices: 1.

Betty's Kitchen Tip

Have some leftover roast beef in the fridge? This recipe is a delicious way to use it. To quickly thaw broccoli, pierce the pouch with a knife; place it on a microwavable plate. Microwave on High 1 to 2 minutes or until warm. Remove broccoli from the pouch; drain well.

mediterranean pizza

Prep Time: 20 Minutes
Start to Finish: 35 Minutes
Servings: 6

Crust

2	tablespoons cornmeal
2-1/2	cups Original Bisquick® mix
1	package fast-acting dry yeast
1/2	cup plus 3 tablespoons warm water (105°F to 115°F)

Topping

1/2	cup basil pesto
1/2	cup sun-dried tomatoes in oil, drained, cut into 1/2-inch pieces
1	can (14 oz) Progresso® artichoke hearts, drained, chopped
1	cup shredded mozzarella cheese (4 oz)
1	package (4 oz) crumbled feta cheese (1 cup)

1 Heat oven to 425°F. Lightly grease a 15x10x1-inch pan with shortening or cooking spray. Sprinkle with cornmeal, tapping off any excess.

2 In a large bowl, blend the Bisquick mix and yeast. Add water; stir until dough leaves the side of the bowl. On a work surface dusted with additional Bisquick mix, lightly knead dough 1 minute. Roll out to a 15x10-inch rectangle. Place dough in a pan; crimp the edges, forming a rim.

3 Spread pesto over the dough. Sprinkle tomatoes, artichokes, mozzarella cheese and feta cheese evenly over the top.

4 Bake 12 to 15 minutes or until cheese is melted and crust is golden brown.

Nutritional Info: 1 Serving: Calories 500; Total Fat 27g (Saturated Fat 10g); Sodium 1270mg; Total Carbohydrate 48g (Dietary Fiber 8g); Protein 15g. Exchanges: 3 Starch, 1 Medium-Fat Meat, 4 Fat. Carbohydrate Choices: 3.

Betty's Kitchen Tip

At the market, you'll find basil pesto in glass jars in the pasta aisle or in plastic containers in the refrigerated pasta section.

king ranch chicken casserole

Prep Time: 20 Minutes
Start to Finish: 1 Hour
Servings: 8

---

2   tablespoons butter or margarine

1-1/4   cups frozen diced celery, onion, and red and green bell peppers (from 10-oz bag)

2   cans (10-3/4 oz each) condensed cream of chicken soup

2   cans (10 oz each) diced tomatoes with green chiles, undrained

1   box (12.5 oz) Old El Paso® taco dinner kit

3   cups shredded deli rotisserie chicken (from 2-lb chicken)

3   cups shredded sharp Cheddar cheese (12 oz)

Chopped fresh cilantro, sour cream and lime wedges, if desired

---

1   Heat oven to 400°F. Spray 13x9-inch (3-quart) baking dish with cooking spray.

2   In a 10-inch skillet, melt butter over medium-high heat. Cook the frozen vegetables in butter 4 to 5 minutes, stirring occasionally, until tender. In a medium bowl, mix the cooked vegetables, soup, tomatoes and 1 teaspoon taco seasoning mix (from dinner kit).

3   Break the taco shells (from dinner kit) into pieces. Layer 1-1/2 cups of the chicken in baking dish. Top with half of the soup mixture and 1 cup of the cheese. Top with half of the tortilla pieces. Repeat layers once. Top with the remaining 1 cup cheese.

4   Bake uncovered 25 to 30 minutes or until hot and bubbly. Let stand 10 minutes before serving. Garnish with cilantro, sour cream and lime wedges.

Nutritional Info: 1 Serving: Calories 490; Total Fat 28g (Saturated Fat 14g); Sodium 1814mg; Total Carbohydrate 27g (Dietary Fiber 3g); Protein 31g. Exchanges: 1-1/2 Starch, 1 Vegetable, 2 Lean Meat, 1-1/2 High-Fat Meat, 2 Fat. Carbohydrate Choices: 1-1/2.

Betty's Kitchen Tip

To make your own diced tomatoes and green chiles, combine two 14.5-ounce cans of plain diced tomatoes with an undrained 4.5-ounce can of Old El Paso® chopped green chiles.

pesto, turkey and pasta

Prep Time: 20 Minutes
Start to Finish: 20 Minutes
Servings: 4

QUICK

- 3 cups uncooked bow-tie (farfalle) pasta (6 oz)
- 2 cups cubed cooked turkey breast
- 1/2 cup basil pesto
- 1/2 cup coarsely chopped roasted red bell peppers (from 7-oz jar)
- 1/4 cup sliced ripe olives, if desired

1 In a 3-quart saucepan, cook and drain the pasta as directed on package. Return pasta to the saucepan.

2 Stir in the turkey, pesto and roasted red peppers. Heat over low heat, stirring constantly, until hot. Garnish with olives.

Nutritional Info: 1 Serving: Calories 440; Total Fat 18g (Saturated Fat 4g); Sodium 470mg; Total Carbohydrate 39g (Dietary Fiber 3g); Protein 30g. Exchanges: 2-1/2 Starch, 3 Lean Meat, 1-1/2 Fat. Carbohydrate Choices: 2-1/2.

Betty's Kitchen Tip

If you don't have bow-tie pasta in your pantry, rotini will work just as well in this recipe.

sesame-peanut chicken lo mein

Prep Time: 25 Minutes
Start to Finish: 25 Minutes
Servings: 4

QUICK

6 oz uncooked fettuccine

2 tablespoons sesame oil

1 package (14 oz) chicken breast tenders (not breaded), cut into 1-inch pieces

2 medium bell peppers (any color), cut into thin strips

1/4 cup creamy peanut butter

3 tablespoons soy sauce

3 tablespoons water

4 medium green onions, chopped (1/4 cup)

Toasted sesame seed, if desired

1 Cook and drain the fettuccine as directed on the package. Rinse with cold water; drain and set aside.

2 Meanwhile, in a 12-inch wok or nonstick skillet, heat oil over medium-high heat. Cook the chicken in oil 3 to 4 minutes, stirring frequently, until no longer pink in center. Add the bell peppers; cook 3 to 4 minutes longer, stirring frequently, until crisp-tender. Reduce heat to low.

3 In a small microwavable bowl, microwave the peanut butter on High 30 seconds to soften. Stir in the soy sauce and water with a whisk until smooth.

4 Add the cooked fettuccine and peanut sauce to the skillet with chicken and bell peppers. Cook and stir until hot. Garnish with onions and sesame seed.

Nutritional Info: 1 Serving: Calories 430; Total Fat 18g (Saturated Fat 3g); Sodium 1050mg; Total Carbohydrate 36g (Dietary Fiber 4g); Protein 31g. Exchanges: 2 Starch, 1 Vegetable, 3 Very Lean Meat, 3 Fat. Carbohydrate Choices: 2-1/2.

Betty's Kitchen Tip

Finish off Sesame-Peanut Chicken Lo Mein with 1 teaspoon toasted sesame seed. Sesame seed and oil have a nutty flavor and are key ingredients in Asian cooking. The oil has a high smoking point, making it a good choice for stir-fry cooking.

spicy chicken and vegetable stir-fry

Prep Time: 15 Minutes
Start to Finish: 15 Minutes
Servings: 4

EASY QUICK

- 2 cups uncooked instant rice
- 1 bag (12 oz) frozen Asian vegetable medley
- 1 package (10 oz) refrigerated grilled chicken breast strips
- 1/2 cup spicy stir-fry sauce
- 1/3 cup chopped dry-roasted peanuts

Chopped green onion, if desired

1 Cook the rice as directed on the package. Meanwhile, in a microwave-safe bowl, microwave vegetables uncovered on High 5 to 6 minutes.

2 Heat a 12-inch skillet over medium-high heat. Add the vegetables, chicken and stir-fry sauce; cook and stir until heated through. Sprinkle with peanuts. Serve over cooked rice. Garnish with chopped green onion, if desired.

Nutritional Info: 1 Serving: Calories 450; Total Fat 11g (Saturated Fat 2g); Sodium 1650mg; Total Carbohydrate 59g (Dietary Fiber 4g); Protein 29g. Exchanges: 3-1/2 Starch, 1/2 Other Carbohydrate, 2-1/2 Very Lean Meat, 1-1/2 Fat. Carbohydrate Choices: 4.

Betty's Kitchen Tip

Use white or brown instant rice in this stir-fry. Want it to be even spicier? Increase the heat level by adding Sriracha sauce, a red-orange chile-based condiment found in the Asian foods section at most supermarkets.

fall pot roast with figs

Prep Time: 40 Minutes
Start to Finish: 3 Hours 40 Minutes
Servings: 8

2 tablespoons olive oil	2 cups Progresso® beef-flavored broth (from 32-oz carton)
10 cloves garlic, peeled	1-1/2 cups water
5 large shallots, cut lengthwise in half	4 cups cubed butternut squash (1-1/2 lb)
2 tablespoons chopped fresh rosemary leaves	8 dried Calimyrna figs, quartered
2 teaspoons kosher (coarse) salt	1/2 cup port or other red wine
2 teaspoons freshly ground pepper	2 tablespoons Gold Medal® all-purpose flour
1 teaspoon sugar	
1 beef rump or chuck roast (4 lb)	

1 In a 6-quart Dutch oven, heat the oil over medium-high heat. Cook the garlic and shallots in oil 3 to 4 minutes or until browned. Remove from pan with a slotted spoon, reserving oil in pan.

2 In a small bowl, mix the rosemary, salt, pepper and sugar. Rub the mixture on all sides of roast. Cook the roast in reserved oil until browned on all sides. Add broth and 1 cup of the water. Scatter garlic and shallots around the roast. Cover tightly; cook over medium-low heat 1 hour. Turn the roast over; cook 1 hour. Turn the roast again; cook covered 1 hour longer or until meat is tender, adding the squash and figs and turning roast during last 30 minutes.

3 Remove roast, fruit and vegetables to a platter. Skim fat from broth, if desired. Heat broth to boiling; boil 5 minutes. Stir in the port; boil 5 minutes. Shake remaining 1/2 cup water and the flour in a tightly covered container; gradually stir into sauce. Heat to boiling, stirring constantly. Boil and stir 1 minute. Serve gravy with the roast.

Nutritional Info: 1 Serving: Calories 409; Total Fat 14g (Saturated Fat 4g); Sodium 819mg; Total Carbohydrate 22g (Dietary Fiber 3g); Protein 46g. Exchanges: 1 Starch, 1/2 Fruit, 6 Lean Meat. Carbohydrate Choices: 1-1/2.

Betty's Kitchen Tip

Calimyrna figs are large, squat, green-skinned, white-fleshed figs grown in California. If you don't have them on hand, use dried apricots or peaches to impart sweetness to the roast.

chicken pot pie

Prep Time: 15 Minutes
Start to Finish: 35 Minutes
Servings: 8 (1-1/4 cups each)

- 1 large onion, chopped (1 cup)
- 2 cloves garlic, finely chopped
- 2 teaspoons chopped fresh thyme leaves
- 1/2 teaspoon salt
- 1/4 teaspoon pepper
- 1 can (10-3/4 oz) condensed cream of chicken soup
- 1-1/2 cups sour cream
- 4 cups chopped cooked chicken
- 2 bags (12 oz each) Green Giant® Valley Fresh Steamers® frozen mixed vegetables, thawed
- 1 can (8 oz) Pillsbury® refrigerated crescent dinner rolls

1. Heat oven to 400°F. Spray bottom and sides of a 13x9-inch (3-quart) glass baking dish with cooking spray.

2. Spray a 10-inch skillet with cooking spray. Heat over medium heat. Add onion; cook 3 minutes. Stir in garlic, thyme, salt and pepper; cook 2 minutes longer or until onion is tender.

3. In a large bowl, mix the onion mixture, soup, sour cream, chicken and vegetables. Spoon into the baking dish.

4. On a lightly floured surface, unroll the dough into a long 13x9-inch rectangle; firmly press the perforations and edges to seal. Place dough over the filling. Fold over the edges to fit inside the casserole dish. Cut small slits in the top of the dough.

5. Bake 20 minutes or until crust is deep golden brown and filling is bubbly.

Nutritional Info: 1 Serving: Calories 426; Total Fat 19g (Saturated Fat 9g); Sodium 731mg; Total Carbohydrate 29g (Dietary Fiber 3g); Protein 31g. Exchanges: 1-1/2 Starch, 1/2 Vegetable, 3 Very Lean Meat, 2-1/2 Fat. Carbohydrate Choices: 2.

Betty's Kitchen Tip

This recipe is perfect for a casual Friday night supper with unexpected guests. The ingredients are easy to keep on hand for emergency meals.

tuna-noodle skillet supper

Prep Time: 20 Minutes
Start to Finish: 25 Minutes
Servings: 6

QUICK

1 tablespoon canola or vegetable oil
1 large onion, coarsely chopped (1 cup)
4 cups water
4 cups uncooked medium egg noodles (8 oz)
1 package (8 oz) sliced fresh mushrooms
 (about 3 cups)

2 cans (5 oz each) solid white tuna
 in water, drained
1 jar (16 oz) Alfredo pasta sauce
1 cup seasoned croutons, coarsely crushed

1 In a 12-inch nonstick skillet, heat canola oil over medium-high heat. Cook the onion in oil 2 to 3 minutes, stirring frequently, until softened.

2 Stir in water and noodles. Cover; heat to boiling. Boil 4 minutes.

3 Stir in the mushrooms, tuna and Alfredo sauce (the sauce will be thin). Reduce the heat to medium; simmer uncovered 4 to 6 minutes or until the mushrooms are tender, sauce has slightly thickened and noodles are tender.

4 Remove from heat; let stand 5 minutes. Just before serving, top with croutons.

Nutritional Info: 1 Serving: Calories 500; Total Fat 30g (Saturated Fat 16g); Sodium 500mg; Total Carbohydrate 38g (Dietary Fiber 2g); Protein 21g. Exchanges: 2 Starch, 1 Vegetable, 2 Very Lean Meat, 5-1/2 Fat. Carbohydrate Choices: 2-1/2.

Betty's Kitchen Tip

To save prep time, use pre-packaged frozen chopped onions. Look for them near the frozen breaded onion rings at your local supermarket.

ground beef chow mein

Prep Time: 25 Minutes
Start to Finish: 25 Minutes
Servings: 6 (1-1/4 cups each)

QUICK LOW FAT

- 1 lb lean (at least 80%) ground beef
- 2 cups thinly sliced celery (3 to 4 medium stalks)
- 1 medium red bell pepper, coarsely chopped (1 cup)
- 1 can (8 oz) sliced water chestnuts, drained
- 1 bottle (12 oz) teriyaki baste and glaze
- 2 cups coleslaw mix (shredded cabbage and carrots)
- 3 cups chow mein noodles

1 In a 12-inch nonstick skillet, cook beef over medium-high heat 5 to 7 minutes, stirring frequently, until thoroughly cooked. Stir in celery and bell pepper. Cook 3 to 4 minutes, stirring frequently, until the vegetables are crisp-tender; drain.

2 Stir water chestnuts and teriyaki glaze into beef mixture. Cook about 2 minutes, stirring frequently, until hot and bubbly. Remove from heat. Stir in coleslaw mix. Serve over noodles.

Nutritional Info: 1 Serving: Calories 350; Total Fat 10g (Saturated Fat 3.5g); Sodium 1480mg; Total Carbohydrate 45g (Dietary Fiber 3g); Protein 19g Exchanges: 1-1/2 Starch, 1 Other Carbohydrate, 1 Vegetable, 1-1/2 Lean Meat, 1/2 Medium Fat Meat, 1/2 Fat Carbohydrate Choices: 3.

Betty's Kitchen Tip

The fat from the ground beef is just enough to cook the vegetables evenly. That's why it's drained off after the vegetables are cooked. Add tropical flair by serving this chow mein with hot cooked rice and a salad of sliced kiwifruit and chunks of fresh pineapple.

thanksgiving dinner pie

Prep Time: 15 Minutes
Start to Finish: 55 Minutes
Servings: 8

EASY

1	lb ground turkey
1	medium onion, chopped (1/2 cup)
1/2	teaspoon salt
1/2	teaspoon pepper
1	bag (24 oz) refrigerated mashed potatoes
2	to 3 teaspoons prepared horseradish
4	oz provolone cheese, shredded (1 cup)

1/2	cup Original Bisquick® mix
1	cup milk
2	eggs
1/4	cup chopped fresh Italian (flat-leaf) parsley
1	can (14 oz) whole berry cranberry sauce

Fresh parsley sprigs, if desired

1 Heat oven to 400°F. Spray a 9-inch glass pie plate with cooking spray. In a 12-inch skillet, cook the turkey, onion, salt and pepper over medium-high heat 6 to 8 minutes or until turkey is no longer pink. Remove from heat. Sprinkle the turkey mixture into the pie plate.

2 Meanwhile, cook the mashed potatoes in the microwave as directed on the package. In a small bowl, mix 2 cups of the potatoes and the horseradish. (Reserve the remaining potatoes for a later use.) Spread the potatoes evenly over the turkey mixture. Sprinkle with cheese.

3 In a small bowl, stir the Bisquick mix, milk, eggs and parsley until blended. Pour over the cheese.

4 Bake 28 to 32 minutes or until a knife inserted in the center comes out clean. Let stand 5 minutes before serving. Top each serving with cranberry sauce. Garnish with parsley sprigs.

Nutritional Info: 1 Serving: Calories 354; Total Fat 14g (Saturated Fat 7g); Sodium 767mg; Total Carbohydrate 37g (Dietary Fiber 2g); Protein 21g. Exchanges: 1-1/2 Starch, 1 Fruit, 3 Very Lean Meat, 1 Fat. Carbohydrate Choices: 2-1/2.

Betty's Kitchen Tip

To quickly reheat in the microwave, cover the pie with microwavable plastic wrap and cut a few slits to vent the steam. Allow some standing time to let the heat equalize throughout the pie.

meat lover's pizza casserole

Prep Time: 20 Minutes
Start to Finish: 1 Hour
Servings: 8 (1-1/2 cups each)

- 1 package (16 oz) ziti pasta (5 cups)
- 1/2 lb bulk Italian pork sausage
- 1 medium onion, chopped (1/2 cup)
- 1 medium green bell pepper, chopped (1 cup)
- 2 cloves garlic, finely chopped
- 2 cans (15 oz each) Muir Glen® organic pizza sauce
- 8 slices bacon, crisply cooked, crumbled
- 1/2 package (3.5-oz size) sliced pepperoni
- 2 cups shredded Italian cheese blend (8 oz)

1 Heat oven to 350°F. Spray a 3-quart casserole with cooking spray. Cook and drain pasta as directed on the package, using the minimum cook time. Return pasta to the saucepan.

2 Meanwhile, in a 12-inch skillet, cook and stir the sausage, onion, bell pepper and garlic over medium-high heat, about 7 minutes or until the sausage is no longer pink and onion is softened. Stir in the pizza sauce, bacon and pepperoni.

3 Pour sausage mixture over the cooked pasta; stir. Spoon half of the pasta mixture (about 4 cups) into the casserole. Sprinkle with 1 cup of the cheese. Spoon the remaining pasta mixture over the top.

4 Bake uncovered 30 minutes. Top with remaining 1 cup cheese. Bake 5 to 10 minutes longer or until hot in the center and cheese is melted and bubbly.

Nutritional Info: 1 Serving: Calories 540; Total Fat 21g (Saturated Fat 9g); Sodium 1350mg; Total Carbohydrate 61g (Dietary Fiber 5g); Protein 27g. Exchanges: 2-1/2 Starch, 1 Other Carbohydrate, 1 Vegetable, 2-1/2 High-Fat Meat. Carbohydrate Choices: 4.

Betty's Kitchen Tip

To give Meat Lover's Pizza Casserole a more authentic Italian flavor, use cooked crumbled pancetta instead of bacon. Pancetta is a cured pork similar to bacon with layers of pink meat and white fat, but it is dried and not smoked.

cantonese chicken chop suey

Prep Time: 35 Minutes
Start to Finish: 35 Minutes
Servings: 4

- 1 cup uncooked regular long-grain rice
- 2-1/2 cups water
- 1 lb boneless skinless chicken breasts, cut into 1/2-inch pieces
- 1/2 teaspoon peppered seasoned salt
- 1 package (16 oz) fresh stir-fry vegetables (4 cups)

- 1/2 cup stir-fry sauce
- 1 tablespoon honey
- 2 cups chow mein noodles
- 1/4 cup cashew pieces

1 Cook rice in 2 cups of the water as directed on the package.

2 Meanwhile, spray 12-inch nonstick skillet or wok with cooking spray; heat over medium-high heat. Add chicken; sprinkle with peppered seasoned salt. Cook 4 to 6 minutes, stirring frequently, until brown.

3 Add vegetables and remaining 1/2 cup water. Heat to boiling; reduce heat to medium. Cover; cook 5 to 7 minutes, stirring occasionally, until vegetables are crisp-tender and chicken is no longer pink in the center. Stir in the stir-fry sauce and honey; heat until hot.

4 Divide cooked rice and chow mein noodles among 4 bowls. Top with chicken mixture. Sprinkle with cashews.

Nutritional Info: 1 Serving: Calories 580; Total Fat 15g (Saturated Fat 3g); Sodium 1930mg; Total Carbohydrate 75g (Dietary Fiber 4g); Protein 35g. Exchanges: 3-1/2 Starch, 1 Other Carbohydrate, 1 Vegetable, 3 Very Lean Meat, 2-1/2 Fat. Carbohydrate Choices: 5.

Betty's Kitchen Tip

Make your own stir-fry veggie combination. Mix 1-1/2 cups sliced celery, 1-1/4 cups sliced carrots, 3/4 cup snow pea pods and 1/2 cup coarsely chopped onion.

stir-fry shrimp

Prep Time: 15 Minutes
Start to Finish: 15 Minutes
Servings: 4 (1 cup shrimp mixture and 1 cup rice each)

EASY QUICK LOW FAT

- 2 cups uncooked instant rice
- 1 red bell pepper, cut into 3/4-inch pieces
- 1 lb fresh asparagus spears, trimmed, cut into 1-inch pieces
- 1 tablespoon water
- 1 lb cooked large deveined peeled shrimp, thawed if frozen, tail shells removed
- 1/2 cup stir-fry sauce

1 Cook rice as directed on package. Meanwhile, heat a 10-inch skillet over medium-high heat. Add the bell pepper, asparagus and 1 tablespoon water. Cook over medium-high heat 3 to 5 minutes, stirring occasionally, until the vegetables are crisp-tender.

2 Add the shrimp and stir-fry sauce to the skillet; cook and stir until heated through. Serve the shrimp mixture over cooked rice.

Nutritional Info: 1 Serving: Calories 350; Total Fat 2g (Saturated Fat 0g); Sodium 1930mg; Total Carbohydrate 54g (Dietary Fiber 3g); Protein 29g. Exchanges: 2 Starch, 1 Other Carbohydrate, 1 Vegetable, 3 Very Lean Meat. Carbohydrate Choices: 3-1/2.

Betty's Kitchen Tip

Use your favorite stir-fry sauce in this handy recipe. Instant brown rice is ready in about 10 minutes and has double the fiber compared to instant white rice.

taco supper skillet

Prep Time: 35 Minutes
Start to Finish: 35 Minutes
Servings: 4

1/2	lb lean (at least 80%) ground beef
1	package (1 oz) Old El Paso® taco seasoning mix
2-1/4	cups water
1-1/2	cups uncooked rotelle (wagon wheel) pasta (about 4 oz)
1-1/2	cups Green Giant® Valley Fresh Steamers™ Niblets® frozen corn (from 12-oz bag)

1	can (15 oz) kidney or pinto beans, drained and rinsed
1	medium tomato, chopped (3/4 cup)
1/2	cup sour cream
1	cup shredded Cheddar cheese (4 oz)
1	tablespoon chopped fresh chives

1 In a 12-inch skillet, cook ground beef over medium-high heat 5 to 7 minutes, stirring frequently, until thoroughly cooked; drain.

2 Stir seasoning mix, water, pasta, corn, beans and tomato into beef. Heat to boiling. Stir; reduce heat to medium-low. Cover; cook 10 to 15 minutes, stirring occasionally, until pasta is desired doneness and most of the liquid has been absorbed.

3 Stir in sour cream. Remove from heat. Sprinkle with cheese and chives. Cover; let stand 2 to 3 minutes or until cheese is melted.

Nutritional Info: 1 Serving: Calories 570; Total Fat 23g (Saturated Fat 12g); Sodium 1100mg; Total Carbohydrate 60g (Dietary Fiber 8g); Protein 30g. Exchanges: 3 Starch, 1/2 Other Carbohydrate, 2 Vegetable, 1 Lean Meat, 1-1/2 Medium-Fat Meat, 2 Fat. Carbohydrate Choices: 4.

Betty's Kitchen Tip

Looking for a more healthful version of this meal? Ground turkey can be used in place of the lean ground beef, and fat-free sour cream can be substituted for the regular sour cream. You'll reduce the fat to 17 grams per serving.

two-cheese chicken and vegetables

Prep Time: 30 Minutes
Start to Finish: 30 Minutes
Servings: 4 (1-1/2 cups each)

QUICK

- 1 cup uncooked rotini pasta (3 oz)
- 2 bags (12 oz each) Green Giant® Valley Fresh Steamers™ frozen broccoli, cauliflower, carrots & cheese sauce
- 1 cup cubed cooked chicken
- 1 cup shredded American-Cheddar cheese blend (4 oz)

1 In a 3-quart saucepan, cook and drain pasta as directed on the package.

2 Meanwhile, in a 2-quart microwavable casserole dish, place the frozen vegetables and cheese sauce. Loosely cover with microwavable plastic wrap. Microwave on High 8 to 10 minutes, stirring twice, until cheese sauce melts and vegetables are just crisp-tender.

3 Return pasta to the saucepan. Stir in the vegetables, chicken and cheese blend. Cover; cook over low heat 2 to 3 minutes or until the cheese is melted. Stir gently before serving.

Nutritional Info: 1 Serving: Calories 330; Total Fat 13g (Saturated Fat 6g); Sodium 1120mg; Total Carbohydrate 31g (Dietary Fiber 4g); Protein 22g. Exchanges: 1-1/2 Starch, 1/2 Other Carbohydrate, 1 Very Lean Meat, 1-1/2 Lean Meat, 1-1/2 Fat. Carbohydrate Choices: 2.

Betty's Kitchen Tip

To complete the meal, pick up a can of Pillsbury® refrigerated breadsticks to bake and a bag of salad greens; toss the greens with chopped tomato and your favorite dressing.

turkey tetrazzini lasagna

Prep Time: 15 Minutes
Start to Finish: 1 Hour 15 Minutes
Servings: 8

EASY

12	uncooked lasagna noodles	2	cups shredded cooked turkey
1	container (15 oz) ricotta cheese	1	cup Green Giant® Valley Fresh Steamers® Select® frozen baby sweet peas, thawed
3	cups shredded Italian cheese blend (12 oz)	1	jar (6 oz) Green Giant® sliced mushrooms, drained
1/4	cup milk	1/3	cup Progresso® Italian style bread crumbs
1-1/2	teaspoons Italian seasoning	2	tablespoons butter, melted
1	egg	2	cups shredded sharp Cheddar cheese (8 oz)
2	jars (16 oz each) Alfredo pasta sauce		

1 Heat oven to 350°F. Spray a 13x9-inch (3-quart) glass baking dish with cooking spray. Cook and drain noodles as directed on the package. Meanwhile, in a medium bowl, mix the ricotta cheese, 1 cup of the Italian cheese, the milk, Italian seasoning and egg.

2 In the baking dish, spread 1 cup of the Alfredo sauce. Top with 4 noodles. Layer with 1 cup of the ricotta mixture, 1 cup of the turkey, 1/2 cup of the peas, half of the mushrooms and 1 cup of the Italian cheese. Top with 1 cup of the Alfredo sauce. Top with 4 more noodles; repeat layers once. Top with the remaining 4 noodles. Spoon remaining 2 cups Alfredo sauce over noodles. In a small bowl, mix the bread crumbs and melted butter; sprinkle over the lasagna.

3 Cover; bake 40 minutes. Uncover; sprinkle with the Cheddar cheese. Bake about 10 minutes longer or until the noodles are tender and the lasagna is bubbly. Let stand 10 minutes.

Nutritional Info: 1 Serving: Calories 770; Total Fat 46g (Saturated Fat 27g); Sodium 1706mg; Total Carbohydrate 43g (Dietary Fiber 2g); Protein 45g. Exchanges: 3 Starch, 2 Very Lean Meat, 3-1/2 High-Fat Meat, 1 Fat. Carbohydrate Choices: 3.

Betty's Kitchen Tip

Bake your frozen one-dish meal slightly longer than one that's baked immediately after being prepared. Most need an extra 10 to 15 minutes; it's a good idea to check it during baking, too.

HOT OFF THE GRILL

p. 113

125

115

128

orange-sage grilled chicken

Prep Time: 50 Minutes
Start to Finish: 50 Minutes
Servings: 4

1/2 cup orange marmalade
1/4 cup balsamic vinegar
  2 tablespoons olive or vegetable oil
  1 teaspoon dried sage leaves
  2 tablespoons chopped fresh chives

  1 cut-up whole chicken (3 to 3-1/2 lb),
     skin removed if desired
1/2 teaspoon garlic salt
1/4 teaspoon coarse ground black pepper

1 Heat gas or charcoal grill. In a 1-quart saucepan, mix marmalade, vinegar, oil and sage. Cook over low heat about 1 minute, stirring occasionally, until well blended. Stir in chives. Reserve 1/3 cup marmalade mixture for serving.

2 Sprinkle the chicken with garlic salt and pepper. Place chicken on the grill over medium heat. Cover the grill; cook 15 minutes. Turn the chicken. Cover the grill; cook 20 to 30 minutes longer, turning occasionally and brushing 2 or 3 times with the marmalade mixture, until juice of the chicken is clear when the thickest pieces are cut to bone (and a thermometer reads at least 165°F).

3 Serve the chicken accompanied by the reserved marmalade mixture.

Nutritional Info: 1 Serving: Calories 440; Total Fat 17g (Saturated Fat 4g); Sodium 260mg; Total Carbohydrate 31g (Dietary Fiber 0g); Protein 40g. Exchanges: 1/2 Starch, 1-1/2 Other Carbohydrate, 3 Very Lean Meat, 2-1/2 Lean Meat, 1-1/2 Fat. Carbohydrate Choices: 2.

Betty's Kitchen Tip

Make this same recipe with 4 to 6 bone-in chicken breasts instead of a whole chicken.

peppercorn t-bones

Prep Time: 25 Minutes
Start to Finish: 25 Minutes
Servings: 6

QUICK

- 6 beef T-bone or sirloin steaks, 1 inch thick (about 1-1/2 lb)
- 3 cloves garlic, cut in half
- 4-1/2 teaspoons black peppercorns, crushed
- 1/3 cup butter or margarine, softened
- 4-1/2 teaspoons Dijon mustard
- 3/4 teaspoon Worcestershire sauce
- 1/4 teaspoon lime juice

Salt and pepper, if desired

1 Heat gas or charcoal grill. Trim the fat on the steaks to 1/4-inch thickness. Rub garlic on the steaks (discard cloves). Press crushed peppercorns into the steaks.

2 In a small bowl, mix the butter, Dijon mustard, Worcestershire sauce and lime juice; set aside.

3 Place steaks on grill over medium heat. Cover grill; cook 12 to 16 minutes for medium doneness, turning once. Sprinkle with salt and pepper. Serve with the butter mixture.

Nutritional Info: 1 Serving: Calories 290; Total Fat 19g (Saturated Fat 10g); Sodium 210mg; Total Carbohydrate 2g (Dietary Fiber 0g); Protein 28g. Exchanges: 4 Medium-Fat Meat. Carbohydrate Choices: 0.

Betty's Kitchen Tip

To crush peppercorns, put them in a resealable freezer plastic bag and use a rolling pin to crush them into smaller pieces.

asian chicken burgers

Prep Time: 25 Minutes
Start to Finish: 25 Minutes
Servings: 4

QUICK

1-1/2 cups coleslaw mix (from 16-oz bag)
1 medium green onion, chopped (1 tablespoon)
3 tablespoons Asian vinaigrette dressing
1 lb ground chicken
1/2 cup Progresso® plain bread crumbs

1 tablespoon soy sauce
2 cloves garlic, finely chopped
2 teaspoons sesame oil
1/4 teaspoon freshly ground pepper
Vegetable oil for grill rack
4 hamburger buns, split

1 Heat gas or charcoal grill. In a small bowl, toss coleslaw mix and green onion with dressing; set aside.

2 In a medium bowl, mix the remaining ingredients except the vegetable oil and buns. Shape the mixture into 4 patties, about 3/4 inch thick.

3 Carefully brush oil on the grill rack. Place patties on the grill over medium heat. Cover the grill; cook 10 to 14 minutes, turning once, until a thermometer inserted in the center of patties reads 165°F. During the last 2 minutes of grilling, place buns, cut sides down, on the grill.

4 Place burgers on the bun bottoms. Using a slotted spoon, top each burger with about 1/3 cup coleslaw mixture. Cover burgers with the bun tops.

Nutritional Info: 1 Serving: Calories 360; Total Fat 15g (Saturated Fat 3.5g); Sodium 610mg; Total Carbohydrate 35g (Dietary Fiber 2g); Protein 20g. Exchanges: 2 Starch, 1/2 Other Carbohydrate, 2 Very Lean Meat, 2-1/2 Fat. Carbohydrate Choices: 2.

Betty's Kitchen Tip

If desired, add 1/4 teaspoon ground ginger to the chicken mixture before shaping the patties. Lean ground chicken is a tasty, healthy meat choice. For the juiciest burgers, avoid pressing the patties while cooking, and do not overcook.

turkey-cheddar-chipotle burgers

Prep Time: 25 Minutes
Start to Finish: 25 Minutes
Servings: 4

QUICK

- 1   package (20 oz) ground turkey
- 2   chipotle chiles in adobo sauce (from 7-oz can), finely chopped
- 3   sticks (1 oz each) Cheddar cheese, cut into 1/2-inch pieces (1/2 cup)
- 1/2   teaspoon salt
- 4   slices Cheddar cheese
- 4   hamburger buns, split
- 4   leaves leaf lettuce, if desired
- 1/4   cup Old El Paso® salsa

1 Heat gas or charcoal grill. In a large bowl, mix turkey, chiles, cheese pieces and salt. Shape mixture into 4 patties, about 3/4 inch thick.

2 Place patties on the grill over medium heat. Cover the grill; cook 13 to 15 minutes, turning once, until a meat thermometer inserted in center of patties reads 165°F. Top each burger with 1 slice cheese. Cover the grill; cook about 30 seconds longer or until the cheese begins to melt.

3 On the bun bottoms, place lettuce and burgers; top each with 1 tablespoon salsa. Cover with the bun tops.

Nutritional Info: 1 Burger: Calories 550; Total Fat 30g (Saturated Fat 14g); Sodium 1160mg; Total Carbohydrate 25g (Dietary Fiber 1g); Protein 41g. Exchanges: 1-1/2 Starch, 3-1/2 Lean Meat, 2 High-Fat Meat, 2 Fat. Carbohydrate Choices: 2.

Betty's Kitchen Tip

To keep burgers from puffing up while grilling, press thumb into center of burger after shaping.

beer can chicken

Prep Time: 10 Minutes
Start to Finish: 1 Hour 55 Minutes
Servings: 6

Basic Barbecue Rub

1	tablespoon paprika
2	teaspoons salt
1/2	teaspoon garlic powder
1/2	teaspoon onion powder
1/2	teaspoon pepper

Chicken

1	whole chicken (4 to 4-1/2 lb)
1	can (12 oz) beer or lemon-lime carbonated beverage

1 Heat gas or charcoal grill for indirect cooking. Combine the barbecue rub ingredients. Fold the wings of the chicken across the back with tips touching. Sprinkle rub inside the cavity and all over the outside of the chicken; rub with fingers. Pour out 1/2 cup of the beer from the can. Hold the chicken upright, with the opening of the body cavity angled downward; insert the beer can into the cavity. Insert an ovenproof meat thermometer in the chicken so the tip is in the thickest part of the inside thigh and does not touch bone.

2 For two-burner gas grill, heat one burner to medium; place the chicken upright over the unheated side. For one-burner gas grill, place the chicken upright on the grill over low heat. For charcoal grill, move medium coals to the edge of the firebox; place the chicken upright over drip pan. Cover grill; cook 1 hour 15 minutes to 1 hour 30 minutes or until the thermometer reads at least 165°F and the legs move easily when lifted or twisted. Using tongs, carefully lift the chicken to a 13x9-inch pan, holding a large metal spatula under the beer can for support. Let stand 15 minutes before carving. Remove the beer can; discard when cool.

Nutritional Info: 1 Serving: Calories 250; Total Fat 9g (Saturated Fat 2.5g); Sodium 890mg; Total Carbohydrate 3g (Dietary Fiber 0g); Protein 35g. Exchanges: 3 Very Lean Meat, 2 Lean Meat, 1/2 Fat. Carbohydrate Choices: 0.

Betty's Kitchen Tip

To bake the chicken instead, place it on the beer can in a 15x10x1-inch baking pan; bake at 375°F on the lowest oven rack using the cooking times above as a guide.

maple and mustard-glazed chicken

Prep Time: 1 Hour 5 Minutes
Start to Finish: 1 Hour 5 Minutes
Servings: 4

- 3/4   cup maple-flavored syrup
- 1/2   cup Dijon mustard
- 2   tablespoons chopped fresh chives
- 1   cut-up whole chicken (3 to 3-1/2 lb)
- 1   teaspoon seasoned salt
- 1/4   teaspoon coarse ground black pepper

1   Heat gas or charcoal grill. In a 1-quart saucepan, mix syrup, mustard and chives.

2   Sprinkle both sides of the chicken pieces with seasoned salt and pepper. Place the chicken, skin sides up, on the grill over medium heat. Cover the grill; cook 15 minutes. Turn the chicken. Cover the grill; cook 20 to 40 minutes longer, turning occasionally and brushing 2 or 3 times with the mustard mixture, until juice of chicken is clear when the thickest pieces are cut to bone (and a thermometer reads at least 165°F).

3   Heat the remaining mustard mixture to boiling; boil 1 minute. Serve sauce alongside the chicken.

Nutritional Info: 1 Serving: Calories 450; Total Fat 12g (Saturated Fat 3g); Sodium 1230mg; Total Carbohydrate 43g (Dietary Fiber 0g); Protein 41g. Exchanges: 1 Starch, 2 Other Carbohydrate, 2 Very Lean Meat, 3-1/2 Lean Meat. Carbohydrate Choices: 3.

Betty's Kitchen Tip

Coleslaw, baked beans, buttermilk biscuits, corn on the cob and strawberry shortcake are perfect accompaniments to this finger-lickin' chicken. And don't forget the lemonade!

lemon-thyme chicken legs

Prep Time: 30 Minutes
Start to Finish: 30 Minutes
Servings: 4

QUICK

1/4 cup honey
1 tablespoon grated lemon peel
1 tablespoon lemon juice
1 teaspoon salt

1/2 teaspoon dried thyme leaves
1/2 teaspoon pepper
8 chicken legs (about 2-1/2 lb)
Lemon wedges

1 Heat gas or charcoal grill. In a small bowl, mix the honey, lemon peel, lemon juice, 1/2 teaspoon of the salt, thyme and 1/4 teaspoon of the pepper; set aside.

2 Sprinkle chicken legs with remaining 1/2 teaspoon salt and 1/4 teaspoon pepper. Place chicken on the grill over medium heat. Cover the grill; cook 16 to 20 minutes, turning once, until juice of chicken is clear when thickest part is cut to bone (and a thermometer reads at least 165°F). Brush the chicken legs generously with lemon-honey sauce, turning to coat evenly. Cover the grill; cook 1 to 2 minutes longer on each side or until the glaze is hot and bubbly.

3 Place the chicken on a serving platter. Garnish with lemon wedges.

Nutritional Info: 1 Serving: Calories 590; Total Fat 31g (Saturated Fat 8g); Sodium 790mg; Total Carbohydrate 18g (Dietary Fiber 0g); Protein 59g. Exchanges: 1 Other Carbohydrate, 8-1/2 Very Lean Meat, 5-1/2 Fat. Carbohydrate Choices: 1.

Betty's Kitchen Tip

The lemon-honey sauce would also taste delicious on other chicken pieces. Prepare as directed, adjusting the grilling time as needed; grill smaller pieces 10 to 15 minutes and larger pieces 20 to 40 minutes. Be sure to grill the chicken until it is completely cooked before brushing with the sauce.

asian chicken kabobs

Prep Time: 20 Minutes
Start to Finish: 20 Minutes
Servings: 4

- 1 lb boneless skinless chicken breasts, cut into 24 (1-inch) cubes
- 1 red bell pepper, cut into 8 (1-inch) pieces
- 1/2 red onion, cut into 8 wedges, separated into layers
- 8 whole fresh mushrooms
- 1/2 cup teriyaki baste and glaze (from 12-oz bottle)

Chopped fresh cilantro, if desired

Lime wedges, if desired

1 Heat gas or charcoal grill. On 4 (12-inch) skewers, alternately thread the chicken and the vegetables.

2 Place skewers on the grill over medium heat. Cover the grill; cook 10 to 11 minutes, turning occasionally, until the chicken is no longer pink in center and vegetables are done as desired. During the last 2 to 3 minutes of grilling, brush the kabobs generously with teriyaki glaze and turn frequently. Sprinkle with cilantro, and serve with lime wedges.

Nutritional Info: 1 Serving: Calories 180; Total Fat 3.5g (Saturated Fat 1g); Sodium 1440mg; Total Carbohydrate 10g (Dietary Fiber 1g); Protein 27g. Exchanges: 1-1/2 Vegetable, 3-1/2 Very Lean Meat, 1/2 Fat. Carbohydrate Choices: 1/2.

Betty's Kitchen Tip

Substitute your favorite vegetables in these savory kabobs. For example, use 1 small zucchini, sliced about 3/4-inch thick, instead of the red onion.

cajun halibut

Prep Time: 25 Minutes
Start to Finish: 25 Minutes
Servings: 4

QUICK LOW FAT

Relish

1   can (7 oz) Green Giant® Niblets®
    whole kernel sweet corn, drained

1   medium plum (Roma) tomato, chopped
    (1/3 cup)

2   tablespoons chopped green onions

1   tablespoon cider vinegar

2   teaspoons honey

3/4   teaspoon dried oregano leaves

1/4   teaspoon ground red pepper (cayenne)

1/4   teaspoon salt

Fish

4   halibut steaks (about 6 oz each)

2   tablespoons Worcestershire sauce

1/2   teaspoon coarse ground black pepper

1/4   teaspoon dried oregano leaves

1 Heat gas or charcoal grill. In a small bowl, mix the relish ingredients; set aside.

2 Brush halibut with Worcestershire sauce; sprinkle with black pepper and 1/4 teaspoon oregano.

3 Place the halibut on the grill over medium heat. Cover the grill; cook 10 to 15 minutes, turning once or twice, until the fish flakes easily with a fork. Serve accompanied by the relish.

Nutritional Info: 1 Serving: Calories 220; Total Fat 2.5g (Saturated Fat 0.5g); Sodium 520mg; Total Carbohydrate 15g (Dietary Fiber 1g); Protein 33g. Exchanges: 1/2 Starch, 1/2 Other Carbohydrate, 4-1/2 Very Lean Meat. Carbohydrate Choices: 1.

Betty's Kitchen Tip

Better safe than sorry! Keep a spray bottle filled with water near the grill. Use it to douse any flare-ups that may occur.

ginger pork with wasabi aioli

Prep Time: 30 Minutes
Start to Finish: 30 Minutes
Servings: 4

QUICK

Pork

2	teaspoons ground ginger
1/2	teaspoon salt
1/2	teaspoon pepper
1	pork tenderloin (about 1 lb)
1	teaspoon vegetable oil

Aioli

1/4	cup mayonnaise
2	teaspoons wasabi powder
1	clove garlic, finely chopped

1 Heat gas or charcoal grill. In a small bowl, mix ginger, salt and pepper. Brush the pork with oil; rub and press ginger mixture on all sides of the pork.

2 Place pork on the grill over medium heat. Cover the grill; cook 17 to 20 minutes, turning several times, until the pork has slight blush of pink in the center and a meat thermometer inserted in center reads 145°F. Remove from grill. Cover; let stand 3 minutes.

3 Meanwhile, in a small bowl, mix aioli ingredients. Cut the pork into thin slices; serve with aioli.

Nutritional Info: 1 Serving: Calories 250; Total Fat 17g (Saturated Fat 3.5g); Sodium 430mg; Total Carbohydrate 2g (Dietary Fiber 0g); Protein 22g. Exchanges: 3 Lean Meat, 1-1/2 Fat. Carbohydrate Choices: 0.

Betty's Kitchen Tip

To ensure the pork cooks evenly, tuck under any thin edges of the tenderloin and secure with kitchen string; remove the string before slicing.

grilled taco-barbecue chicken

Prep Time: 25 Minutes
Start to Finish: 25 Minutes
Servings: 4

QUICK LOW FAT

2 tablespoons Old El Paso® taco seasoning mix (from 1-oz package)

1 teaspoon dried oregano leaves

4 boneless skinless chicken breasts (about 1-1/4 lb)

1 tablespoon olive or vegetable oil

1/4 cup barbecue sauce

2 tablespoons chili sauce

1/2 teaspoon ground cumin

1 Heat gas or charcoal grill. In a small bowl, combine the taco seasoning mix and the oregano.

2 Brush both sides of chicken with oil; sprinkle with taco seasoning mixture.

3 Place chicken on the grill over medium heat. Cover the grill; cook about 10 to 15 minutes, turning once, until the juice of chicken is clear when center of thickest part is cut (and a thermometer reads at least 165°F).

4 In a small microwavable bowl, mix the barbecue sauce, chili sauce and cumin. Microwave on High 30 to 60 seconds or until hot. Serve over the chicken.

Nutritional Info: 1 Serving: Calories 250; Total Fat 8g (Saturated Fat 2g); Sodium 790mg; Total Carbohydrate 11g (Dietary Fiber 0g); Protein 32g. Exchanges: 1/2 Other Carbohydrate, 4-1/2 Very Lean Meat, 1 Fat. Carbohydrate Choices: 1.

Betty's Kitchen Tip

To make Grilled Taco-Barbecue Chicken in the oven, heat oven to 375°F. Line a shallow baking pan with foil or spray with cooking spray. Place coated chicken in the pan. Bake uncovered 25 to 30 minutes or until juice of the chicken is clear when center of thickest part is cut (and a thermometer reads at least 165°F).

veggie-stuffed portabellas

Prep Time: 30 Minutes
Start to Finish: 30 Minutes
Servings: 2

QUICK

1/2 lb fresh asparagus, trimmed, cut into 1-inch pieces
3/4 cup Green Giant® Valley Fresh Steamers™ Niblets® frozen corn (from 12-oz bag)
1 cup fresh bread crumbs
1/4 cup finely shredded Parmesan cheese (1 oz)

2 tablespoons chopped fresh chives
2 tablespoons vegetable or chicken broth
1/2 teaspoon salt
1/8 teaspoon pepper
4 large portabella mushrooms, stems removed
1 tablespoon olive oil

1 Heat gas or charcoal grill. In a 1-quart saucepan, heat 1/4 cup water to boiling. Add asparagus. Cover; cook 4 minutes or until crisp-tender, adding corn during the last 2 minutes of cooking time. Drain.

2 In a medium bowl, mix the asparagus, corn, bread crumbs, cheese, chives, broth, 1/4 teaspoon of the salt and the pepper. Set aside.

3 Brush the mushroom caps with oil; sprinkle with remaining 1/4 teaspoon salt. Place mushrooms, gill sides down, on the grill over medium heat. Cover grill; cook 5 minutes. Turn the mushrooms over; mound about 1/2 cup vegetable mixture into each mushroom. Cover grill; cook 5 to 7 minutes longer or until stuffing is golden brown and cheese is melted.

Nutritional Info: 1 Serving: Calories 450; Total Fat 14g (Saturated Fat 4g); Sodium 1280mg; Total Carbohydrate 62g (Dietary Fiber 8g); Protein 19g. Exchanges: 1-1/2 Starch, 1 Other Carbohydrate, 5 Vegetable, 1/2 Lean Meat, 2-1/2 Fat. Carbohydrate Choices: 4.

Betty's Kitchen Tip

Instead of fresh chives, consider using any combination of herbs you wish, such as thyme, oregano, basil and/or rosemary.

paprika chicken dinner packets

Prep Time: 1 Hour
Start to Finish: 1 Hour
Servings: 4

4	boneless skinless chicken breasts (about 1-1/4 lb)
2	cups quartered small red potatoes (4 or 5 potatoes)
1-1/2	cups ready-to-eat baby-cut carrots, cut lengthwise in half
1	cup Green Giant® Valley Fresh Steamers™ frozen cut green beans (from 12-oz bag)
1	cup chicken gravy (from 12-oz jar)
2	tablespoons Gold Medal® all-purpose flour
1	teaspoon paprika
1/2	teaspoon dried thyme leaves
2	tablespoons finely chopped fresh parsley

1 Heat gas or charcoal grill. Cut 4 (18x12-inch) sheets of heavy-duty foil. Place 1 chicken breast on the center of each sheet; top with potatoes, carrots and frozen green beans.

2 In a small bowl, combine gravy and flour until well blended. Drizzle over the chicken mixture. Sprinkle with paprika and thyme.

3 Bring up 2 sides of foil so edges meet. Seal the edges, making a tight 1/2-inch fold; fold again. Allow space on the sides for heat circulation and expansion. Fold the other sides to seal.

4 Place packets on the grill over medium heat. Cover the grill; cook 30 to 40 minutes, rotating packets a half-turn after 15 minutes, until the juice of chicken is clear when center of thickest part is cut (and a thermometer reads at least 165°F) and vegetables are tender. Place the packets on plates. Cut a large X across top of each packet; carefully fold back the foil. Sprinkle with parsley.

Nutritional Info: 1 Serving: Calories 320; Total Fat 8g (Saturated Fat 2g); Sodium 460mg; Total Carbohydrate 26g (Dietary Fiber 4g); Protein 36g. Exchanges: 1-1/2 Starch, 1 Vegetable, 4 Very Lean Meat, 1 Fat. Carbohydrate Choices: 2.

Belly's Kitchen Tip

If your family prefers dark meat, substitute 2 boneless skinless chicken thighs for each chicken breast.

chicken with chipotle-peach glaze

Prep Time: 30 Minutes
Start to Finish: 30 Minutes
Servings: 8

1/2 cup peach preserves
1/4 cup lime juice
1 chipotle chile in adobo sauce (from 7-oz can), seeded and chopped
1 teaspoon adobo sauce (from can of chiles)
2 tablespoons chopped fresh cilantro
8 boneless skinless chicken breasts (about 2-1/2 lb)

1 teaspoon garlic-pepper blend
1/2 teaspoon ground cumin
1/2 teaspoon salt
4 peaches, cut in half and pitted, if desired
Cilantro sprigs

1 Heat gas or charcoal grill. In a 1-quart saucepan, mix preserves, lime juice, chile and adobo sauce. Heat over low heat, stirring occasionally, until preserves are melted. Stir in chopped cilantro; set aside.

2 Sprinkle chicken with garlic-pepper blend, cumin and salt. Place chicken on the grill over medium heat. Cover grill; cook 15 to 20 minutes, turning once or twice and brushing with preserves mixture during last 2 minutes of grilling, until juice of chicken is clear when center of thickest part is cut (and a thermometer reads at least 165°F). Add peach halves to grill last 2 to 3 minutes of grilling, until heated.

3 Heat any remaining preserves mixture to boiling; boil and stir 1 minute. Serve with chicken and peaches. Garnish with cilantro sprigs.

Nutritional Info: 1 Serving: Calories 230; Total Fat 5g (Saturated Fat 1.5g); Sodium 340mg; Total Carbohydrate 15g (Dietary Fiber 0g); Protein 32g. Exchanges: 1 Other Carbohydrate, 4-1/2 Very Lean Meat, 1/2 Fat. Carbohydrate Choices: 1.

Betty's Kitchen Tip

Make your own garlic-pepper blend by mixing 1/2 teaspoon each garlic powder and coarse ground black pepper.

crispy-coated lemon-pepper salmon

Prep Time: 20 Minutes
Start to Finish: 20 Minutes
Servings: 4

QUICK

- 1/4   cup buttermilk
- 3   tablespoons butter or margarine, melted
- 1/2   cup Progresso® lemon pepper panko crispy bread crumbs
- 4   salmon fillets, about 1 inch thick (1-1/2 lb)

1 Heat gas or charcoal grill. In a shallow dish, place the buttermilk. In a small bowl, mix butter and bread crumbs. Dip salmon in buttermilk. Press the crumb mixture evenly on tops of salmon.

2 Carefully brush oil on the grill rack. Place the salmon, skin side down, on the grill over medium heat. Cover the grill; cook 10 to 14 minutes or until the fish flakes easily with a fork.

Nutritional Info: 1 Serving: Calories 380; Total Fat 21g (Saturated Fat 8g); Sodium 390mg; Total Carbohydrate 9g (Dietary Fiber 0g); Protein 38g. Exchanges: 1/2 Starch, 5-1/2 Lean Meat, 1 Fat. Carbohydrate Choices: 1/2.

Betty's Kitchen Tip

Get in the habit of serving fish at least once a week. Wild salmon is high in heart-friendly omega-3 fatty acids, plus it's tasty! Serve it with a fresh cucumber and red onion salad.

garlic-rosemary grilled chicken

Prep Time: 20 Minutes
Start to Finish: 50 Minutes
Servings: 4

3 tablespoons olive oil	1/2 teaspoon salt
1/4 cup fresh lemon juice	1/4 teaspoon pepper
3 cloves garlic, finely chopped	4 boneless skinless chicken breasts (1-1/4 lb)
2 tablespoons chopped fresh rosemary leaves	

1 In a shallow glass or plastic dish or a resealable food-storage plastic bag, mix oil, lemon juice, garlic, rosemary, salt and pepper. Add the chicken, turning to coat with marinade. Cover the dish or seal the bag; refrigerate 30 minutes to marinate.

2 Heat gas or charcoal grill. Remove chicken from the marinade; discard the marinade. Place chicken on the grill over medium heat. Cover the grill; cook 12 to 15 minutes, turning once, until juice of the chicken is clear when center of the thickest part is cut (and a thermometer reads at least 165°F).

Nutritional Info: 1 Serving: Calories 270; Total Fat 15g (Saturated Fat 2.5g); Sodium 380mg; Total Carbohydrate 2g (Dietary Fiber 0g); Protein 32g. Exchanges: 4-1/2 Very Lean Meat, 2-1/2 Fat. Carbohydrate Choices: 0.

Betty's Kitchen Tip

If you have more time, you may marinate the chicken for a longer period for more intense flavor. Use fresh thyme leaves instead of the rosemary. Lime juice can be substituted for lemon juice.

grilled pork chops with peach salsa

Prep Time: 25 Minutes
Start to Finish: 25 Minutes
Servings: 4

QUICK LOW FAT

3	ripe medium peaches, peeled and chopped (about 1-1/2 cups)
1/4	cup finely chopped red bell pepper
2	tablespoons finely chopped red onion
1	tablespoon chopped fresh cilantro
2	teaspoons packed brown sugar
2	teaspoons fresh lime juice
1/4	teaspoon finely chopped serrano or jalapeño chile
4	bone-in pork loin chops, 1/2 inch thick (1 lb)
1	tablespoon chili powder

1 Heat gas or charcoal grill. In a medium bowl, mix peaches, bell pepper, onion, cilantro, brown sugar, lime juice and chile; set aside.

2 Rub both sides of the pork chops with chili powder. Place pork on the grill over medium heat. Cover the grill; cook 6 to 9 minutes, turning once, until the pork is no longer pink in the center. Serve the pork chops with salsa.

Nutritional Info: 1 Serving: Calories 240; Total Fat 9g (Saturated Fat 3g); Sodium 60mg; Total Carbohydrate 15g (Dietary Fiber 2g); Protein 24g. Exchanges: 1 Other Carbohydrate, 3-1/2 Very Lean Meat, 1-1/2 Fat. Carbohydrate Choices: 1.

Betty's Kitchen Tip

If ripe peaches are not available, substitute about 1-1/2 cups of another chopped fruit such as mango or pineapple. To avoid irritated skin, wear gloves when chopping the chile.

grilled pork 'n nectarine spinach salad

Prep Time: 25 Minutes
Start to Finish: 25 Minutes
Servings: 6

QUICK LOW FAT

1   peppercorn-flavored pork tenderloin (1 lb)

3   nectarines, cut in half

2   bags (6 oz each) fresh baby spinach leaves

1/4   cup light balsamic vinaigrette dressing

1/4   cup crumbled feta cheese (1 oz)

Black pepper

1 Heat gas or charcoal grill. Using a sharp knife, cut tenderloin in half horizontally, cutting to, but not through, the other side; open flat as you would a book.

2 Carefully brush oil on grill rack. Place nectarine halves, cut sides down, and pork on the grill over medium heat. Cover grill; cook 8 to 10 minutes, turning once, until the nectarines are thoroughly heated and the pork has a slight blush of pink in the center. Remove nectarines and pork from grill. Cover the pork; let stand 5 minutes.

3 Cut the nectarine halves into slices. Thinly slice the pork. In a large bowl, gently toss the spinach and dressing.

4 On each of 6 plates, evenly divide spinach, nectarine slices, pork slices and cheese. Sprinkle with pepper, if desired.

Nutritional Info: 1 Serving: Calories 180; Total Fat 6.8g (Saturated Fat 2g); Sodium 692mg; Total Carbohydrate 16g (Dietary Fiber 4g); Protein 16g. Exchanges: 1/2 Fruit, 1 Vegetable, 2 Lean Meat, 1/2 Fat. Carbohydrate Choices: 1.

Betty's Kitchen Tip

Look for bright golden-yellow nectarines that have generous blushes of red. Ripe fruit will be slightly soft to the touch and fragrant. Nectarines will ripen at room temperature and should be refrigerated and used within 5 days.

honey-mustard chicken sandwiches

Prep Time: 30 Minutes
Start to Finish: 30 Minutes
Servings: 4

1/4 cup Dijon mustard
2 tablespoons honey
1 teaspoon dried oregano leaves
1/8 to 1/4 teaspoon ground red pepper (cayenne)
4 boneless skinless chicken breasts (about 1-1/4 lb)
4 whole-grain sandwich buns, split
4 slices tomato
4 leaves leaf lettuce

1 Heat gas or charcoal grill. In a small bowl, mix the mustard, honey, oregano and red pepper. Brush mixture onto both sides of the chicken.

2 Place the chicken on the grill over medium heat. Cover the grill; cook 12 to 15 minutes, brushing frequently with the mustard mixture and turning occasionally, until juice of the chicken is clear when the center of the thickest part is cut (and a thermometer reads at least 165°F). Discard any remaining mustard mixture. Serve the chicken in buns with tomato and lettuce.

Nutritional Info: 1 Serving: Calories 320; Total Fat 7g (Saturated Fat 1.5g); Sodium 630mg; Total Carbohydrate 26g (Dietary Fiber 3g); Protein 38g. Exchanges: 1/2 Starch, 1 Other Carbohydrate, 5 Very Lean Meat, 1 Fat. Carbohydrate Choices: 2.

Betty's Kitchen Tip

This is the ideal recipe for using up mustard that's been "hiding" in the refrigerator. Just about any variety you have—spicy brown, honey or coarse-grained—will blend with the honey, oregano and ground red pepper flavors you add.

spiced-up california burgers

Prep Time: 25 Minutes
Start to Finish: 25 Minutes
Servings: 4

QUICK

- -

1 lb lean (at least 80%) ground beef	4 slices pepper Jack cheese
5 medium green onions, sliced (1/3 cup)	4 hamburger buns, split
1/2 teaspoon salt	4 leaves romaine lettuce
1/4 teaspoon pepper	4 slices tomato
1/4 cup barbecue sauce	1/2 cup French-fried onions (from 2.8-oz can)

- -

1 Heat gas or charcoal grill. In a large bowl, mix the beef, green onions, salt and pepper. Shape the mixture into 4 patties, about 1/2 inch thick.

2 Place patties on the grill over medium-high heat. Cover the grill; cook 8 to 12 minutes, turning once, until a meat thermometer inserted in center of patties reads 160°F. Top each of the burgers with 1 tablespoon barbecue sauce and 1 slice cheese. Cover the grill; cook about 30 seconds longer or until cheese begins to melt.

3 Remove burgers from the grill; cover to keep warm. Place the buns, cut sides down, on the grill. Cover the grill; cook about 1 minute or until golden brown.

4 On the bun bottoms, layer lettuce and tomato. Top with burgers and French-fried onions. Cover with bun tops.

Nutritional Info: 1 Serving: Calories 490; Total Fat 25g (Saturated Fat 11g); Sodium 990mg; Total Carbohydrate 35g (Dietary Fiber 2g); Protein 31g. Exchanges: 1-1/2 Starch, 1/2 Other Carbohydrate, 1/2 Vegetable, 3-1/2 Medium-Fat Meat, 1-1/2 Fat. Carbohydrate Choices: 2.

Betty's Kitchen Tip

For a change of pace, swap steak sauce for the barbecue sauce, or serve on onion or kaiser rolls instead of traditional hamburger buns.

grilled chicken soft tacos

Prep Time: 25 Minutes
Start to Finish: 55 Minutes
Servings: 4 (2 tacos each)

- 1/4 cup lime juice
- 1/4 cup vegetable oil
- 2 cloves garlic, finely chopped
- 1 teaspoon ground cumin
- 1/2 teaspoon salt
- 1 lb boneless skinless chicken breasts, cut into 1-inch cubes
- 1/2 red onion, cut into 1-inch wedges, separated into layers
- 1 large red or green bell pepper, cut into 1-inch squares
- 8 Old El Paso® flour tortillas for soft tacos & fajitas (8 inch; from 8.2-oz package), heated as directed on package
- 1/2 cup Old El Paso® Thick 'n Chunky Salsa

Shredded lettuce, if desired

1 In a small bowl, mix lime juice, oil, garlic, cumin and salt. In a large resealable food-storage plastic bag, place the chicken and 1/4 cup of the lime juice mixture. Seal the bag; shake to coat chicken evenly. Refrigerate 30 minutes to marinate. Set remaining lime juice mixture aside until serving time.

2 Heat gas or charcoal grill. Remove the chicken from marinade; discard marinade. On 8 (12-inch) skewers, alternately thread chicken, onion and bell pepper. Place skewers on the grill over medium heat. Cover the grill; cook 10 to 11 minutes, turning occasionally, until chicken is no longer pink in the center and vegetables are done as desired. Place the kabobs on a large plate; drizzle with reserved lime juice mixture and turn to coat evenly. Slide chicken and vegetables off each skewer onto 1 tortilla; serve with salsa.

Nutritional Info: 1 Serving: Calories 360; Total Fat 18g (Saturated Fat 3.5g); Sodium 770mg; Total Carbohydrate 26g (Dietary Fiber 1g); Protein 24g. Exchanges: 1-1/2 Starch, 1/2 Vegetable, 2-1/2 Very Lean Meat, 3 Fat. Carbohydrate Choices: 2.

Betty's Kitchen Tip

Top each tortilla with about 1/4 cup shredded iceberg lettuce, then top with chicken and vegetables. Serve with a dollop of guacamole or sour cream and sprinkle with fresh cilantro.

greek burgers

Prep Time: 30 Minutes
Start to Finish: 30 Minutes
Servings: 4 (2 pita pockets each)

1   lb lean (at least 90%) ground beef
1/2 cup crumbled herb-flavored feta cheese (2 oz)
1/4 cup chopped kalamata olives
1   tablespoon chopped fresh oregano leaves
2   teaspoons chopped fresh mint leaves

4   pita (pocket) breads (6 inch), cut in half to form pockets
1/2 medium cucumber, thinly sliced
4   thin slices red onion, cut in half
1   medium tomato, sliced
1/4 cup Yoplait® Greek Fat Free plain yogurt

1 Heat gas or charcoal grill. In large bowl, mix beef, cheese, olives, oregano and mint. Shape the mixture into 4 patties, about 1/2 inch thick.

2 Place patties on the grill over medium heat. Cover grill; cook 10 to 12 minutes, turning once, until a meat thermometer inserted in center of patties reads 160°F.

3 Cut the burgers in half. Fill each pita pocket with burger half, cucumber, onion and tomato slices; drizzle with yogurt.

Nutritional Info: 1 Serving: Calories 420; Total Fat 17g (Saturated Fat 7g); Sodium 620mg; Total Carbohydrate 38g (Dietary Fiber 2g); Protein 29g. Exchanges: 2-1/2 Starch, 3 Medium-Fat Meat. Carbohydrate Choices: 2-1/2.

Betty's Kitchen Tip

Add chopped tomatoes and additional chopped mint, if desired, with the cucumber and onion. Serve with a Greek pasta salad and watermelon slices. Or if you're really in a hurry, your favorite potato chips will do just fine!

grilled brats with mustard relish

Prep Time: 30 Minutes
Start to Finish: 30 Minutes
Servings: 4

1-1/2	cups apple cider, beer or water
4	uncooked bratwurst (about 1 lb), thawed if frozen
1/2	teaspoon vegetable oil
1	slice (1/2 inch thick) sweet onion
1/3	cup chunky applesauce
2	tablespoons spicy brown mustard
4	brat or hot dog buns, split

1 Heat gas or charcoal grill. In a 2-quart saucepan, heat the cider to boiling. Add the bratwurst; reduce heat to low. Cover; simmer 15 minutes.

2 Meanwhile, brush oil on the cut side of the onion. Place onion, oil side up, on the grill over medium heat. Cover grill; cook 9 to 12 minutes, turning once, until the onion is soft and the edges are golden brown. Remove onion from the grill; coarsely chop. In a small bowl, mix the onion, applesauce and mustard; set aside.

3 Drain the bratwurst. Place on the grill over medium heat. Cover grill; cook 6 minutes, turning once, until brown.

4 In each bun, place 1 bratwurst and about 2 tablespoons relish.

Nutritional Info: 1 Serving: Calories 550; Total Fat 34g (Saturated Fat 12g); Sodium 1450mg; Total Carbohydrate 44g (Dietary Fiber 2g); Protein 17g. Exchanges: 2 Starch, 1 Other Carbohydrate, 1-1/2 High-Fat Meat, 4 Fat. Carbohydrate Choices: 3.

Betty's Kitchen Tip

To save time, use fully cooked bratwurst and skip the simmering step. Serve with coleslaw and some fresh fruit.

sirloin steaks with cilantro chimichurri

Prep Time: 25 Minutes
Start to Finish: 25 Minutes
Servings: 4

QUICK LOW FAT

- 1 cup loosely packed fresh cilantro
- 1 small onion, cut into quarters
- 2 cloves garlic, cut in half
- 1 jalapeño chile, cut in half, seeded
- 2 teaspoons lime juice
- 2 teaspoons oil

- 1-1/4 teaspoons salt
- 2 teaspoons ground cumin
- 1/2 teaspoon pepper
- 4 beef sirloin steaks, 1 inch thick (about 1-1/2 lb)

1 Heat gas or charcoal grill. In a food processor, place the cilantro, onion, garlic, chile, lime juice, oil and 1/4 teaspoon of the salt. Cover; process until finely chopped. Blend in 2 to 3 teaspoons water to thin the sauce, if desired. Transfer to a small bowl; set aside until serving time.

2 In a small bowl, combine the cumin, pepper and remaining 1 teaspoon salt; rub evenly over steaks. Place steaks on the grill over medium heat. Cover the grill; cook 7 to 10 minutes for medium-rare (145°F), turning once halfway through cooking.

3 Serve 2 tablespoons chimichurri over each sirloin steak.

Nutritional Info: 1 Serving: Calories 290; Total Fat 9g (Saturated Fat 2.5g); Sodium 800mg; Total Carbohydrate 3g (Dietary Fiber 0g); Protein 48g. Exchanges: 1/2 Vegetable, 4-1/2 Very Lean Meat, 2 Lean Meat. Carbohydrate Choices: 0.

Betty's Kitchen Tip

For freshest flavor, purchase whole cumin seed and grind using a mortar and pestle or spice grinder just before cooking.

SALADS & SANDWICHES

p. 135

142

151

153

asian steak salad

Prep Time: 25 Minutes
Start to Finish: 25 Minutes
Servings: 6

QUICK LOW FAT

- 1/4 cup citrus vinaigrette dressing
- 1/4 cup teriyaki marinade and sauce (from 10-oz bottle)
- 1 lb beef strips for stir-fry
- 1 package (3 oz) Oriental-flavor ramen noodle soup mix

- 1 bag (10 oz) romaine and leaf lettuce mix
- 1 cup fresh snow pea pods, strings removed
- 1/2 cup julienne carrots (from 10-oz bag)
- 1 can (11 oz) mandarin orange segments, drained

1 In a small bowl, mix dressing and teriyaki marinade; set aside.

2 Spray a 12-inch skillet with cooking spray; heat over medium-high heat. Add beef; sprinkle with 1 teaspoon seasoning from soup mix (discard remaining seasoning packet or save for another use). Cook 4 to 6 minutes, stirring occasionally, until beef is brown. Stir in 1 tablespoon of dressing mixture.

3 Into a large bowl, break the block of noodles into small pieces. Add the lettuce, pea pods, carrots and orange segments. Add the remaining dressing mixture; toss until well coated. Divide the mixture among 6 serving plates; top with beef.

Nutritional Info: 1 Serving: Calories 250; Total Fat 7g (Saturated Fat 2g); Sodium 880mg; Total Carbohydrate 25g (Dietary Fiber 2g); Protein 23g. Exchanges: 1 Other Carbohydrate, 1-1/2 Vegetable, 2-1/2 Lean Meat. Carbohydrate Choices: 1-1/2.

Betty's Kitchen Tip

For a stylish Asian dinner, set the table with chopsticks and brew a pot of jasmine tea. For dessert, set out a plate of pineapple chunks or fresh orange wedges. You can substitute sugar snap peas or cut broccoli for the pea pods.

smoky chicken melt paninis

Prep Time: 20 Minutes
Start to Finish: 20 Minutes
Servings: 4 (1/2 sandwich each)

QUICK

4	large slices (1/2 inch thick) sourdough bread
2	tablespoons butter or margarine, softened
4	oz smoky Cheddar cheese, sliced
1-1/2	cups shredded cooked chicken
1/4	cup cooked real bacon bits (from 3-oz jar)
6	thin slices tomato
2	thin slices onion, separated into rings

1 Heat panini maker or closed contact grill 5 minutes. Spread 1 side of each bread slice with butter. On the unbuttered side of 2 slices, arrange half of the cheese. Top evenly with the chicken, bacon, tomato, onion and remaining cheese. Top with the remaining 2 bread slices, buttered sides facing up.

2 Place sandwiches on the grill. Close the grill; cook 3 to 5 minutes or until bread is toasted and cheese is melted. Cut each sandwich in half to serve.

Nutritional Info: 1 Serving: Calories 570; Total Fat 22g (Saturated Fat 12g); Sodium 1110mg; Total Carbohydrate 56g (Dietary Fiber 2g); Protein 36g. Exchanges: 3 Starch, 1/2 Other Carbohydrate, 1-1/2 Very Lean Meat, 1-1/2 Lean Meat, 1 Medium-Fat Meat, 2 Fat. Carbohydrate Choices: 4.

Betty's Kitchen Tip

If you don't have a panini maker or closed contact grill, you can cook the sandwiches in a 10-inch nonstick skillet. Heat the skillet over medium heat; cook the sandwiches about 2 to 3 minutes on each side or until bread is toasted and cheese is melted.

steak and feta spinach salad

Prep Time: 30 Minutes
Start to Finish: 30 Minutes
Servings: 4

1 beef sirloin steak, 1-1/2 inches thick (1 lb)	1-1/2 cups halved cherry tomatoes
2/3 cup balsamic vinaigrette dressing	3/4 cup crumbled tomato and basil feta cheese (3 oz)
1 bag (6 oz) fresh baby spinach leaves	

1 Set oven control to broil. Spray a broiler pan with cooking spray. Place steak on the broiler pan; brush with 1 tablespoon of the dressing. Broil with the top about 4 to 6 inches from the heat 10 minutes. Turn the steak over; brush with another 1 tablespoon of dressing. Broil 5 to 10 minutes longer or until the meat reaches the desired doneness (145°F for medium-rare). Cover; let stand 5 minutes.

2 Meanwhile, on each of 4 serving plates, evenly divide the spinach and tomatoes. Thinly slice the steak across the grain; arrange over the salads. Top with cheese. Drizzle with the remaining dressing, about 2 tablespoons on each salad.

Nutritional Info: 1 Serving: Calories 360; Total Fat 19g (Saturated Fat 4g); Sodium 810mg; Total Carbohydrate 14g (Dietary Fiber 2g); Protein 35g. Exchanges: 1/2 Starch, 1/2 Other Carbohydrate, 4-1/2 Lean Meat, 1 Fat. Carbohydrate Choices: 1.

Betty's Kitchen Tip

Flat iron, flank steak or another tender cut can be used instead of the sirloin. Broiling times may vary if your cut of steak is thinner or thicker than 1-1/2 inches.

open-face chicken crostini

Prep Time: 10 Minutes
Start to Finish: 10 Minutes
Servings: 4 (2 crostini each)

EASY QUICK

- 3/4 cup fig spread or preserves
- 1/3 cup finely chopped shallots
- 3 tablespoons balsamic vinegar
- 2 tablespoons olive oil
- 2 cups mixed baby salad greens
- 2 cups shredded cooked chicken
- 8 slices rustic Italian bread, toasted
- 1/2 cup crumbled goat cheese (2 oz)

1. In a small bowl, mix the fig spread, shallots, vinegar and oil. In a medium bowl, toss the salad greens with 1/2 cup of the fig dressing.

2. Divide the greens and chicken mixture evenly among toasted bread slices; drizzle with the remaining fig dressing and top with goat cheese.

Nutritional Info: 1 Serving: Calories 580; Total Fat 18g (Saturated Fat 6g); Sodium 490mg; Total Carbohydrate 75g (Dietary Fiber 3g); Protein 28g. Exchanges: 2-1/2 Starch, 2 Other Carbohydrate, 1 Vegetable, 2-1/2 Lean Meat, 2 Fat. Carbohydrate Choices: 5.

Betty's Kitchen Tip

Two crostini make a perfect portion for lunch. If you'd like to serve Open-Face Chicken Crostini as part of a brunch or lunch buffet, plan to serve just one crostini per person.

sweet 'n spicy chicken salad

Prep Time: 25 Minutes
Start to Finish: 25 Minutes
Servings: 8 (1-1/2 cups each)

QUICK

2 boxes (5.9 oz each) Betty Crocker® Suddenly Salad® chipotle ranch pasta salad mix

1/2 cup sweet-and-sour sauce

1/3 cup mayonnaise

1/3 cup sour cream

4 cups chopped cooked chicken

1 ripe mango, seed removed, peeled and chopped (about 1-1/2 cups)

1 medium red bell pepper, chopped (about 1 cup)

3 medium green onions, chopped (3 tablespoons)

1 can (15 oz) Progresso® black beans, drained, rinsed

1/4 cup chopped fresh cilantro

1 Fill a 3-quart saucepan two-thirds full of water; heat to boiling. Empty the pasta mix (from Suddenly Salad boxes) into boiling water. Gently boil uncovered 12 minutes, stirring occasionally. Drain; rinse the pasta with cold water. Shake to drain well.

2 In a large serving bowl, combine the seasoning mixes (from Suddenly Salad boxes), sweet-and-sour sauce, mayonnaise and sour cream. Add the chicken, mango, bell pepper, onions, beans and cooked pasta; toss until ingredients are evenly coated. Sprinkle with the cilantro.

Nutritional Info: 1 Serving: Calories 460; Total Fat 16g (Saturated Fat 3.5g); Sodium 580mg; Total Carbohydrate 51g (Dietary Fiber 6g); Protein 28g. Exchanges: 2 Starch, 1 Other Carbohydrate, 1 Vegetable, 3 Lean Meat, 1 Fat. Carbohydrate Choices: 3-1/2.

Betty's Kitchen Tip

This salad can be prepared ahead of time, but refrigerate the dressing separately. When you're ready to serve, just toss everything together!

loaded potato salad

Prep Time: 10 Minutes
Start to Finish: 30 Minutes
Servings: 6 (2/3 cup each)

EASY **QUICK**

1	package (20 oz) refrigerated red potato wedges with skins (4 cups)
1/3	cup water
1/4	cup chopped fresh chives
2	tablespoons butter or margarine, melted
1/4	teaspoon salt
1/4	teaspoon pepper
1/4	cup sour cream
1/4	cup mayonnaise
1	tablespoon milk
1/4	cup cooked real bacon bits (from 3-oz jar)
1/4	cup chopped red bell pepper
1/4	cup shredded Cheddar cheese (1 oz)

1 In a large microwavable bowl, place the potatoes and water. Cover; microwave on High 8 to 10 minutes or just until the potatoes are tender. Drain.

2 Stir in the chives, butter, salt and pepper. Refrigerate uncovered 10 minutes.

3 In a small bowl, mix the sour cream, mayonnaise and milk. Stir the sour cream mixture, bacon, bell pepper and cheese into the potatoes. Serve immediately, or cover and refrigerate until serving time.

Nutritional Info: 1 Serving: Calories 220; Total Fat 16g (Saturated Fat 6g); Sodium 460mg; Total Carbohydrate 13g (Dietary Fiber 2g); Protein 6g. Exchanges: 1 Starch, 1/2 Medium-Fat Meat, 2-1/2 Fat. Carbohydrate Choices: 1.

Betty's Kitchen Tip

If the salad dressing dries out while it's in the refrigerator, stir in another tablespoon of milk before serving. If you prefer smaller potato pieces, cut each wedge in half after cooking.

greek-style tuna salad sandwiches

Prep Time: 10 Minutes
Start to Finish: 10 Minutes
Servings: 4 sandwiches

EASY QUICK

1   can (12 oz) tuna, drained and flaked

1/2   cup chopped drained roasted red bell peppers (from 7-oz jar)

1/2   cup crumbled feta cheese or shredded mozzarella cheese (2 oz)

1   medium stalk celery, chopped (1/2 cup)

1   loaf (1 lb) French bread

1/4   cup Italian dressing

1 In a medium bowl, mix the tuna, roasted peppers, cheese and celery.

2 Cut bread into 4 (4-inch) pieces; cut each piece in half horizontally. Remove some of the bread from the center of each slice; discard the removed bread or save for another use.

3 Drizzle the dressing on cut sides of the bread. Spoon 1/2 cup tuna mixture on each bread bottom; cover with the bread tops. Serve immediately, or wrap each sandwich in plastic wrap and refrigerate up to 24 hours.

Nutritional Info: 1 Sandwich: Calories 520; Total Fat 11g (Saturated Fat 4g); Sodium 1520mg; Total Carbohydrate 71g (Dietary Fiber 4g); Protein 35g. Exchanges: 3-1/2 Starch, 1 Other Carbohydrate, 3-1/2 Very Lean Meat, 1-1/2 Fat. Carbohydrate Choices: 5.

 Kitchen Tip

Use 1/2 cup chopped drained pepperoncini peppers (bottled Italian peppers, shown in the photo at left) instead of the roasted bell peppers for a slightly sweet and spicy-hot flavor.

not your mother's grilled cheese sandwich

Prep Time: 10 Minutes
Start to Finish: 10 Minutes
Servings: 2 sandwiches

EASY QUICK

- 4 slices sourdough or other rustic whole-grain bread
- 2 tablespoons apple butter
- 4 slices (3/4 to 1 oz each) sharp Cheddar cheese
- 4 oz thin slices cooked chicken breast
- 2 tablespoons butter, softened

1 On one side of 2 bread slices, evenly spread the apple butter. Top each with 1 slice of cheese, half of the chicken, a second slice of cheese and the remaining bread slices.

2 In a 10-inch nonstick skillet, melt 1 tablespoon of the butter over medium-low heat. Place sandwiches in the skillet. Spread tops of the bread with remaining 1 tablespoon butter. Cook 5 minutes, turning once, until cheese is melted and bread is golden brown.

Nutritional Info: 1 Sandwich: Calories 740; Total Fat 30g (Saturated Fat 17g); Sodium 1850mg; Total Carbohydrate 83g (Dietary Fiber 3g); Protein 35g. Exchanges: 4-1/2 Starch, 1 Other Carbohydrate, 3 Lean Meat, 3-1/2 Fat. Carbohydrate Choices: 5-1/2.

Betty's Kitchen Tip

Cut the fat in this sandwich by choosing one of the low-fat pre-sliced cheeses available in the dairy section of your supermarket.

dijon chicken and pasta salad

Prep Time: 20 Minutes
Start to Finish: 20 Minutes
Servings: 4

QUICK

1 box (7.75 oz) Betty Crocker® Suddenly Salad® classic pasta salad mix

2 tablespoons vegetable oil

3 tablespoons cold water

2 tablespoons Dijon mustard

1 cup cubed cooked chicken

1 Fill a 3-quart saucepan two-thirds full of water; heat to boiling. Empty the pasta mix (from Suddenly Salad box) into boiling water. Gently boil uncovered 12 minutes, stirring occasionally. Drain; rinse pasta with cold water. Shake to drain well.

2 In a large bowl, stir the seasoning mix (from Suddenly Salad box), oil, water and mustard until blended. Stir in the cooked pasta and chicken.

Nutritional Info: 1 Serving: Calories 330; Total Fat 11g (Saturated Fat 2g); Sodium 1270mg; Total Carbohydrate 41g (Dietary Fiber 1g); Protein 16g. Exchanges: 2-1/2 Starch, 1 Lean Meat, 1-1/2 Fat. Carbohydrate Choices: 3.

Betty's Kitchen Tip

If you're an artichoke lover, stir in a 14-ounce can of artichoke hearts, drained and quartered, with the chicken. Or, one cup of cooked frozen (thawed) imitation crabmeat chunks instead of chicken turns this into a seafood delight.

crunchy sesame chicken salad

Prep Time: 15 Minutes
Start to Finish: 15 Minutes
Servings: 8 (1-1/2 cups each)

EASY QUICK

4	cups shredded deli rotisserie chicken (from 2-lb chicken)
1	bag (16 oz) coleslaw mix (about 8 cups)
2	cups chow mein noodles (from 6-oz bag)
1	bag (8 oz) fresh sugar snap peas, strings removed (about 2 cups)
1	cup shredded carrots (from 10-oz bag)
1-1/4	cups Asian toasted sesame dressing (from 16-oz bottle)
3	medium green onions, sliced (3 tablespoons)

1 In a large serving bowl, toss all ingredients except onions until evenly coated. Sprinkle with the green onions.

Nutritional Info: 1 Serving: Calories 370; Total Fat 21g (Saturated Fat 4g); Sodium 810mg; Total Carbohydrate 24g (Dietary Fiber 3g); Protein 22g. Exchanges: 1/2 Starch, 1 Other Carbohydrate, 3 Lean Meat, 2-1/2 Fat. Carbohydrate Choices: 1-1/2.

 Kitchen Tip

For a tasty topping, try chopped wasabi- or soy sauce-flavored almonds. Look for them in the snack section of your grocery store.

turkey taco layered salad

Prep Time: 15 Minutes
Start to Finish: 15 Minutes
Servings: 6

EASY QUICK

- 1/2 cup Old El Paso® Thick 'n Chunky salsa
- 1/2 cup French dressing
- 2 tablespoons chopped fresh cilantro
- 6 cups torn lettuce
- 2 cups diced cooked turkey
- 1 can (11 oz) Green Giant® Mexicorn® whole kernel corn with red and green peppers, drained
- 2 large tomatoes, chopped (2 cups)
- 1 cup shredded Colby-Monterey Jack cheese blend (4 oz)
- 4 medium green onions, chopped (1/4 cup)
- 1 cup tortilla chips

1 In a small bowl, mix the salsa, dressing and cilantro.

2 In a deep 3-quart salad bowl, layer the lettuce, turkey, corn, tomatoes and cheese. Top with the dressing mixture. Serve immediately, or cover and refrigerate up to 24 hours.

3 Just before serving, sprinkle onions over the salad and arrange tortilla chips around the edge of the bowl.

Betty's Kitchen Tip

If you are transporting this salad, package the tortilla chips in plastic wrap to put on the salad just before you serve it.

Nutritional Info: 1 Serving: Calories 350; Total Fat 19g (Saturated Fat 6g); Sodium 640mg; Total Carbohydrate 23g (Dietary Fiber 2g); Protein 20g. Exchanges: 1/2 Starch, 1 Other Carbohydrate, 2-1/2 Very Lean Meat, 3-1/2 Fat. Carbohydrate Choices: 1-1/2.

caesar chicken subs

Prep Time: 15 Minutes
Start to Finish: 15 Minutes
Servings: 4

EASY QUICK

- 1   baguette French bread (8 oz) or 4 submarine sandwich rolls (about 6 inch)
- 1/3   cup Caesar dressing
- 1/2   package (3.5-oz size) sandwich sliced pepperoni
- 3/4   lb deli rotisserie chicken (from 2-lb chicken), cut into about 1/4-inch slices
- 4   slices (1 oz each) Colby-Monterey Jack cheese blend
- 4   slices tomato, cut in half
- 4   lettuce leaves
- 1/2   medium red onion, thinly sliced

1 Cut the baguette or rolls in half horizontally (if using the baguette, first cut into fourths). Spread dressing over the cut sides.

2 On the bread bottoms, layer pepperoni, chicken, cheese, tomato, lettuce and onion; cover with the bread tops. Press gently; secure with toothpicks. Cut each sandwich diagonally in half.

Nutritional Info: 1 Serving: Calories 620; Total Fat 35g (Saturated Fat 12g); Sodium 960mg; Total Carbohydrate 36g (Dietary Fiber 2g); Protein 41g. Exchanges: 2 Starch, 1/2 Other Carbohydrate, 5 Very Lean Meat, 6 Fat. Carbohydrate Choices: 2-1/2.

Betty's Kitchen Tip

You can make these sandwiches ahead, but add the tomato slices just before serving.

orzo with chicken and fresh herbs

Prep Time: 25 Minutes
Start to Finish: 25 Minutes
Servings: 4

QUICK

1/2	cup uncooked orzo or rosamarina pasta (about 3.5 oz)
1	pint (2 cups) cherry or grape tomatoes, cut in half
2	cloves garlic, finely chopped
1/4	cup olive oil
3	tablespoons white wine vinegar
1/2	teaspoon salt
1/8	teaspoon pepper
3	tablespoons chopped fresh basil, oregano, marjoram or thyme leaves (or a combination)
2	cups cut-up cooked chicken
1	cup small fresh mozzarella cheese balls (about 6 oz)
4	large leaves butter lettuce

1 Cook and drain pasta as directed on the package. Rinse pasta with cold water to cool; drain.

2 In a large bowl, mix the tomatoes, garlic, oil, vinegar, salt, pepper and herbs. Add the chicken, cheese and cooked pasta; toss until evenly coated. To serve, spoon 1-1/4 cups of the salad onto each lettuce leaf.

Nutritional Info: 1 Serving: Calories 490; Total Fat 28g (Saturated Fat 9g); Sodium 580mg; Total Carbohydrate 25g (Dietary Fiber 2g); Protein 35g. Exchanges: 1-1/2 Starch, 1 Vegetable, 4 Lean Meat, 3 Fat. Carbohydrate Choices: 1-1/2.

Betty's Kitchen Tip

This salad is delicious served at room temperature or chilled. It is a perfect recipe for when you have leftover rotisserie chicken.

open-face egg salad sandwiches

Prep Time: 15 Minutes
Start to Finish: 30 Minutes
Servings: 4

EASY QUICK

Bread

- 1 cup Original Bisquick® mix
- 1/2 cup milk
- 1 egg, slightly beaten
- 1 tablespoon ground mustard
- 1/2 teaspoon celery seed

Egg Salad

- 8 hard-cooked eggs, peeled and chopped

- 1/4 cup mayonnaise
- 2 tablespoons finely chopped onion
- 2 tablespoons finely chopped celery
- 2 tablespoons finely chopped red bell pepper
- 1/2 teaspoon salt
- 1/2 teaspoon pepper
- 1 cup shredded lettuce

1 Heat oven to 350°F. Spray an 8-inch square pan with cooking spray. In a large bowl, stir all bread ingredients. Spread in the pan. Bake 15 to 17 minutes or until a toothpick inserted in the center comes out clean (top will not brown). Cool.

2 Meanwhile, in a medium bowl, combine all egg salad ingredients except the lettuce.

3 Cut the bread into 4 squares; top each square with 1/2 cup egg salad and 1/4 cup lettuce. Season with additional salt and pepper, if desired.

Nutritional Info: 1 Serving: Calories 420; Total Fat 28g (Saturated Fat 7g); Sodium 900mg; Total Carbohydrate 24g (Dietary Fiber 1g); Protein 18g. Exchanges: 1-1/2 Other Carbohydrate, 1/2 Vegetable, 2-1/2 Medium-Fat Meat, 3 Fat. Carbohydrate Choices: 1-1/2.

Betty's Kitchen Tip

Hard-cook the eggs 1 or 2 days before making this recipe. Or to save even more time, look for hard-cooked eggs in the deli or dairy section of the grocery store. For a fancier version with a different flavor profile, substitute roasted red bell pepper for the fresh bell pepper.

salad with pears and maple vinaigrette

Prep Time: 15 Minutes
Start to Finish: 15 Minutes
Servings: 6 (1-1/3 cups each)

EASY QUICK

Vinaigrette

1/4	cup real maple syrup or maple-flavored syrup
2	tablespoons balsamic vinegar
1/2	teaspoon Dijon mustard
1/4	teaspoon salt
1/4	teaspoon pepper
1/4	cup canola or vegetable oil

Salad

1/3	cup pecan halves
8	cups torn mixed salad greens
3	medium pears, peeled, cut into wedges
1/3	cup sweetened dried cranberries

1 In a small bowl, mix all the vinaigrette ingredients except oil with a wire whisk. Beat in the oil until blended.

2 Place pecans in a 1-cup glass measuring cup. Microwave on High 2 minutes to 2 minutes 30 seconds, stirring every 30 seconds, until browned.

3 Divide the salad greens among 6 serving plates. Arrange pear wedges on the greens; sprinkle with pecans and cranberries. Drizzle vinaigrette over the salads.

Nutritional Info: 1 Serving: Calories 240; Total Fat 14g (Saturated Fat 1g); Sodium 130mg; Total Carbohydrate 26g (Dietary Fiber 5g); Protein 2g. Exchanges: 1/2 Fruit, 1 Other Carbohydrate, 1/2 High-Fat Meat, 2 Fat. Carbohydrate Choices: 2.

Betty's Kitchen Tip

This salad is also delicious topped with sliced leftover turkey. If the pears you purchase are very firm, place them in a brown bag on your counter for a day or two to help them ripen.

cobb salad wraps

Prep Time: 15 Minutes
Start to Finish: 15 Minutes
Servings: 2 wraps

EASY **QUICK**

1 cup chopped deli rotisserie chicken (from 2-lb chicken)	2 tablespoons cooked real bacon bits (from 3-oz jar)
1-1/2 cups torn romaine lettuce	1 hard-cooked egg, chopped
1/4 cup blue cheese dressing	2 flour tortillas (10 inch)
1 small tomato, chopped (1/2 cup)	1/2 avocado, peeled and sliced

1 In a medium bowl, toss the chicken, lettuce and dressing to coat. Stir in the tomato, bacon and egg.

2 Place the tortillas on a large microwavable plate; cover with microwavable plastic wrap. Microwave on High 15 to 30 seconds to soften.

3 Spoon the chicken mixture down the center of each tortilla to within 1 inch of edges. Top with the avocado slices. Fold opposite sides of the tortilla up toward the center about 1 inch over filling (sides will not meet in center); roll up the tortilla, beginning at one open end. Cut diagonally in half. Secure with a toothpick, if necessary. Serve immediately.

Nutritional Info: 1 Wrap: Calories 590; Total Fat 35g (Saturated Fat 7g); Sodium 930mg; Total Carbohydrate 38g (Dietary Fiber 5g); Protein 32g. Exchanges: 2-1/2 Starch, 1-1/2 Very Lean Meat, 1 Lean Meat, 1 Medium-Fat Meat, 5 Fat. Carbohydrate Choices: 2-1/2.

Betty's Kitchen Tip

For a more intense flavor, sprinkle crumbled blue cheese over the sandwich mixture before rolling up the wraps.

white barbecue chicken sandwiches

Prep Time: 10 Minutes
Start to Finish: 10 Minutes
Servings: 6 sandwiches

White Barbecue Sauce

1	cup light mayonnaise
3/4	cup cider vinegar
2	tablespoons fresh lemon juice
1	tablespoon freshly ground black pepper
1/4	teaspoon ground red pepper (cayenne)

Sandwiches

6	hamburger buns, split
2	cups angel hair coleslaw (from 16-oz bag)
3	cups shredded deli rotisserie chicken (from 2-lb chicken)
12	hamburger dill pickle slices

1 In a small bowl, mix mayonnaise, vinegar, lemon juice, black pepper and red pepper with a wire whisk.

2 On each bun bottom, place 1/3 cup coleslaw, 1/2 cup chicken, 2 tablespoons white barbecue sauce and 2 pickle slices; cover with the bun tops. Refrigerate the remaining white barbecue sauce in a covered container up to 1 week.

Nutritional Info: 1 Sandwich: Calories 386; Total Fat 18g (Saturated Fat 3g); Sodium 705mg; Total Carbohydrate 27g (Dietary Fiber 2g); Protein 26g. Exchanges: 1-1/2 Starch, 2-1/2 Lean Meat, 2-1/2 Fat. Carbohydrate Choices: 1-1/2.

Betty's Kitchen Tip

White barbecue sauce, widely used in traditional Alabama-style barbecue, is known for its vinegary taste and use of mayonnaise as its base, rather than the usual tomato sauce. To make the sauce ahead of time, combine all the ingredients, store the sauce in the refrigerator, and bring it to room temperature before serving.

chicken wedge salad

Prep Time: 20 Minutes
Start to Finish: 20 Minutes
Servings: 6

- 6 slices bacon
- 3/4 cup mayonnaise
- 1/3 cup plain yogurt
- 2 tablespoons red wine vinegar
- 3 oz crumbled blue cheese (3/4 cup)
- 1 head iceberg lettuce, cored, cut into 6 wedges

- 2 packages (6 oz each) refrigerated cooked chicken breast strips
- 1 large apple, chopped (about 2 cups)
- 3/4 cup chopped red onion
- 3/4 cup glazed walnuts (from 3.5-oz bag)

1 In a 10-inch nonstick skillet, cook the bacon over medium-high heat until crisp; drain on paper towels. Crumble the bacon; set aside. Meanwhile, in a small bowl, combine the mayonnaise, yogurt, vinegar and blue cheese.

2 On each of 6 serving plates, place 1 lettuce wedge. Arrange the chicken, apple, onion and walnuts around each wedge. Drizzle with blue cheese dressing; sprinkle with the bacon.

Nutritional Info: 1 Serving: Calories 540; Total Fat 42g (Saturated Fat 9g); Sodium 600mg; Total Carbohydrate 14g (Dietary Fiber 3g); Protein 27g. Exchanges: 1/2 Other Carbohydrate, 1 Vegetable, 3-1/2 Lean Meat, 6-1/2 Fat. Carbohydrate Choices: 1.

Betty's Kitchen Tip

Glazed nuts can be found in the crouton or baking aisle of your supermarket. The sweetness adds a nice dimension to the flavors in Chicken Wedge Salad, but you can also use regular walnuts or even pecans, if desired.

lemon-pepper chicken salad

Prep Time: 20 Minutes
Start to Finish: 20 Minutes
Servings: 4

QUICK

- 3/4 cup Progresso® lemon pepper panko crispy bread crumbs
- 1 package (14 oz) chicken breast tenders (not breaded)
- 1 bag (9 oz) romaine lettuce (6 cups)
- 2 oranges, peeled, sectioned and chopped
- 1/2 cup tropical mango-olive oil vinaigrette dressing

Sliced almonds, if desired

1 Heat oven to 400°F. Line a cookie sheet with a piece of cooking parchment paper or spray with cooking spray.

2 Place bread crumbs in a shallow dish. Add chicken tenders to a dish; press crumbs into the chicken to coat well. Place chicken on the cookie sheet. Bake 12 to 15 minutes or until no longer pink. Cut chicken into 1-inch pieces.

3 Divide the lettuce among 4 salad plates or shallow bowls. Top evenly with chicken and orange pieces. Drizzle each salad with 2 tablespoons dressing. Garnish with sliced almonds.

Nutritional Info: 1 Serving: Calories 320; Total Fat 13g (Saturated Fat 0.5g); Sodium 750mg; Total Carbohydrate 27g (Dietary Fiber 3g); Protein 24g. Exchanges: 1-1/2 Starch, 1/2 Other Carbohydrate, 2-1/2 Very Lean Meat, 2 Fat. Carbohydrate Choices: 2.

Betty's Kitchen Tip

If you can't find a bottled mango vinaigrette, look for other fruit vinaigrettes such as orange, lemon or raspberry.

summer layered chicken salad

Prep Time: 15 Minutes
Start to Finish: 15 Minutes
Servings: 6

EASY QUICK

Salad

7	cups torn romaine lettuce
1	package (9 oz) frozen cooked chicken breast strips, thawed
1/2	cup crumbled Gorgonzola cheese (2 oz)
1/2	cup pecan halves
1	quart fresh strawberries, quartered (3 cups)

Dressing

2	tablespoons sugar
3	tablespoons red wine vinegar
2	tablespoons olive or vegetable oil
1	teaspoon Dijon mustard
1/2	teaspoon salt
1	clove garlic, finely chopped

1 In a deep 3-quart salad bowl, place half of the lettuce. Layer with the chicken, cheese, pecans, the remaining lettuce and the strawberries.

2 In a small bowl or a glass measuring cup, mix the dressing ingredients with a wire whisk until *f*well blended. Just before serving, pour dressing over the salad.

Nutritional Info: 1 Serving: Calories 240; Total Fat 13g (Saturated Fat 2g); Sodium 470mg; Total Carbohydrate 18g (Dietary Fiber 4g); Protein 14g. Exchanges: 1 Other Carbohydrate, 2 Very Lean Meat, 2-1/2 Fat. Carbohydrate Choices: 1.

Betty's Kitchen Tip

The salad and dressing can be made ahead, separately. Cover each with plastic wrap and refrigerate up to 4 hours before serving.

BREADS&BAKED GOODS

p. 159

156

158

169

monkey bread

Prep Time: 20 Minutes
Start to Finish: 1 Hour 5 Minutes
Servings: 12

- 3 cups Original Bisquick® mix
- 2 tablespoons granulated sugar, divided
- 1/4 cup butter (do not use margarine), melted
- 1/4 cup milk
- 1 teaspoon vanilla

- 3 eggs
- 1/4 cup granulated sugar
- 1/2 teaspoon ground cinnamon
- 1 cup butter (do not use margarine)
- 3/4 cup packed brown sugar

1 Heat oven to 350°F. Spray a 12-cup fluted tube cake pan with cooking spray.

2 In a large bowl, stir the Bisquick mix, 2 tablespoons granulated sugar, 1/4 cup butter, the milk, vanilla and eggs until a soft dough forms. Divide the dough into 24 pieces. With greased hands, roll the dough into balls.

3 In a small bowl, mix 1/4 cup granulated sugar and the cinnamon. Roll each dough ball in the sugar mixture; place balls randomly in the pan. Sprinkle with any remaining sugar mixture.

4 In a 2-quart saucepan, melt 1 cup butter. Stir in the brown sugar; heat to boiling over medium heat, stirring constantly. Boil 2 minutes; remove from heat. Pour the caramel mixture over dough balls in pan.

5 Bake 22 to 28 minutes or until lightly browned on top. Cool 3 to 5 minutes. Place a heatproof serving plate upside down over the pan; turn the plate and pan over. Remove pan; cool 10 minutes. Serve warm.

Nutritional Info: 1 Serving: Calories 380; Total Fat 22g (Saturated Fat 12g); Sodium 510mg; Total Carbohydrate 40g (Dietary Fiber 0g); Protein 4g. Exchanges: 2 Starch, 1/2 Other Carbohydrate, 4 Fat. Carbohydrate Choices: 2-1/2.

Betty's Kitchen Tip

Make sure you always have the ingredients for this recipe in your pantry and refrigerator, so you can bake up this family favorite as a weekend surprise. Be sure to firmly pack the brown sugar when measuring it for the caramel mixture.

bacon biscuits
with orange-honey butter

Prep Time: 20 Minutes
Start to Finish: 30 Minutes
Servings: 8 (1 biscuit and 1 tablespoon butter each)

8	slices bacon, cut into 1/2-inch pieces
1-1/4	cups Original Bisquick® mix
1/2	cup yellow cornmeal
1/4	cup sugar
1/2	cup milk
1/4	cup butter, softened
3	tablespoons orange marmalade
1	tablespoon honey

1. Heat oven to 425°F. In a 10-inch nonstick skillet, cook bacon over medium-high heat, stirring frequently, until crisp. Drain on paper towels.

2. In a medium bowl, stir the Bisquick mix, cornmeal, sugar and bacon. Stir in the milk until a soft dough forms. On an ungreased cookie sheet, drop dough by 8 spoonfuls. Bake 7 to 9 minutes or until golden brown.

3. In a small bowl, beat butter, marmalade and honey with a whisk until blended. Serve the warm biscuits with the orange-honey butter.

Nutritional Info: 1 Serving: Calories 260; Total Fat 12g (Saturated Fat 6g); Sodium 450mg; Total Carbohydrate 34g (Dietary Fiber 1g); Protein 5g. Exchanges: 1 Starch, 1 Other Carbohydrate, 1/2 Medium-Fat Meat, 2 Fat. Carbohydrate Choices: 2.

Betty's Kitchen Tip

Try serving these biscuits with other flavored butters. Simply substitute your favorite flavor of jam, jelly or preserves for the orange marmalade. Save time by purchasing cooked real bacon pieces in a jar or package rather than cooking sliced bacon.

rosemary-lemon cream scones

Prep Time: 25 Minutes
Start to Finish: 50 Minutes
Servings: 8 scones

Tammy Love
Dallas, NC
Better with Bisquick® Recipe Contest

Scones

2-1/2	cups Original Bisquick® mix
1/3	cup granulated sugar
2	tablespoons cold butter
1	egg, beaten
1	container (6 oz) Yoplait® 99% Fat Free Original lemon burst yogurt
1/4	cup heavy whipping cream

1	tablespoon grated lemon peel
1	tablespoon finely chopped fresh rosemary leaves
1	tablespoon heavy whipping cream
1	tablespoon granulated sugar

Lemon Drizzle

1/2	cup powdered sugar
1	tablespoon lemon juice

1 Heat oven to 400°F. Generously spray a cookie sheet with cooking spray.

2 In a large bowl, combine Bisquick mix and 1/3 cup granulated sugar. Cut in butter, using a pastry blender (or pulling 2 table knives through ingredients in opposite directions), until mixture looks like coarse crumbs. In a small bowl, mix the egg, yogurt and 1/4 cup whipping cream. Stir into crumb mixture just until combined. Stir in lemon peel and rosemary.

3 Place dough on a cookie sheet; using greased hands, pat the dough into an 8-inch round. Brush the dough with 1 tablespoon whipping cream; sprinkle with 1 tablespoon granulated sugar. Cut into 8 wedges with a sharp knife dipped in additional Bisquick mix, but do not separate into wedges.

4 Bake 15 to 20 minutes or until light golden brown. Carefully cut into wedges and immediately remove from a cookie sheet to the cooling rack. Cool 5 minutes. Meanwhile, in a small bowl, mix powdered sugar and lemon juice. Drizzle over scones. Serve warm.

Nutritional Info: 1 Scone: Calories 320; Total Fat 13g (Saturated Fat 6g); Sodium 500mg; Total Carbohydrate 46g (Dietary Fiber 1g); Protein 4g. Exchanges: 1-1/2 Starch, 1-1/2 Other Carbohydrate, 2-1/2 Fat. Carbohydrate Choices: 3.

Betty's Kitchen Tip

The flavor combination of rosemary and lemon is both unexpected and refreshing. Serve these at any time of day.

pear and ginger muffins

Prep Time: 15 Minutes
Start to Finish: 35 Minutes
Servings: 12 muffins

EASY

2	cups Bisquick Heart Smart® mix
2/3	cup milk
1	egg
1/3	cup packed brown sugar
2	tablespoons vegetable oil
1	teaspoon ground cinnamon
1	teaspoon grated gingerroot
1	cup chopped unpeeled pear

1 Heat oven to 400°F. Place a paper baking cup in each of 12 regular-size muffin cups.

2 In a medium bowl, combine all ingredients except pear. Fold in the pear. Divide batter evenly among muffin cups.

3 Bake 17 to 20 minutes or until golden brown. Immediately remove from pan to a wire rack. Serve warm, if desired.

Nutritional Info: 1 Muffin: Calories 140; Total Fat 4.5g (Saturated Fat 0.5g); Sodium 180mg; Total Carbohydrate 22g (Dietary Fiber 0g); Protein 2g. Exchanges: 1 Starch, 1/2 Other Carbohydrate, 1 Fat. Carbohydrate Choices: 1-1/2.

Betty's Kitchen Tip

Gingerroot can be found in the produce section at the grocery store. Peel before grating. Wrap the unused portion tightly in foil and store in the freezer. Freeze leftover muffins and reheat in the microwave when ready to eat.

cranberry-lemon tea bread

Prep Time: 20 Minutes
Start to Finish: 2 Hours 45 Minutes
Servings: 16 (1 slice each)

- 1 tablespoon granulated sugar
- 1 box Betty Crocker® SuperMoist® lemon cake mix
- 1 cup sweetened dried cranberries
- 1 box (4-serving size) cheesecake instant pudding and pie filling mix
- 1 cup water

- 1/3 cup vegetable oil
- 4 eggs
- 1 oz cream cheese, softened
- 1-1/2 cups powdered sugar
- 2 tablespoons milk
- 1 tablespoon fresh lemon juice
- 1 tablespoon grated lemon peel, if desired

1 Heat oven to 350°F. Coat 2 (8x4-inch) loaf pans with cooking spray; sprinkle 1-1/2 teaspoons granulated sugar in each pan.

2 In a small bowl, toss 2 tablespoons of the cake mix with cranberries. In a large bowl, beat the remaining cake mix, dry pudding mix, water, oil and eggs with an electric mixer on low speed until moistened; beat 2 minutes on high speed, scraping the bowl occasionally. Stir in the cranberries. Divide the batter evenly between the pans.

3 Bake 40 to 45 minutes or until a toothpick inserted in the center comes out clean. Cool 10 minutes; remove from pans to a cooling rack. Cool completely, about 1 hour 30 minutes.

4 In a medium bowl, beat the cream cheese, powdered sugar, milk and lemon juice until smooth and thin enough to drizzle. Pour glaze over the bread, allowing some to drizzle down the sides. Sprinkle with lemon peel.

Nutritional Info: 1 Slice: Calories 289; Total Fat 9g (Saturated Fat 2g); Sodium 326mg; Total Carbohydrate 50g (Dietary Fiber 0g); Protein 3g. Exchanges: 3 Other Carbohydrate, 1-1/2 Fat. Carbohydrate Choices: 3.

Betty's Kitchen Tip

Grated orange peel would also be a nice topping for this sweet and moist snack loaf.

spiced blueberry muffins

Prep Time: 10 Minutes
Start to Finish: 30 Minutes
Servings: 12 muffins

EASY QUICK

2	cups Original Bisquick® mix
2/3	cup milk
1/4	cup butter or margarine, melted
1	egg
1/3	cup sugar
3/4	teaspoon ground cinnamon
1/2	teaspoon ground ginger
1/4	teaspoon ground nutmeg
3/4	cup fresh or frozen blueberries

1 Heat oven to 400°F. Place a paper baking cup in each of 12 regular-size muffin cups.

2 In a large bowl, combine all ingredients except the blueberries. Gently fold in the blueberries. Divide the batter evenly among the muffin cups.

3 Bake 17 to 20 minutes or until golden brown. Remove from the pan to a cooling rack. Serve warm, if desired.

Nutritional Info: 1 Muffin: Calories 160; Total Fat 7g (Saturated Fat 3.5g); Sodium 280mg; Total Carbohydrate 21g (Dietary Fiber 0g); Protein 2g. Exchanges: 1 Starch, 1/2 Other Carbohydrate, 1-1/2 Fat. Carbohydrate Choices: 1-1/2.

Betty's Kitchen Tip

Fill each of the muffin cups with scant 1/4 cup of batter. If you use frozen blueberries, don't thaw them before folding into the batter.

lemon-blueberry scones

Prep Time: 15 Minutes
Start to Finish: 45 Minutes
Servings: 8 scones

EASY

2	cups Gold Medal® all-purpose flour	2	teaspoons grated lemon peel
3	teaspoons baking powder	1/2	cup dried blueberries
1/4	cup sugar, divided	1	cup whipping cream
1/3	cup cold butter, cut into small pieces	1/2	teaspoon vanilla

1 Heat oven to 425°F. Line cookie sheet with cooking parchment paper.

2 In a food processor bowl with a metal blade, place the flour, baking powder and 3 tablespoons of the sugar. Cover; process with on-and-off pulses 6 times or until blended. Add the butter, scattering evenly over the dry ingredients, and lemon peel. Cover; process with on-and-off pulses 12 times or until mixture is the consistency of coarse crumbs.

3 Transfer crumb mixture to a large bowl. Add the blueberries, tossing with a fork until blended. Add the whipping cream and vanilla, tossing with a fork just until dough begins to form, about 30 seconds (do not overmix).

4 On a cookie sheet, press dough into an 8-inch round. Cut into 8 wedges; separate wedges slightly. Sprinkle the remaining 1 tablespoon sugar evenly over wedges.

5 Bake scones 14 to 16 minutes or until golden brown. Cool on a cooling rack about 10 minutes. Serve scones warm or at room temperature.

Nutritional Info: 1 Scone: Calories 322; Total Fat 18g (Saturated Fat 11g); Sodium 232mg; Total Carbohydrate 37g (Dietary Fiber 1g); Protein 3g. Exchanges: 1-1/2 Starch, 1/2 Fruit, 1/2 Other Carbohydrate, 3 Fat. Carbohydrate Choices: 2-1/2.

Betty's Kitchen Tip

Want tender, evenly baked scones? Place the dough between two 1/2-inch-thick dowel rods. Roll the dough to an even thickness without over-handling it.

banana-rum raisin mini loaves

Prep Time: 15 Minutes
Start to Finish: 3 Hours 50 Minutes
Servings: 16

EASY

2/3	cup light rum
1/2	cup golden raisins
4	(5x3-inch) foil loaf pans
1	box (15.5 oz) Betty Crocker® banana nut muffin quick bread mix
1/2	cup canned coconut milk (not cream of coconut)
3	tablespoons vegetable oil
2	eggs
3	tablespoons flaked coconut
2/3	cup powdered sugar

1 Reserve 2 tablespoons rum. In a 1-quart saucepan, heat the raisins and remaining rum to boiling over medium-high heat. Remove from heat. Cover; let stand 1 hour. Heat oven to 375°F. Spray bottoms only of foil loaf pans with cooking spray.

2 In a medium bowl, stir the quick bread mix, raisin-rum mixture, coconut milk, oil and eggs just until moistened. Pour into the mini loaf pans.

3 Bake 30 minutes or until a toothpick inserted in center comes out clean. Cool 5 minutes. Run a knife around the sides of the pans to loosen the loaves; remove from pans to cooling racks. Cool completely, about 1 hour. Return loaves to the pans. Heat oven to 350°F. Bake the coconut in a shallow pan 5 to 7 minutes, stirring occasionally, until golden brown.

4 In a small bowl, mix the powdered sugar and reserved 2 tablespoons rum. Drizzle over tops of loaves; sprinkle with coconut. Let stand 1 hour or until glaze is set.

Nutritional Info: 1 Serving: Calories 209; Total Fat 7g (Saturated Fat 2g); Sodium 172mg; Total Carbohydrate 30g (Dietary Fiber 0g); Protein 3g. Exchanges: 1/2 Starch, 1-1/2 Other Carbohydrate, 1-1/2 Fat. Carbohydrate Choices: 2.

Betty's Kitchen Tip

If you're wrapping up these mini loaves as gifts, be sure that the bread is cooled completely and the glaze is firmly set before packaging. Doing so will avoid a messy presentation.

coffee-crunch banana bread

Prep Time: 25 Minutes
Start to Finish: 2 Hours 40 Minutes
Servings: 16 (1 slice each)

1/4 cup packed brown sugar	1/3 cup butter, softened
1/4 cup quick-cooking oats	1 cup granulated sugar
1/4 cup chopped walnuts	2 eggs
2 tablespoons cold butter, cut into small pieces	1-1/2 cups mashed very ripe bananas (3 large)
1 teaspoon instant coffee granules or crystals	1 teaspoon vanilla
2 cups Gold Medal® all-purpose flour	1/3 cup Yoplait® Light Fat Free creamy vanilla yogurt (from 2-lb container)
3/4 teaspoon baking soda	1/2 cup powdered sugar
1/2 teaspoon salt	2 teaspoons milk

1 Heat oven to 350°F. Spray bottom only of a 9x5-inch loaf pan with cooking spray.

2 For the coffee crunch topping, in a small bowl, mix first 5 ingredients with fingers until mixture holds together in clumps.

3 In a small bowl, mix flour, baking soda and salt. In a large bowl, beat 1/3 cup butter and the granulated sugar with an electric mixer on medium speed until blended. Add the eggs, one at a time, beating well after each addition. Add the bananas, vanilla and yogurt; beat on low speed. Slowly add the flour mixture, beating just until blended. Pour into pan. Sprinkle coffee-crunch topping over the batter.

4 Bake 60 to 65 minutes or until a toothpick inserted in the center comes out clean. Remove from the pan to a cooling rack. Cool completely.

5 For the glaze, mix powdered sugar and milk until thin enough to drizzle over loaf.

Nutritional Info: 1 Slice: Calories 219; Total Fat 8g (Saturated Fat 4g); Sodium 183mg; Total Carbohydrate 36g (Dietary Fiber 1g); Protein 3g. Exchanges: 1 Starch, 1 Other Carbohydrate, 1 Fat. Carbohydrate Choices: 2.

Betty's Kitchen Tip

Stir 1/2 cup dark or milk chocolate chips into the banana bread batter for a mouthwatering flavor combination.

irish yogurt bread

Prep Time: 10 Minutes
Start to Finish: 30 Minutes
Servings: 8

1-3/4   cups Gold Medal® all-purpose flour
 1/2   cup currants or raisins
1-1/2   teaspoons baking powder
 1/4   teaspoon baking soda
 1/4   teaspoon salt
   1   container (6 oz) Yoplait® lemon burst, orange crème or French vanilla yogurt
   2   tablespoons vegetable oil

1 Heat oven to 375°F. Lightly grease bottom and side of 9-inch round cake pan with shortening.

2 In a medium bowl, mix flour, currants, baking powder, baking soda and salt. In a small bowl, mix the yogurt and oil; stir into flour mixture just until moistened. Spread dough in the pan.

3 Bake about 20 minutes or until a toothpick inserted in the center comes out clean. Cut into wedges. Serve warm or cool.

Nutritional Info: 1 Serving: Calories 173; Total Fat 4g (Saturated Fat 1g); Sodium 206mg; Total Carbohydrate 30g (Dietary Fiber 1g); Protein 4g. Exchanges: 1-1/2 Starch, 1/2 Other Carbohydrate, 1/2 Fat. Carbohydrate Choices: 2.

Betty's Kitchen Tip

For a quick, fruity topping for these tasty wedges, mix equal parts of plain or flavored yogurt and your favorite preserves and spread over the top.

glazed orange-ginger scones

Prep Time: 20 Minutes
Start to Finish: 40 Minutes
Servings: 8 scones

---

2 cups Gold Medal® all-purpose flour	3/4 cup whipping cream
1/3 cup granulated sugar	2 tablespoons fresh orange juice
2 tablespoons chopped crystallized ginger	2 tablespoons whipping cream
1 tablespoon baking powder	1/2 cup powdered sugar
1 tablespoon grated orange peel	3 to 4 teaspoons milk or whipping cream
1/2 teaspoon salt	
1/2 cup cold butter or margarine, cut into small pieces	

---

1 Heat oven to 425°F. Line a cookie sheet with cooking parchment paper.

2 In a large bowl, combine the flour, granulated sugar, ginger, baking powder, orange peel and salt until blended. Cut in the butter, using a pastry blender (or pulling 2 table knives through mixture in opposite directions), until mixture looks like fine crumbs. Stir in 3/4 cup whipping cream and the orange juice until a soft dough forms.

3 On a lightly floured surface, pat the dough into a 7-inch circle. Cut into 8 wedges. Place wedges 2 inches apart on the cookie sheet. Brush the dough with 2 tablespoons whipping cream.

4 Bake 15 to 18 minutes or until golden brown. In a small bowl, mix the powdered sugar and enough milk until it is thin enough to drizzle. Drizzle over the scones. Serve warm.

Nutritional Info: 1 Scone: Calories 395; Total Fat 23g (Saturated Fat 14g); Sodium 392mg; Total Carbohydrate 46g (Dietary Fiber 1g); Protein 4g. Exchanges: 1-1/2 Starch, 1 Other Carbohydrate, 4-1/2 Fat. Carbohydrate Choices: 3.

Betty's Kitchen Tip

To shape the scones, push a scone cutter (dipped in flour) straight into the dough. Try not to twist as you cut so that scones are of equal size. Cut scones as close together as possible.

sour cream-butter muffins

Prep Time: 10 Minutes
Start to Finish: 40 Minutes
Servings: 36 muffins

EASY

2-1/2	cups Original Bisquick® mix
3/4	cup butter, melted
2	tablespoons chopped fresh chives
1	container (8 oz) sour cream

1 Heat oven to 350°F. Lightly spray 36 mini muffin cups with cooking spray.

2 In a large bowl, mix all ingredients just until moistened. Divide batter evenly among the muffin cups, filling almost to the top.

3 Bake 25 minutes or until lightly browned. Cool 2 minutes; remove the muffins from pans. Serve warm.

Nutritional Info: 1 Muffin: Calories 80; Total Fat 6g (Saturated Fat 4g); Sodium 133mg; Total Carbohydrate 6g (Dietary Fiber 0g); Protein 1g. Exchanges: 1/2 Starch, 1 Fat. Carbohydrate Choices: 1/2.

Betty's Kitchen Tip

These mini biscuit-type treats are a blank canvas for just about any fresh herb that's available in your grocer's produce section— or in your herb garden!

streusel pumpkin muffins

Prep Time: 20 Minutes
Start to Finish: 45 Minutes
Servings: 12 muffins

1-1/2	cups Gold Medal® all-purpose flour	2	tablespoons vegetable oil
1	cup packed brown sugar	1	egg
1	teaspoon baking soda	3/4	cup crushed gingersnaps (about 13 cookies)
1	teaspoon pumpkin pie spice	3	tablespoons Gold Medal® all-purpose flour
1/4	teaspoon salt	3	tablespoons packed brown sugar
1	cup canned pumpkin (not pumpkin pie mix)	3	tablespoons butter, softened
1/2	cup buttermilk		Sliced almonds, if desired

1 Heat oven to 350°F. Place a paper baking cup in each of 12 regular-size muffin cups. Spray baking cups with cooking spray.

2 In a large bowl, mix 1-1/2 cups flour, 1 cup brown sugar, the baking soda, pumpkin pie spice and salt. Stir in the pumpkin, buttermilk, oil and egg just until mixture is moistened. Divide the batter evenly among muffin cups.

3 In a small bowl, mix the gingersnaps, 3 tablespoons flour, 3 tablespoons brown sugar and the butter with a fork until crumbly. Sprinkle evenly over the batter in each cup.

4 Bake 24 minutes or until a toothpick inserted in the center comes out clean. Remove muffins from the pan to a cooling rack. Sprinkle with the sliced almonds, if desired. Serve warm.

Nutritional Info: 1 Muffin: Calories 218; Total Fat 6g (Saturated Fat 2g); Sodium 213mg; Total Carbohydrate 38g (Dietary Fiber 1g); Protein 3g. Exchanges: 1 Starch, 1 Other Carbohydrate, 1 Fat. Carbohydrate Choices: 2.

Betty's Kitchen Tip

Use a spring-handled #20 or #24 ice-cream scoop to fill regular-size muffin cups about three-quarters full with batter—just the right amount to give muffins nicely rounded tops.

harvest bread

Prep Time: 15 Minutes
Start to Finish: 2 Hours 20 Minutes
Servings: 16 (1 slice each)

EASY

1	can (8 oz) crushed pineapple in juice, drained, juice reserved
1/4	cup fat-free egg product or 1 egg, beaten
2	tablespoons canola or soybean oil
2	cups Gold Medal® all-purpose flour
3/4	cup packed brown sugar
1/2	cup raisins
1	teaspoon baking powder
1/2	teaspoon baking soda
1/2	teaspoon salt
1/2	teaspoon ground cinnamon
1	cup shredded carrots (2 small)
1	cup chopped walnuts

1 Heat oven to 350°F. Spray an 8x4-inch loaf pan with cooking spray.

2 Discard 3 tablespoons of the pineapple juice. In a medium bowl, mix remaining juice, the pineapple, egg product and oil. Stir in remaining ingredients until blended. Spread batter in pan.

3 Bake 50 to 60 minutes or until toothpick inserted in center comes out clean. Cool in the pan 10 minutes; remove from pan to cooling rack. Cool completely, about 1 hour, before slicing.

Nutritional Info: 1 Slice: Calories 180; Total Fat 7g (Saturated Fat 0.5g); Sodium 160mg; Total Carbohydrate 27g (Dietary Fiber 1g); Protein 3g. Exchanges: 1 Starch, 1 Other Carbohydrate, 1 Fat. Carbohydrate Choices: 2.

Betty's Kitchen Tip

Wrap the cooled loaf tightly in plastic wrap and store at room temperature up to 4 days.

garlic-rosemary french rolls

Prep Time: 10 Minutes
Start to Finish: 20 Minutes
Servings: 10 rolls

EASY QUICK

1   bag (12.4 oz) Pillsbury® frozen crusty French dinner rolls (10 rolls)

3   tablespoons olive or vegetable oil

1   teaspoon finely crushed dried rosemary leaves

1/2   teaspoon garlic powder

1   tablespoon shredded Asiago or Parmesan cheese, if desired

1 Heat oven to 425°F. Place rolls on an ungreased cookie sheet. Bake 4 minutes.

2 Meanwhile, in a small bowl, mix the olive oil, rosemary and garlic powder. Remove rolls from the oven. With a serrated knife, carefully cut an X shape in each of the rolls, cutting about halfway through. Generously brush the oil mixture over and into each roll. Sprinkle with cheese.

3 Bake 2 to 3 minutes longer or until golden brown. Serve warm.

Nutritional Info: 1 Roll: Calories 140; Total Fat 6g (Saturated Fat 0.5g); Sodium 200mg; Total Carbohydrate 18g (Dietary Fiber 0g); Protein 4g. Exchanges: 1 Starch, 1 Fat. Carbohydrate Choices: 1.

Betty's Kitchen Tip

If you are really in a hurry, you can omit the cutting step and brush the tops of the rolls with the olive oil mixture.

SAVORY SIDES

p. 173

174

182

175

swiss chard gratin

Prep Time: 1 Hour 30 Minutes
Start to Finish: 1 Hour 55 Minutes
Servings: 6 (1/2 cup each)

2	large bunches Swiss chard
1	cup soft bread crumbs, lightly toasted
1	cup shredded Parmesan or Gruyère cheese (4 oz)
2	tablespoons butter or margarine, melted
1	cup whipping cream

3	cloves garlic, crushed
1/4	cup butter or margarine
1	large red onion, finely chopped (1 cup)
1/2	teaspoon salt
1/4	teaspoon pepper

1 Heat oven to 400°F. Spray a shallow 1-1/2-quart casserole or gratin dish with cooking spray. Rinse the Swiss chard; shake to remove excess moisture and pat dry. Cut leaves from the stalks; finely chop the stalks and leaves and keep separate.

2 In a small bowl, combine bread crumbs, cheese and melted butter; set aside. In a 1-quart saucepan, heat the cream and garlic to boiling. Reduce heat; simmer 2 minutes. Remove from heat.

3 In a 4-quart Dutch oven, melt 1/4 cup butter over medium heat. Cook onion in butter 3 minutes or until tender. Stir in chopped chard stalks; cook 12 to 14 minutes, stirring occasionally, until tender and beginning to brown. Increase heat to medium-high. Add chopped chard leaves, salt and pepper; cook 4 minutes or until wilted. Drain well, pressing with back of spoon. Spread mixture in casserole.

4 Strain the cream, discarding garlic. Pour cream over the chard. Sprinkle with the bread crumb mixture. Bake uncovered 20 to 25 minutes or until bubbly and the top is golden brown.

Nutritional Info: 1 Serving: Calories 345; Total Fat 31g (Saturated Fat 19g); Sodium 729mg; Total Carbohydrate 11g (Dietary Fiber 2g); Protein 8g. Exchanges: 1/2 Starch, 1 Vegetable, 1 High-Fat Meat, 4 Fat. Carbohydrate Choices: 1.

Betty's Kitchen Tip

Not actually Swiss, chard originated in the Mediterranean. When deciding what to buy, look for bright stalks with deep-green, unblemished leaves. Wash it immediately before using.

maple-orange sweet potatoes

Prep Time: 10 Minutes
Start to Finish: 1 Hour 25 Minutes
Servings: 8 (2/3 cup each)

EASY

6	medium-large sweet potatoes (3 lb)
1/2	cup butter or margarine, melted
1/2	cup real maple syrup
1	teaspoon grated orange peel

Juice of 1 medium orange

1/2	teaspoon salt

Fresh rosemary sprig, if desired

1 Heat oven to 375°F. Line a cookie sheet with foil. Place sweet potatoes on the cookie sheet; prick several times with a fork. Bake 1 hour or until very tender. Let stand 15 minutes.

2 Cut the potatoes in half lengthwise; scoop pulp into a large bowl. Mash the pulp well. Add butter, syrup, orange peel, orange juice and salt; mash well. Garnish with a rosemary sprig.

Nutritional Info: 1 Serving: Calories 255; Total Fat 12g (Saturated Fat 7g); Sodium 293mg; Total Carbohydrate 37g (Dietary Fiber 3g); Protein 2g. Exchanges: 1-1/2 Starch, 1/2 Other Carbohydrate, 2 Fat. Carbohydrate Choices: 2.

Betty's Kitchen Tip

To reduce the cooking time, microwave the sweet potatoes, two at a time, on microwavable paper towels on High 8 to 10 minutes or until tender; proceed to step 2.

crescent-cornbread dressing

Prep Time: 20 Minutes
Start to Finish: 1 Hour 30 Minutes
Servings: 10 (1 cup each)

2 cans (8 oz each) Pillsbury® refrigerated crescent dinner rolls	1 container (8 oz) refrigerated chopped onion, celery and pepper mix
2 pouches (6.5 oz each) Betty Crocker® cornbread & muffin mix	2 cloves garlic, finely chopped
2/3 cup milk	1/4 cup butter or margarine, melted
1/4 cup butter or margarine	1 teaspoon dried sage leaves
3 eggs	1 carton (32 oz) Progresso® chicken broth (4 cups)
4 slices bacon	1 egg

1 Heat oven to 375°F. Bake the crescent rolls as directed on the package.

2 Increase the oven temperature to 400°F. Make and bake cornbread as directed on the package, using milk, 1/4 cup butter and 3 eggs. Cool completely.

3 Spray a 13x9-inch (3-quart) baking dish with cooking spray. In a 10-inch skillet, cook bacon until crisp; drain on paper towels. Crumble the bacon; set aside. Add onion, celery and pepper mix and garlic to bacon drippings; cook over medium-high heat, stirring occasionally, until tender.

4 In a large bowl, crumble the crescent rolls and cornbread. Stir in the onion mixture, bacon, melted butter, sage, broth and 1 egg until blended. Spoon into the baking dish.

5 Bake uncovered 45 to 50 minutes or until browned.

Nutritional Info: 1 Serving: Calories 526; Total Fat 30g (Saturated Fat 14g); Sodium 1153mg; Total Carbohydrate 50g (Dietary Fiber 1g); Protein 14g. Exchanges: 3-1/2 Starch, 1/2 Medium-Fat Meat, 5 Fat. Carbohydrate Choices: 3-1/2.

Betty's Kitchen Tip

Turn leftovers of this well-loved side dish into stuffing for mushrooms: Heat oven to 350°F. Remove stems from fresh mushrooms; reserve caps. Spoon about 1 teaspoon stuffing into each mushroom cap. Bake on an ungreased cookie sheet until heated through, about 10 minutes.

roasted red potatoes

Prep Time: 15 Minutes
Start to Finish: 1 Hour 30 Minutes
Servings: 4

EASY

- 12 small unpeeled red potatoes (about 1-1/2 lb)
- 2 tablespoons olive or vegetable oil
- 2 medium green onions with tops, sliced (2 tablespoons)
- 2 tablespoons chopped fresh or 2 teaspoons dried rosemary leaves, crushed

1 Heat oven to 350°F. In an ungreased 8- or 9-inch square pan or 13x9-inch pan, place potatoes. Drizzle oil over the potatoes; turn potatoes so all sides are coated.

2 Sprinkle the onions and rosemary over the potatoes; stir.

3 Roast uncovered about 1 hour 15 minutes, stirring occasionally, until the potatoes are tender when pierced with a fork.

Nutritional Info: 1 Serving: Calories 200; Total Fat 7g (Saturated Fat 1g); Sodium 10mg; Total Carbohydrate 31g (Dietary Fiber 4g); Protein 3g. Exchanges: 1-1/2 Starch, 1/2 Other Carbohydrate, 1 Fat. Carbohydrate Choices: 2.

Betty's Kitchen Tip

Most small red potatoes are about 2 inches in diameter. If they are much bigger, cut them in half so they will roast more quickly.

butternut squash spoon bread

Prep Time: 20 Minutes
Start to Finish: 1 Hour 45 Minutes
Servings: 8

2	packages (12 oz each) refrigerated chopped butternut squash (5 cups)
1/2	cup freshly grated Parmesan cheese
1/4	cup Gold Medal® all-purpose flour
1/2	cup butter or margarine, melted
1	cup milk

1	tablespoon chopped fresh or 1 teaspoon dried sage leaves
1/2	teaspoon salt
4	eggs, separated
1/4	cup finely chopped walnuts, toasted

1 Heat oven to 425°F. Spray a 15x10x1-inch pan with cooking spray. Place squash in a single layer in the pan. Bake 40 minutes, stirring after 20 minutes, or until tender. Cool 5 minutes. Reduce oven temperature to 350°F.

2 Spray 8 (4-oz) custard cups or ramekins with cooking spray. Place cups on a cookie sheet. In a food processor, place squash, cheese, flour, butter, milk, sage, salt and egg yolks. Cover; process, using quick on-and-off pulses, until well blended. Spoon squash mixture into a large bowl.

3 In a medium bowl, beat egg whites with an electric mixer on high speed until stiff peaks form. Fold into the squash mixture. Divide evenly among custard cups.

4 Bake 35 to 40 minutes or until slightly puffed and golden brown. Sprinkle with walnuts. Serve warm.

Nutritional Info: 1 Serving: Calories 259; Total Fat 19g (Saturated Fat 10g); Sodium 390mg; Total Carbohydrate 16g (Dietary Fiber 2g); Protein 9g. Exchanges: 1/2 Starch, 1-1/2 Vegetable, 1 Medium-Fat Meat, 2-1/2 Fat. Carbohydrate Choices: 1.

Betty's Kitchen Tip

Butternut squash is a tan-skinned, orange-fleshed vegetable with a long neck and a bulbous end. When selecting a butternut squash at the market, look for one with a hard, tough rind that feels heavy for its size.

roasted candied carrots

Prep Time: 15 Minutes
Start to Finish: 45 Minutes
Servings: 6 (1 cup each)

EASY

2	tablespoons olive oil
1/4	cup honey
1	teaspoon ground cumin
1/2	teaspoon smoked paprika
1/2	teaspoon seasoned salt
1	bag (2 lb) fresh carrots, cut into 2-1/2-inch pieces

1 Heat oven to 450°F. Place a 15x10x1-inch pan in the oven 10 minutes to preheat. Meanwhile, in a large bowl, mix all the ingredients except carrots until blended. Add the carrots; toss to coat.

2 Spray the hot pan with cooking spray. Place the carrots in single layer in pan.

3 Roast uncovered 30 minutes, stirring once, until golden brown. Immediately remove carrots from the pan.

Nutritional Info: 1 Serving: Calories 118; Total Fat 4g (Saturated Fat 1g); Sodium 149mg; Total Carbohydrate 21g (Dietary Fiber 3g); Protein 1g. Exchanges: 1/2 Other Carbohydrate, 2 Vegetable, 1 Fat. Carbohydrate Choices: 1-1/2.

Betty's Kitchen Tip

Preheating the pan 10 minutes while you're preparing the ingredients gives the carrots a jump start on roasting.

ciabatta-sausage stuffing

Prep Time: 45 Minutes
Start to Finish: 1 Hour 30 Minutes
Servings: 10

1	large loaf ciabatta bread (1 lb), cut into 1-inch cubes (8 cups)
1	lb bulk maple-flavored pork sausage
1/4	cup butter or margarine
1-1/2	cups chopped onions
1-1/2	cups chopped peeled apples
1	cup chopped celery

2	tablespoons chopped fresh parsley
1	tablespoon chopped fresh sage leaves
1/2	teaspoon salt
1/4	teaspoon coarse ground black pepper
2	to 2-1/2 cups Progresso® chicken broth (from 32-oz carton)

1 Heat oven to 350°F. Spray bottom and sides of a 13x9-inch (3-quart) glass baking dish with cooking spray.

2 On a large, ungreased cookie sheet, place the bread cubes in a single layer. Bake 20 minutes, stirring occasionally, until dry and lightly golden. Cool 15 minutes.

3 Meanwhile, in a 12-inch skillet, cook the sausage over medium heat 6 to 8 minutes or until no longer pink. With a slotted spoon, remove the sausage. Add 2 tablespoons of the butter to drippings in the skillet. Add onions, apples and celery; cook 15 minutes, stirring occasionally, until tender. Remove from heat.

4 In a large bowl, toss the apple mixture, parsley, sage, salt, pepper, sausage and bread cubes. Mix in 2 cups broth; add 1/2 cup more broth if mixture looks dry. Spoon stuffing into the baking dish. Dot with remaining 2 tablespoons butter.

5 Bake uncovered 40 to 45 minutes or until golden brown.

Nutritional Info: 1 Serving: Calories 369; Total Fat 21g (Saturated Fat 9g); Sodium 942mg; Total Carbohydrate 36g (Dietary Fiber 2g); Protein 11g. Exchanges: 2-1/2 Starch, 1 High-Fat Meat, 2 Fat. Carbohydrate Choices: 2-1/2.

Betty's Kitchen Tip

Just about any kind of bread makes great stuffing! Try whole grain, sourdough, rye, herb or cornbread. You can even mix and match bread varieties if you'd like.

maple-glazed brussels sprouts

Prep Time: 30 Minutes
Start to Finish: 30 Minutes
Servings: 8 (1/2 cup each)

QUICK

6 slices maple-flavored bacon	1/3 cup real maple syrup
1-3/4 lb Brussels sprouts, trimmed, halved (6 cups)	3/4 teaspoon salt
2 shallots, finely chopped	3/4 teaspoon freshly ground pepper
1/2 cup chicken broth	1/2 cup chopped pecans, toasted

1 In a 12-inch nonstick skillet, cook bacon until crisp; drain on paper towels. Crumble bacon; set aside. Add Brussels sprouts and shallots to drippings in skillet; cook over medium-high heat, stirring occasionally, until browned.

2 Add broth to the skillet. Heat to boiling; reduce heat. Cover; simmer 5 to 10 minutes. Stir in syrup, salt and pepper. Cook uncovered over medium-high heat 2 to 4 minutes, stirring frequently, until Brussels sprouts are glazed. Sprinkle with bacon and pecans.

Nutritional Info: 1 Serving: Calories 151; Total Fat 8g (Saturated Fat 1g); Sodium 403mg; Total Carbohydrate 17g (Dietary Fiber 3g); Protein 6g. Exchanges: 1/2 Other Carbohydrate, 1 Vegetable, 1-1/2 Fat. Carbohydrate Choices: 1.

Betty's Kitchen Tip

Prep the fresh Brussels sprouts in advance and store in a resealable food-storage plastic bag in the refrigerator up to a day ahead.

corn amandine

Prep Time: 20 Minutes
Start to Finish: 20 Minutes
Servings: 6 (2/3 cup each)

QUICK

2	tablespoons butter or margarine
1/2	cup slivered almonds
2	cans (15.25 oz each) Green Giant® whole kernel sweet corn
1/4	cup water
1	teaspoon chicken bouillon granules
1/8	teaspoon garlic powder
1/8	teaspoon pepper
1	tablespoon chopped fresh parsley

1 In a 10-inch nonstick skillet, melt the butter over medium heat. Cook almonds in butter about 2 minutes, stirring frequently, until golden.

2 Stir in the corn, water, bouillon granules, garlic powder and pepper. Heat to boiling, stirring occasionally, reduce heat. Cover; simmer 3 to 5 minutes or until corn is tender. Sprinkle with parsley.

Nutritional Info: 1 Serving: Calories 190; Total Fat 9g (Saturated Fat 3g); Sodium 490mg; Total Carbohydrate 23g (Dietary Fiber 3g); Protein 5g. Exchanges: 1-1/2 Starch, 1/2 Vegetable, 1-1/2 Fat. Carbohydrate Choices: 1-1/2.

Betty's Kitchen Tip

Sliced almonds or pecan halves can be substituted for the slivered almonds.

cheesy cauliflower and broccoli

Prep Time: 35 Minutes
Start to Finish: 35 Minutes
Servings: 4 (1 cup each)

7 cups fresh cauliflower florets	2 tablespoons Gold Medal® all-purpose flour
5 cups fresh broccoli florets	1 cup milk
2 tablespoons olive oil	3/4 cup shredded sharp white Cheddar cheese (3 oz)
1/2 teaspoon salt	1/4 cup pine nuts, toasted
1/2 teaspoon freshly ground pepper	
2 tablespoons butter or margarine	

1 Heat oven to 425°F. In a large roasting pan, toss the cauliflower and broccoli with oil, salt and pepper. Roast uncovered 25 minutes, stirring occasionally, until the vegetables are browned and tender.

2 Meanwhile, in a 1-quart saucepan, melt the butter over medium-low heat. Stir in the flour. Cook and stir until the mixture is smooth and bubbly. Gradually add the milk, stirring constantly until the mixture boils and thickens. Stir in the cheese until it has melted.

3 Spoon the roasted vegetables into 4 single-size serving dishes. Pour cheese sauce over the vegetables; sprinkle with pine nuts.

Nutritional Info: 1 Serving: Calories 389; Total Fat 27g (Saturated Fat 10g); Sodium 602mg; Total Carbohydrate 26g (Dietary Fiber 10g); Protein 17g. Exchanges: 1/2 Starch, 3 Vegetable, 1 High-Fat Meat, 4 Fat. Carbohydrate Choices: 1-1/2.

Betty's Kitchen Tip

Omit the pine nuts, if desired, and add a sprinkle of fresh herbs instead. It will cut down on the fat and brighten up the flavor.

minted cranberry relish

Prep Time: 5 Minutes
Start to Finish: 3 Hours 5 Minutes
Servings: 8 (1/4 cup each)

EASY LOW FAT

- 1 small seedless orange, quartered
- 2 cups fresh or frozen (thawed) cranberries
- 1/2 cup sugar
- 3 tablespoons chopped walnuts
- 2 tablespoons chopped fresh mint leaves
- 1 tablespoon orange-flavored liqueur, if desired

1 In a food processor bowl with a metal blade, place orange pieces. Cover; process, using quick on-and-off pulses, about 15 seconds or until finely chopped. Add the cranberries; process until finely chopped.

2 In a nonmetal container, combine the cranberry mixture, sugar, walnuts and mint. Stir in the liqueur. Let mixture stand at least 3 hours before serving to allow flavors to blend. Store in the refrigerator up to 1 week.

Nutritional Info: 1 Serving: Calories 87; Total Fat 2g (Saturated Fat 0g); Sodium 1mg; Total Carbohydrate 18g (Dietary Fiber 2g); Protein 1g. Exchanges: 1/2 Other Carbohydrate, 1/2 Fruit. Carbohydrate Choices: 1.

Betty's Kitchen Tip

Fresh cranberries should be bright red and shiny; discard any that are shriveled or discolored.

cheese straw-spinach casserole

Prep Time: 25 Minutes
Start to Finish: 1 Hour
Servings: 12

3 tablespoons butter or margarine	1/4 teaspoon pepper
1 large onion, finely chopped (1-1/2 cups)	1-1/2 cups half-and-half or milk
2 cloves garlic, finely chopped	5 boxes (9 oz each) Green Giant® frozen chopped spinach, thawed, squeezed to drain
2 packages (8 oz each) cream cheese, softened	
2 tablespoons Gold Medal® all-purpose flour	2 cups shredded Cheddar cheese (8 oz)
2 eggs	2 cups cheese straws, coarsely crushed
1/2 teaspoon salt	

1 Heat oven to 350°F. Spray a 13x9-inch (3-quart) baking dish with cooking spray. In a 10-inch skillet, melt the butter over medium-high heat. Cook onion and garlic in butter, stirring frequently, until golden.

2 In a large bowl, mix cream cheese and flour until smooth. Add eggs, one at a time. Stir in salt and pepper. Beat in half-and-half with a wire whisk until blended. Add spinach, Cheddar cheese and onion mixture. Spoon the mixture into a baking dish. Sprinkle with cheese straws.

3 Bake uncovered 30 to 35 minutes or until hot and bubbly.

Nutritional Info: 1 Serving: Calories 384; Total Fat 31g (Saturated Fat 18g); Sodium 714mg; Total Carbohydrate 12g (Dietary Fiber 1g); Protein 12g. Exchanges: 1/2 Starch, 1 Vegetable, 1 High-Fat Meat, 4 Fat. Carbohydrate Choices: 1.

Betty's Kitchen Tip

Use your favorite brand of cheese straws for this casserole. For a kid-friendly version, use cheese-flavored tiny fish-shaped crackers.

golden mashed potatoes

Prep Time: 25 Minutes
Start to Finish: 45 Minutes
Servings: 10 (1/2 cup each)

LOW FAT

3   lb unpeeled Yukon gold potatoes (about 8 medium), cut into 1-inch pieces
1   tablespoon butter or olive oil
1/2   teaspoon salt
1   container (6 oz) Yoplait® Greek Fat Free plain yogurt
1/4   teaspoon fresh ground black pepper
2   tablespoons chopped fresh chives, if desired

1 In a 3-quart saucepan, place potatoes. Add enough water just to cover. Heat to boiling; reduce heat to low. Cover; simmer 15 to 20 minutes or until the potatoes are tender when pierced with a fork. Drain.

2 In the same saucepan, mash the potatoes, butter and salt with a potato masher. Gradually add the yogurt, mashing until blended and fluffy (leave some lumps in the potatoes, if desired). Stir in the pepper and chives.

Nutritional Info: 1 Serving: Calories 130; Total Fat 1.5g (Saturated Fat 1g); Sodium 150mg; Total Carbohydrate 24g (Dietary Fiber 2g); Protein 4g. Exchanges: 1-1/2 Starch. Carbohydrate Choices: 1 1/2.

Betty's Kitchen Tip

For garlic mashed potatoes, add a couple of peeled garlic cloves to the water before boiling the potatoes, then mash the garlic along with the potatoes. You can substitute chopped green onions for the fresh chives if you like.

roasted autumn vegetables

Prep Time: 20 Minutes
Start to Finish: 1 Hour 5 Minutes
Servings: 8

1   small butternut squash (about 1-1/2 lb), peeled, seeded and cut into 1-inch pieces

2   medium unpeeled Yukon gold or red potatoes, cut into 1-inch pieces

1   medium red onion, cut into thin wedges

1   large dark-orange sweet potato (about 1/2 lb), cut into 1-inch pieces

1   lb baby-cut carrots

2   tablespoons olive or vegetable oil

1   clove garlic, chopped

1   tablespoon chopped fresh or 1 teaspoon dried sage leaves

1   tablespoon chopped fresh or 1 teaspoon crushed dried rosemary leaves

1/2   teaspoon salt

1   Heat oven to 425°F. Spray a 15x10x1-inch pan with cooking spray. Place the squash, potatoes, onion, sweet potato and carrots in the pan.

2   Pour oil over the vegetables. Sprinkle with garlic, sage, rosemary and salt. Stir to coat the vegetables.

3   Bake uncovered 35 to 45 minutes, stirring occasionally, until the vegetables are crisp-tender when pierced with a fork.

Nutritional Info: 1 Serving: Calories 150; Total Fat 3.5g (Saturated Fat 0.5g); Sodium 200mg; Total Carbohydrate 26g (Dietary Fiber 4g); Protein 3g. Exchanges: 1 Starch, 1/2 Other Carbohydrate, 1/2 Fat. Carbohydrate Choices: 2

Betty's Kitchen Tip

To cut butternut squash, first remove the bottom and stem ends of the squash. Then remove the narrow part and cut the rounded bottom in half; peel and chop into pieces as desired. Other types of winter squash work well for this recipe, too, such as Hubbard or buttercup.

cakes,
CUPCAKES & CHEESECAKES

p. 195

188

194

206

salted caramel cheesecake

Prep Time: 50 Minutes
Start to Finish: 9 Hours 15 Minutes
Servings: 16

1-3/4   cups graham cracker crumbs
        (about 28 squares)
1/4   cup packed brown sugar
1/2   cup butter, melted
3   packages (8 oz each) cream
        cheese, softened
1   cup packed brown sugar
3   eggs

3/4   cup whipping cream
1/4   cup caramel-flavored coffee syrup
1/2   cup butter
1-1/4   cups packed brown sugar
2   tablespoons caramel-flavored coffee syrup
1/2   cup whipping cream
1-1/2   teaspoons flaked sea salt

1 Heat oven to 350°F. Wrap the outside bottom and side of a 9-inch springform pan with foil. Grease inside of pan with shortening. In a bowl, mix the crumbs, 1/4 cup brown sugar and 1/2 cup butter; press in bottom of pan. Bake 8 to 10 minutes or until set. Reduce temperature to 300°F. Cool 10 minutes.

2 In a large bowl, beat the cream cheese and 1 cup brown sugar with electric mixer on medium speed until smooth. Beat in eggs, one at a time, until blended. Add the 3/4 cup cream and the 1/4 cup syrup; beat until blended. Pour over crust.

3 Bake at 300°F 1 hour 10 minutes to 1 hour 20 minutes or until cheesecake edge is set 2 inches from the edge of the pan but the center still jiggles slightly. Turn the oven off; open the door 4 inches. Leave in the oven 30 minutes. Run a metal spatula around the edge. Cool on a cooling rack 30 minutes. Refrigerate 6 hours or overnight.

4 In a 2-quart saucepan, melt 1/2 cup butter over medium heat. Add 1-1/4 cups brown sugar and 2 tablespoons syrup. Heat to boiling; cook 1 minute, stirring frequently, until the sugar dissolves. Stir in 1/2 cup cream; return to boiling. Remove from heat. Cool 10 minutes. Run a metal spatula around the edge of pan; remove the side of the pan. Drizzle sauce over the slices; sprinkle with salt. Store covered in the refrigerator.

Nutritional Info: 1 Serving: Calories 510; Total Fat 34g (Saturated Fat 20g); Sodium 520mg; Total Carbohydrate 47g (Dietary Fiber 0g); Protein 5g. Exchanges: 1 Starch, 2 Other Carbohydrate, 6-1/2 Fat. Carbohydrate Choices: 3.

lemon-white chocolate cheesecake bites

Prep Time: 25 Minutes
Start to Finish: 2 Hours 25 Minutes
Servings: 18 cheesecake bites

. . . .

Crust

1/2	cup graham cracker crumbs
1	teaspoon sugar
2	tablespoons unsalted butter, melted, slightly cooled

Filling

1	package (8 oz) cream cheese, softened
1/4	cup sugar
1	egg
1	teaspoon grated lemon peel
4-1/2	teaspoons fresh lemon juice
1/2	cup white vanilla baking chips
1	teaspoon vegetable oil

. . . .

1 Heat oven to 300°F. Place a mini paper baking cup in each of 18 mini muffin cups; spray paper cups with cooking spray. In a medium bowl, mix crust ingredients until crumbs are moist. Spoon and lightly press 1 teaspoon mixture in bottom of each cup.

2 In large bowl, beat the cream cheese and 1/4 cup sugar with an electric mixer on medium speed until well blended. On low, beat in egg until smooth. Add lemon peel and juice; beat until smooth. Spoon about 1 teaspoon cream cheese mixture into each paper cup. Place 5 to 6 of the white baking chips on top of each (using 1/4 cup total). Divide remaining cream cheese mixture evenly among cups (about 2 heaping teaspoons each). Bake 25 to 30 minutes or just until filling looks set. Cool on cooling racks 30 minutes. Refrigerate 1 hour.

3 In a small microwavable bowl, microwave remaining 1/4 cup white baking chips and the oil uncovered on High 30 to 40 seconds until the mixture can be stirred smooth.

Drizzle over cheesecakes. Store covered in the refrigerator.

Nutritional Info: 1 Cheesecake Bite: Calories 120; Total Fat 8g (Saturated Fat 5g); Sodium 70mg; Total Carbohydrate 9g (Dietary Fiber 0g); Protein 1g. Exchanges: 1/2 Other Carbohydrate, 1-1/2 Fat. Carbohydrate Choices: 1/2

Betty's Kitchen Tip

The cheesecakes will continue to set once out of the oven, so it's better to take them out before the tops begin to brown.

spiced apple cupcakes with salted caramel frosting

Prep Time: 30 Minutes
Start to Finish: 1 Hour 30 Minutes
Servings: 12 cupcakes

Edwina Gadsby
Great Falls, MT
Better with Bisquick® Recipe Contest

Cupcakes

1-1/2	cups Original Bisquick® mix
1/2	cup sugar
1	teaspoon apple pie spice
1/2	cup apple cider or juice
2	tablespoons butter or shortening, softened
1	teaspoon vanilla
1	egg

1-1/4	cups chopped peeled apple (about 1 medium)

Salted Caramel Frosting

3/4	cup Betty Crocker® Rich & Creamy Vanilla frosting (from 1-lb container)
1/4	cup caramel topping
1/4	teaspoon kosher (coarse) salt

1 Heat oven to 375°F. Place a paper baking cup in each of 12 regular-size muffin cups.

2 In a large bowl, beat all the cupcake ingredients except apple with an electric mixer on low speed 30 seconds, scraping the bowl constantly. Beat on medium speed 4 minutes, scraping the bowl occasionally. Fold in the apple. Fill the muffin cups about three-fourths full.

3 Bake 17 to 22 minutes or until a toothpick inserted in the center comes out clean. Immediately remove cupcakes from the pan to a cooling rack; cool completely.

4 In a small bowl, mix the frosting and caramel topping until smooth and spreadable. Frost the cupcakes. Sprinkle with kosher salt.

Nutritional Info: 1 Cupcake: Calories 220; Total Fat 7g (Saturated Fat 2.5g); Sodium 290mg; Total Carbohydrate 37g (Dietary Fiber 0g); Protein 2g. Exchanges: 1 Starch, 1-1/2 Other Carbohydrate, 1-1/2 Fat. Carbohydrate Choices: 2-1/2.

Betty's Kitchen Tip

Any crisp, sweet-tart apple would work well in this recipe. We like varieties such as Gala, Braeburn and Cortland.

mimosa cupcakes

Prep Time: 35 Minutes
Start to Finish: 1 Hour 35 Minutes
Servings: 24 cupcakes

1	box Betty Crocker® SuperMoist® white cake mix
3/4	cup Champagne or ginger ale
1/2	cup orange juice
1/3	cup vegetable oil
3	egg whites
1	teaspoon grated orange peel
6	cups powdered sugar
1/2	cup butter or margarine, softened
3	tablespoons Champagne or ginger ale
3	tablespoons orange juice
1	teaspoon grated orange peel

Edible glitter or coarse white sparkling sugar
Grated orange peel

Nutritional Info: 1 Cupcake: Calories 270; Total Fat 8g (Saturated Fat 3.5g); Sodium 180mg; Total Carbohydrate 49g (Dietary Fiber 0g); Protein 1g. Exchanges: 3-1/2 Other Carbohydrate, 1-1/2 Fat. Carbohydrate Choices: 3.

1 Heat oven to 350°F (325°F for dark or nonstick pans). Place a paper baking cup in each of 24 regular-size muffin cups. In a large bowl, beat the cake mix, 3/4 cup Champagne, 1/2 cup orange juice, the oil, egg whites and 1 teaspoon orange peel with an electric mixer on low speed 30 seconds. Beat on medium speed 2 minutes, scraping the bowl occasionally. Divide the batter evenly among muffin cups, filling each about two-thirds full.

2 Bake 18 to 23 minutes or until a toothpick inserted in center of the cupcake comes out clean. Cool 10 minutes. Remove cupcakes from the pans to cooling racks. Cool completely, about 30 minutes.

3 In a large bowl, beat the powdered sugar, butter, 3 tablespoons Champagne, 3 tablespoons orange juice and 1 teaspoon orange peel with an electric mixer on medium speed until smooth and creamy. Spoon into a decorating bag with a large star tip (#5). Pipe frosting onto cupcakes. Sprinkle with glitter and orange peel. Store in the refrigerator.

Betty's Kitchen Tip

You can find edible glitter and sparkling sugars at some supermarkets, craft stores and online baking supply stores.

creamy lemon-iced citrus cake

Prep Time: 30 Minutes
Start to Finish: 2 Hours 15 Minutes
Servings: 12 to 16

Cake

- 1 box Betty Crocker® SuperMoist® lemon cake mix
- 1/2 cup water
- 1/2 cup orange juice
- 1/2 cup vegetable oil
- 3 eggs

Filling and Frosting

- 2 cups whipping cream
- 1/4 cup powdered sugar
- 1 can (15.75 oz) lemon pie filling
- 2 teaspoons grated orange peel

Strips of lemon and orange peel

1 Heat oven to 350°F (325°F for dark or nonstick pans). Grease the bottoms and sides of 2 (8- or 9-inch) round cake pans with shortening; lightly flour.

2 In a large bowl, beat the cake mix, water, juice, oil and eggs with an electric mixer on low speed 30 seconds. Beat on medium speed 2 minutes. Pour into the cake pans. Bake and cool as directed on the box for 8- or 9-inch round pans.

3 In a chilled medium bowl, beat the whipping cream and powdered sugar on high speed until stiff peaks form. Fold in 1/2 cup of the pie filling and the grated orange peel.

4 On a serving plate, place 1 cake layer, rounded side down. Spread the remaining pie filling over layer to within 1 inch of edge. Top with the second layer, rounded side up. Spread whipped cream mixture over the side and top of cake. Garnish the top of the cake with strips of lemon and orange peel. Store in the refrigerator.

Nutritional Info: 1 Serving: Calories 430; Total Fat 27g (Saturated Fat 12g); Sodium 410mg; Total Carbohydrate 43g (Dietary Fiber 0g); Protein 4g. Exchanges: 1 Starch, 2 Other Carbohydrate, 5-1/2 Fat. Carbohydrate Choices: 3.

Betty's Kitchen Tip

Instead of using pie filling, try lemon, lime or orange curd. Look for 10-ounce jars of it near the jams and jellies at your supermarket.

rhu-berry snack cake

Prep Time: 20 Minutes
Start to Finish: 1 Hour 25 Minutes
Servings: 9

Cake

1-3/4	cups Betty Crocker® SuperMoist® white cake mix (from 1 lb 2.25-oz box)
2	tablespoons Gold Medal® all-purpose flour
1/2	cup sour cream
1/4	cup water
1	tablespoon vegetable oil
2	egg whites
1	cup chopped fresh or frozen rhubarb, thawed and patted dry
1/3	cup fresh blueberries

Topping

1/2	cup sugar
1/4	cup Gold Medal® all-purpose flour
3	tablespoons butter or margarine, melted

1 Heat oven to 350°F (325°F for dark or nonstick pan). Spray the bottom and sides of a 9- or 8-inch square pan with baking spray with flour.

2 In large bowl, beat cake mix, 2 tablespoons flour, the sour cream, water, oil and egg whites with an electric mixer on low speed 30 seconds. Beat on medium speed about 2 minutes, scraping the bowl occasionally. Spread batter in the pan. Top evenly with rhubarb and blueberries.

3 In a small bowl, stir the topping ingredients until well mixed. Sprinkle evenly over the batter and fruit.

4 Bake 40 to 45 minutes or until a toothpick inserted in the center comes out clean. Cool 20 minutes. Serve warm or cool. Garnish with sweetened whipped cream and fresh mint leaves, if desired.

Nutritional Info: 1 Serving: Calories 250; Total Fat 9g (Saturated Fat 5g); Sodium 250mg; Total Carbohydrate 40g (Dietary Fiber 0g); Protein 3g. Exchanges: 2-1/2 Other Carbohydrate, 2 Fat. Carbohydrate Choices: 2-1/2.

Betty's Kitchen Tip

Although eaten as a fruit, rhubarb is really a vegetable. The plant's stalks mature to a bright red color and are usually harvested between April and June. Due to the stalks' tartness, sugar is added to give the rhubarb a more pleasant flavor.

lime cupcakes with strawberry frosting

Prep Time: 35 Minutes
Start to Finish: 2 Hours 35 Minutes
Servings: 24 cupcakes

- 2-3/4 cups Gold Medal® all purpose flour
- 3 teaspoons baking powder
- 1/2 teaspoon salt
- 1 cup shortening
- 1-2/3 cups granulated sugar
- 5 egg whites
- 3 tablespoons grated lime peel
- 1 teaspoon vanilla

- 1 cup milk
- 2 tablespoons lime juice
- 1 package (8 oz) cream cheese, softened
- 1/2 cup butter, softened
- 3-1/2 cups powdered sugar
- 1/2 cup mashed strawberries, well drained
- Small strawberries

1 Heat oven to 350°F (325°F for dark or nonstick pans). Place paper baking cup in each of 24 regular-size muffin cups. In a medium bowl, mix the flour, baking powder and salt.

2 In a large bowl, beat shortening with electric mixer on medium speed 30 seconds. Gradually add granulated sugar, about 1/3 cup at a time, beating after each addition. Beat 2 minutes longer. Add egg whites, one at a time, beating well after

each. Beat in lime peel and vanilla. On low speed, alternately add flour mixture, about one-third at a time, with milk, about half at a time, beating just until blended. Stir in lime juice. Divide batter evenly among muffin cups. Bake 20 to 25 minutes or until toothpick comes out clean. Cool about 5 minutes. Remove from pans to cooling racks. Cool completely.

3 In a large bowl, beat cream cheese, butter and powdered sugar until fluffy. Beat in mashed strawberries until blended. Frost cooled cupcakes. Top each cupcake with a strawberry. Store in refrigerator.

Nutritional Info: 1 Cupcake: Calories 330; Total Fat 16g (Saturated Fat 7g); Sodium 180mg; Total Carbohydrate 44g (Dietary Fiber 0g); Protein 3g. Exchanges: 3 Other Carbohydrate, 3 Fat. Carbohydrate Choices: 3.

Betty's Kitchen Tip

Place frosting in disposable decorating bag or large resealable freezer bag with 1 bottom corner cut off to create a 1-inch opening. Pipe frosting in a circular motion over cupcakes for a bakery-shop look.

chocolate cupcakes with white truffle frosting

Prep Time: 35 Minutes
Start to Finish: 1 Hour 10 Minutes
Servings: 24 cupcakes

Cupcakes

1   box Belly Crocker® SuperMoist® devil's food cake mix

Water, vegetable oil and eggs called for on cake mix box

White Truffle Frosting

1   cup white vanilla baking chips (6 oz)

1   container (1 lb) Betty Crocker® Rich & Creamy vanilla frosting

1 Heat oven to 350°F (325°F for dark or nonstick pans). Following directions on the cake mix box, make and bake 24 cupcakes, using water, oil and eggs. Cool 10 minutes. Remove from the pans to cooling racks. Cool completely, about 30 minutes.

2 In a medium microwavable bowl, microwave baking chips, uncovered, on High 45 seconds. Stir. If necessary, microwave in 15-second increments, stirring after each, until melted and smooth. Cool 5 minutes. Stir in the frosting until well blended. Immediately frost or pipe frosting on the cupcakes. If desired, tie ribbons around cupcakes for decoration. Store loosely covered.

Nutritional Info: 1 Cupcake: Calories 260; Total Fat 12g (Saturated Fat 4.5g); Sodium 250mg; Total Carbohydrate 36g (Dietary Fiber 0g); Protein 2g. Exchanges: 2-1/2 Other Carbohydrate, 2-1/2 Fat. Carbohydrate Choices: 2-1/2.

Betty's Kitchen Tip

To make Chocolate Truffle Frosting, use semisweet chocolate chips and Betty Crocker® Rich & Creamy chocolate frosting.

praline-pumpkin cake

Prep Time: 25 Minutes
Start to Finish: 2 Hours 20 Minutes
Servings: 16

1/2 cup butter or margarine
1/4 cup whipping cream
1 cup packed brown sugar
3/4 cup coarsely chopped pecans
1 box Betty Crocker® SuperMoist® yellow cake mix
1 cup canned pumpkin (not pumpkin pie mix)
1/2 cup water

1/3 cup vegetable oil
4 eggs
1-1/2 teaspoons pumpkin pie spice
1 container (1 lb) Betty Crocker® Rich & Creamy cream cheese frosting

Caramel topping, if desired
Additional coarsely chopped pecans, if desired

1 Heat oven to 325°F. In a heavy 1-quart saucepan, cook butter, whipping cream and brown sugar over low heat, stirring occasionally just until butter is melted. Pour into 2 (9- or 8-inch) round cake pans; sprinkle evenly with 3/4 cup pecans.

2 In a large bowl, beat the cake mix, pumpkin, water, oil, eggs and 1 teaspoon of the pumpkin pie spice with an electric mixer on low speed until moistened. Beat 2 minutes on medium speed; carefully spoon batter over pecan mixture in pans.

3 Bake 41 to 47 minutes or until the cake springs back when touched lightly in the center. Cool 5 minutes; remove from pans to a cooling rack. Cool completely, about 1 hour.

4 Stir the remaining 1/2 teaspoon pumpkin pie spice into the frosting. To assemble the cake, place 1 layer, praline side up, on serving plate. Spread with about 1 cup of the frosting. Top with second layer, praline side up; spread with remaining frosting to the edge of the layer. Drizzle with caramel topping; sprinkle with pecans. Store loosely covered in the refrigerator.

Nutritional Info: 1 Serving: Calories 440; Total Fat 22g (Saturated Fat 7g); Sodium 310mg; Total Carbohydrate 57g (Dietary Fiber 1g); Protein 3g. Exchanges: 4 Other Carbohydrate, 1/2 High-Fat Meat, 3-1/2 Fat. Carbohydrate Choices: 4.

Betty's Kitchen Tip

Cool layer cakes in their pans on cooling racks 5 minutes. This keeps the cake from breaking apart while it's too warm and tender.

mexican chocolate cheesecake

Prep Time: 20 Minutes
Start to Finish: 8 Hours 20 Minutes
Servings: 16

- 1-1/2 cups crushed vanilla wafers
- 3/4 teaspoon ground cinnamon
- 3 tablespoons butter or margarine, melted
- 1-1/2 cups semisweet chocolate chips (9 oz)
- 1/2 cup whipping cream
- 3 packages (8 oz each) cream cheese, softened
- 1/2 cup sugar
- 1/2 teaspoon chili powder, if desired
- 1 teaspoon ground cinnamon
- 1 teaspoon vanilla
- 3 eggs
- 2 cups sweetened whipped cream

1 Heat oven to 350°F. Wrap the outside bottom and side of an 8-inch springform pan with heavy-duty foil. Spray the inside of the pan with cooking spray. In a small bowl, mix the wafers, 3/4 teaspoon cinnamon and butter; press into the bottom of the pan. Bake 8 to 10 minutes until set. Reduce oven temperature to 300°F. Cool crust 10 minutes.

2 In a 2-quart saucepan, melt the chocolate chips and cream over medium-low heat; stir until smooth. In a large bowl, beat the cream cheese, sugar, chili powder, 1/2 teaspoon cinnamon and vanilla with an electric mixer on medium speed until fluffy. Beat in the eggs, one at a time, just until blended. Stir in the chocolate mixture. Pour over the crust. Bake at 300°F 1 hour or until the edge of the cheesecake is set 2 inches from the edge of the pan but the center still jiggles slightly. Turn the oven off; open the oven door about 4 inches. Leave the cheesecake in the oven 30 minutes. Run a metal spatula around the edge of the pan. Cool on a cooling rack 30 minutes. Refrigerate 6 hours or overnight.

3 Run the metal spatula around the edge of the pan; remove the side of the pan. Slice. Top slices with whipped cream; sprinkle with remaining 1/2 teaspoon cinnamon. Garnish with chocolate shavings, if desired. Store covered in the refrigerator.

Nutritional Info: 1 Serving: Calories 450; Total Fat 33g (Saturated Fat 18g); Sodium 250mg; Total Carbohydrate 32g (Dietary Fiber 1g); Protein 5g. Exchanges: 1 Starch, 1 Other Carbohydrate, 6-1/2 Fat. Carbohydrate Choices: 2.

Betty's Kitchen Tip

For clean, even slices, cut the cheesecake with a hot, wet knife; wipe it off after each cut.

chocolate-berry cheesecake

Prep Time: 18 Minutes
Start to Finish: 3 Hours 50 Minutes
Servings: 15

- 1 box Betty Crocker® SuperMoist® chocolate fudge cake mix
- 1/2 cup butter or margarine, softened
- 2 packages (8 oz each) cream cheese, softened
- 1 container (6 oz) Yoplait® Original 99% Fat Free red raspberry yogurt

- 1 container (1 lb) Betty Crocker® Rich & Creamy chocolate frosting
- 3 eggs
- 1-1/2 cups sliced fresh strawberries
- 1/2 cup fresh blueberries
- 1 can (21 oz) strawberry pie filling

1 Heat oven to 325°F. Grease the bottom only of a 13x9-inch pan with shortening or spray with cooking spray. In a large bowl, beat cake mix and butter with an electric mixer on low speed until crumbly; reserve 3/4 cup. Press the remaining crumbly mixture in the bottom of the pan.

2 In the same bowl, beat the cream cheese, yogurt and frosting on medium speed until smooth. Beat in the eggs, one at a time, just until blended. Pour over the crust. Sprinkle evenly with the reserved crumb mixture.

3 Bake 40 to 45 minutes or until center is set. Cool 30 minutes. Refrigerate at least 2 hours until chilled.

4 Just before serving, stir the strawberries and blueberries into the pie filling. Cut the cheesecake into squares; top each with berry mixture. Store cheesecake covered in the refrigerator.

Nutritional Info: 1 Serving: Calories 480; Total Fat 24g (Saturated Fat 12g); Sodium 530mg; Total Carbohydrate 62g (Dietary Fiber 1g); Protein 5g. Exchanges: 1 Starch, 3 Other Carbohydrate, 4-1/2 Fat. Carbohydrate Choices: 4.

Betty's Kitchen Tip

Did you forget to take the butter and cream cheese out of the refrigerator to soften? Just give each package a couple of light whacks with a rolling pin, and they'll blend easily with the other ingredients.

molten butterscotch cakes

Prep Time: 15 Minutes
Start to Finish: 35 Minutes
Servings: 6

6	teaspoons graham cracker crumbs
1	cup butterscotch chips (6 oz)
2/3	cup butter or margarine
3	whole eggs
3	egg yolks
3/4	cup packed brown sugar
1/2	cup Gold Medal® all-purpose flour

1 Heat oven to 450°F. Spray the sides and bottoms of 6 (6-oz) custard cups or ramekins with baking spray with flour. Sprinkle 1 teaspoon cracker crumbs onto the bottom and around the side of each cup.

2 In a 1-quart saucepan, melt butterscotch chips and butter over medium heat, stirring constantly. Remove from heat; cool slightly, about 5 minutes.

3 Meanwhile, in a large bowl, beat the whole eggs and egg yolks with a whisk until well blended. Beat in brown sugar. Beat in butterscotch mixture and flour until well blended. Divide the batter evenly among custard cups. Place the cups on a cookie sheet with sides.

4 Bake 12 to 14 minutes or until the sides are set and the centers are still soft (tops will be puffed and cracked). Let the cakes stand 3 minutes. Run a small knife or metal spatula along the sides of the cups to loosen cakes. Immediately place a dessert plate upside down on top of each cup; turn the plate and cup over. Remove the cup. Serve cakes warm.

Nutritional Info: 1 Serving: Calories 550; Total Fat 34g (Saturated Fat 21g); Sodium 220mg; Total Carbohydrate 56g (Dietary Fiber 0g); Protein 6g. Exchanges: 2 Starch, 1-1/2 Other Carbohydrate, 6-1/2 Fat. Carbohydrate Choices: 4.

Betty's Kitchen Tip

This luscious dessert tastes even better with a scoop of ice cream on top.

raspberry-filled lemon cupcakes

Prep Time: 40 Minutes
Start to Finish: 1 Hour 40 Minutes
Servings: 24 cupcakes

Cupcakes

1 box Betty Crocker® SuperMoist® French vanilla cake mix

Water, vegetable oil and eggs called for on cake mix box

2 tablespoons grated lemon peel (2 medium lemons)

Filling and Frosting

1 container (6 oz) fresh raspberries (1 to 1-1/4 cups)

2 containers (12 oz each) Betty Crocker® Whipped fluffy white frosting

2 tablespoons grated lemon peel (2 medium lemons)

1 tablespoon fresh lemon juice

Grated lemon peel strips

1 Heat oven to 350°F (325°F for dark or nonstick pans). Place a paper baking cup in each of 24 regular-size muffin cups. Following directions on the cake mix box, make and bake cupcakes, using water, oil, eggs and adding 2 tablespoons lemon peel. Cool 10 minutes. Remove to cooling racks. Cool completely.

2 Reserve 24 raspberries for the garnish; set aside. In a small bowl, beat the remaining raspberries, 1 cup of the frosting and 2 tablespoons lemon peel until well blended.

3 Fit a 1/4-inch diameter round tip into a decorating bag. Spoon the raspberry mixture into the bag. Insert the tip into the center of each cupcake, roughly two-thirds of the way down; gently squeeze the bag, pulling upwards until the cupcake swells slightly and filling comes to the top. (Do not let the filling spill out over the top of the cupcake.)

4 In a small bowl, mix the remaining frosting and the lemon juice until smooth and shiny. Pipe or spread frosting on the cupcakes. Garnish each with a fresh raspberry and lemon peel strips.

Nutritional Info: 1 Cupcake: Calories 240; Total Fat 10g (Saturated Fat 3g); Sodium 180mg; Total Carbohydrate 36g (Dietary Fiber 0g); Protein 1g. Exchanges: 2-1/2 Other Carbohydrate, 2 Fat. Carbohydrate Choices: 2-1/2.

Betty's Kitchen Tip

One jar (9 to 10 oz) of lemon curd can be substituted for the raspberries and frosting filling. Or try a lime twist on this recipe. Replace the lemon peel with lime peel and lemon juice with lime juice.

cherry cheesecake with ganache

Prep Time: 30 Minutes
Start to Finish: 9 Hours 40 Minutes
Servings: 16

1-1/2   cups finely crushed creme-filled chocolate sandwich cookies (about 15 cookies)
1/4   cup butter, melted
4   packages (8 oz each) cream cheese, softened
1-1/4   cups sugar
4   eggs
1/2   cup whipping cream

1   teaspoon almond extract
1   bag (16 oz) or 3 cups frozen dark sweet cherries, thawed, drained and patted dry

Ganache
1/2   cup dark chocolate chips (about 3 oz)
1/4   cup whipping cream
3   tablespoons corn syrup

1 Heat oven to 325°F. Wrap the outside bottom and side of a 10-inch springform pan with foil. Spray the inside with cooking spray. In a bowl, mix the cookies and butter; press in bottom of pan. Bake 8 minutes or until set. Reduce the temperature to 300°F. Cool the crust 10 minutes.

2 In a large bowl, beat the cream cheese and sugar with a mixer on medium speed until fluffy. Beat in the eggs, one at a time, just until blended. Beat in 1/2 cup cream and extract. Pour 4 cups cream cheese mixture over the crust. Top with cherries. Top with remaining mixture, covering cherries. Bake at 300°F 1 hour 25 minutes or until the edge of the cheesecake is set 2 inches from the edge of the pan but the center still jiggles slightly. Turn the oven off; open door 4 inches. Leave the cheesecake in the oven 30 minutes. Run a metal spatula around the edge of the pan. Cool on a cooling rack 30 minutes. Refrigerate 6 hours or overnight.

3 In a microwavable bowl, microwave ganache ingredients on High 1 minute 30 seconds, stirring once, until smooth. Spread over the cheesecake. Chill 30 minutes. Run the metal spatula around the edge of the pan; remove the side of the pan. Store covered in the refrigerator.

Nutritional Info: 1 Serving: Calories 460; Total Fat 31g (Saturated Fat 17g); Sodium 280mg; Total Carbohydrate 39g (Dietary Fiber 1g); Protein 6g. Exchanges: 2 Starch, 1/2 Other Carbohydrate, 6 Fat. Carbohydrate Choices: 2-1/2.

Betty's Kitchen Tip

Some cracking may occur while the cheesecake cools. This will not affect the quality of the cheesecake and it will not be noticeable once topped with ganache.

gingerbread poke cake

Prep Time: 15 Minutes
Start to Finish: 2 Hours
Servings: 12

EASY

3-1/2	cups Gold Medal® all-purpose flour
2	tablespoons chopped crystallized ginger
1	tablespoon ground ginger
2	teaspoons ground cinnamon
1/2	teaspoon salt
1	cup molasses
1	cup sugar
1	cup canola oil
2	eggs
1	cup boiling water
1	tablespoon baking soda
1	cup whipping cream
4	pasteurized egg yolks (see tip below)
1/4	cup sugar

Whipped cream, if desired

1 Heat oven to 350°F. Spray a 13x9-inch pan with cooking spray. In a large bowl, mix flour, crystallized ginger, ground ginger, cinnamon and salt; set aside.

2 In a medium bowl, mix the molasses, 1 cup sugar and the oil with wire whisk until blended. Add eggs, one at a time, stirring with whisk until blended. Add molasses mixture to flour mixture, stirring with a whisk until blended.

3 In a small bowl, mix boiling water and baking soda until soda is dissolved. Add to the batter, stirring until blended. Pour into the pan. Bake 40 to 45 minutes or until a toothpick inserted in the center comes out clean.

4 In a 1-quart saucepan, heat the whipping cream to simmering. In a small bowl, mix the pasteurized egg yolks and 1/4 cup sugar; add to cream, stirring with a whisk. Strain mixture through a fine strainer. Poke the warm cake every inch with a wooden skewer halfway into the cake.

Slowly drizzle the cream mixture over the cake. Cool completely, about 1 hour. Store covered in the refrigerator. Garnish with whipped cream.

Nutritional Info: 1 Serving: Calories 568; Total Fat 28g (Saturated Fat 6g); Sodium 459mg; Total Carbohydrate 73g (Dietary Fiber 1g); Protein 7g. Exchanges: 2 Starch, 3 Other Carbohydrate, 5 Fat. Carbohydrate Choices: 5.

Betty's Kitchen Tip

Pasteurized eggs are uncooked eggs that have been heat-treated to kill bacteria which can cause food poisoning.

mini key lime cupcakes

Prep Time: 40 Minutes
Start to Finish: 1 Hour 50 Minutes
Servings: 48 cupcakes

Topping

1	box (4-serving size) vanilla instant pudding and pie filling mix
1-1/2	cups whipping cream
1/4	cup Key lime or regular lime juice
4	drops green food color
1-1/2	cups powdered sugar

Cupcakes

48	regular-size paper baking cups

1	box Betty Crocker® SuperMoist® yellow cake mix
	Water, vegetable oil and eggs called for on cake mix box

Frosting

1	container Betty Crocker® Whipped fluffy white frosting
1	tablespoon Key lime or regular lime juice
1/2	teaspoon grated Key lime or regular lime peel

1 In a large bowl, beat pudding mix and whipping cream with whisk 2 minutes. Let stand 3 minutes. Beat in 1/4 cup Key lime juice and the food color; stir in powdered sugar until smooth. Cover and refrigerate.

2 Heat oven to 350°F (325°F for dark or nonstick pans). Place paper baking cup in each of 24 regular-size muffin cups.

3 Make cake batter as directed on box. Spoon about 1 rounded tablespoonful batter into each muffin cup, using about half of the batter. (Muffin cups will be about one-third full.) Refrigerate remaining batter. Bake 11 to 15 minutes (14 to 20 minutes for dark or nonstick pan) or until a toothpick inserted in center comes out clean. Remove from pan to cooling rack. Repeat with remaining baking cups and batter. Cool cupcakes completely, about 15 minutes.

3 Remove paper baking cups from cupcakes. Swirl about 2 teaspoons topping on top of each cupcake.

4 Stir frosting in container 20 times. Gently stir in 1 tablespoon Key lime juice and the lime peel. Spoon frosting into 1-quart resealable food-storage plastic bag. Cut 1/2-inch opening from bottom corner of bag. Squeeze 1 rounded teaspoonful frosting from bag onto topping. Garnish with a fresh lime wedge, if desired. Store in refrigerator.

Nutritional Info: 1 Cupcake: Calories 140; Total Fat 7g (Saturated Fat 3g); Cholesterol 25mg; Sodium 110mg; Total Carbohydrate 18g (Dietary Fiber 0g); Protein 0g. Exchanges: 1 Other Carbohydrate, 1-1/2 Fat. Carbohydrate Choices: 1

maple-walnut mini cupcakes

Prep Time: 20 Minutes
Start to Finish: 55 Minutes
Servings: 36 cupcakes

- 1-1/3   cups Gold Medal® all-purpose flour
- 1/2   teaspoon baking powder
- 1/8   teaspoon salt
- 1/2   cup butter, softened
- 3/4   cup granulated sugar
- 2   eggs
- 1/2   cup milk
- 3/4   cup chopped walnuts, toasted
- 1   teaspoon maple flavor

Maple-Cream Cheese Frosting
- 4   oz (half of 8-oz package) cream cheese, softened
- 1/4   cup butter, softened
- 1-3/4   cups powdered sugar
- 1/2   teaspoon maple flavor

Turbinado sugar (raw sugar) or maple sugar, if desired

Chopped walnuts or walnut halves, if desired

1 Heat oven to 350°F. Place a mini paper baking cup in each of 36 mini muffin cups.

2 In a medium bowl, mix flour, baking powder and salt; set aside. In a large bowl, beat 1/2 cup butter and the granulated sugar with an electric mixer on medium speed 2 to 4 minutes or until light and fluffy. Add eggs, one at a time, beating well after each addition. Beat in the flour mixture alternately with the milk. Stir in 3/4 cup walnuts and 1 teaspoon maple flavor. Divide batter evenly among muffin cups, filling each almost full.

3 Bake 17 to 18 minutes or until a toothpick inserted in the center comes out clean. Remove from pans to cooling racks; cool completely, about 15 minutes.

4 In a medium bowl, beat the cream cheese and 1/4 cup butter until blended. Gradually add the powdered sugar and 1/2 teaspoon maple flavor, beating until smooth. Frost cupcakes. Garnish with turbinado sugar and walnuts.

Nutritional Info: 1 Cupcake: Calories 122; Total Fat 7g (Saturated Fat 3g); Sodium 115mg; Total Carbohydrate 14g (Dietary Fiber 0g); Protein 2g. Exchanges: 1/2 Starch, 1/2 Other Carbohydrate, 1 Fat. Carbohydrate Choices: 1.

lemon-zucchini pound cake

Prep Time: 30 Minutes
Start to Finish: 3 Hours 15 Minutes
Servings: 16

Cake

3	cups Gold Medal® all-purpose flour
1	teaspoon baking powder
1/4	teaspoon baking soda
1/4	teaspoon salt
1	cup butter or margarine, softened
2	cups powdered sugar
4	eggs
2/3	cup milk
2	teaspoons grated lemon peel
2	tablespoons lemon juice
1	cup shredded zucchini (about 1 medium), squeezed to drain

Glaze

1	cup powdered sugar
1	tablespoon butter or margarine, softened
1	tablespoon half-and-half
1	teaspoon grated lemon peel
2	tablespoons lemon juice

1 Heat oven to 350°F. Grease a 12-cup fluted tube cake pan with shortening; lightly flour. In a medium bowl, mix flour, baking powder, baking soda and salt.

2 In a large bowl, beat 1 cup butter with electric mixer on medium speed about 2 minutes or until creamy. Beat in 2 cups powdered sugar. Add eggs, one at a time, beating well after each addition. Add the flour mixture alternately with the milk, beating well on low speed. Stir in 2 teaspoons lemon peel, 2 tablespoons lemon juice and the zucchini. Spoon the batter into the pan.

3 Bake 50 to 60 minutes or until a toothpick inserted in the center comes out clean. Cool 15 minutes; remove from the pan to cooling rack. Cool completely, about 1 hour.

4 In a 1-quart saucepan, heat all the glaze ingredients just to boiling over medium heat, stirring constantly; remove from heat. Let stand about 30 minutes. Drizzle over the cake.

Nutritional Info: 1 Serving: Calories 310; Total Fat 14g (Saturated Fat 7g); Sodium 190mg; Total Carbohydrate 42g (Dietary Fiber 0g); Protein 5g. Exchanges: 2 Starch, 1 Other Carbohydrate, 2 Fat. Carbohydrate Choices: 3.

Betty's Kitchen Tip

Shredded zucchini in the batter keeps this pound cake moist and tender.

spiced apple cake with maple glaze

Prep Time: 30 Minutes
Start to Finish: 2 Hours 35 Minutes
Servings: 16

Cake

3	cups chopped peeled apples (3 medium)
3	cups Gold Medal® all-purpose flour
1	teaspoon baking powder
1/2	teaspoon baking soda
1/2	teaspoon salt
2	teaspoons ground cinnamon
1/2	teaspoon ground nutmeg
1/4	teaspoon ground cloves
2	cups packed brown sugar
1	cup vegetable oil
4	eggs
1	teaspoon vanilla

Glaze

1-1/2	cups powdered sugar
3	to 4 tablespoons whipping cream
1/4	teaspoon maple flavor

1 Heat oven to 350°F. Grease a 12-cup fluted tube cake pan with shortening; then lightly flour.

2 In a medium bowl, toss apples with 2 tablespoons of the flour. In another medium bowl, mix the baking powder, baking soda, salt, cinnamon, nutmeg, cloves and remaining flour. In a large bowl, beat the brown sugar, oil, eggs and vanilla with an electric mixer on medium speed until mixed. On low speed, beat in the flour mixture just until blended. Stir in the apples. Spoon batter into the pan.

3 Bake 55 minutes or until a toothpick inserted in the center comes out clean. Cool 10 minutes; remove from pan to cooling rack. Cool completely, about 1 hour.

4 In a medium bowl, mix glaze ingredients until smooth and thick. Drizzle glaze over the cake.

Nutritional Info: 1 Serving: Calories 392; Total Fat 17g (Saturated Fat 3g); Sodium 165mg; Total Carbohydrate 59g (Dietary Fiber 1g); Protein 4g. Exchanges: 1 Starch, 2 Other Carbohydrate, 3 Fat. Carbohydrate Choices: 4.

Betty's Kitchen Tip

Be sure to follow directions for greasing and flouring the pan. Shortening plus flour works well, as does baking spray with flour. However, plain baking spray is often not enough.

lemon buttercream cake with blueberries

Prep Time: 40 Minutes
Start to Finish: 4 Hours 40 Minutes
Servings: 12

2-3/4 cups Gold Medal® all-purpose flour	1/3 cup fresh lemon juice
2-1/2 teaspoons baking powder	1-1/2 cups butter, softened
1 teaspoon salt	4 cups powdered sugar
1-1/2 cups granulated sugar	3 tablespoons milk
3/4 cup butter, softened	2 tablespoons fresh lemon juice
3 eggs	3 cups fresh blueberries
1-1/4 cups milk	3 teaspoons grated lemon peel
1 cup powdered sugar	

1 Heat oven to 350°F. Grease and flour 2 (8- or 9-inch) round cake pans. In a medium bowl, mix flour, baking powder and salt. In a large bowl, beat granulated sugar and 3/4 cup butter with an electric mixer on medium speed until fluffy. Add the eggs, one at a time, beating well. On low alternately beat in flour mixture and milk until blended. Pour into pans. Bake 25 to 35 minutes or until a toothpick comes out clean. Cool 10 minutes. With fork, poke tops every 1 inch. Mix 1 cup powdered sugar and 1/3 cup lemon juice until smooth. Spoon over the cakes. Let stand 10 minutes. Remove from pans; place top side up on cooling racks. Cool.

2 In a large bowl, beat 1-1/2 cups butter, 4 cups powdered sugar, 3 tablespoons milk and 2 tablespoons lemon juice on low until blended. Beat 3 minutes on medium speed until fluffy. On a plate, place 1 cake layer, rounded side up. Spread with 1/2 cup frosting. Top with 1-1/2 cups berries. Spoon 3/4 cup frosting over the berries; carefully spread to cover. Place the remaining layer, top side up, over berries. Frost top and side. Arrange remaining berries on the cake. Sprinkle with lemon peel. Chill 2 hours. Before serving, let cake stand at room temperature 15 minutes. Cover; refrigerate remaining cake.

Nutritional Info: 1 Serving: Calories 770; Total Fat 37g (Saturated Fat 23g); Sodium 570mg; Total Carbohydrate 104g (Dietary Fiber 2g); Protein 6g. Exchanges: 2 Starch, 5 Other Carbohydrate, 7 Fat. Carbohydrate Choices: 7.

mini almond butter tea cakes

Prep Time: 35 Minutes
Start to Finish: 2 Hours 35 Minutes
Servings: 24 tea cakes

1/2	cup butter (do not use margarine)
1/2	cup slivered almonds
1	cup powdered sugar
1/2	cup Gold Medal® all-purpose flour
1/4	teaspoon salt
1	teaspoon vanilla
1/4	teaspoon almond extract
4	egg whites
1/2	cup sliced almonds
2	teaspoons white decorator sugar crystals

1 Heat oven to 375°F. Line an 8-inch square pan with foil; spray foil with cooking spray. In a 2-quart saucepan, heat butter over medium-high heat about 5 minutes, stirring frequently, until it becomes a rich hazelnut-brown color. Remove from heat; cool 5 minutes.

2 Meanwhile, in a food processor, process slivered almonds until finely ground. In a large bowl, stir together ground almonds, powdered sugar, flour and salt. Add the vanilla, almond extract and egg whites; beat about 1 minute or until blended.

3 On medium speed, beat in the browned butter until smooth, about 1 minute. Pour batter into the pan. Sprinkle sliced almonds evenly over the batter; sprinkle sugar crystals evenly over the almonds.

4 Bake 20 to 25 minutes or until golden brown. Cool completely in the pan on a cooling rack, about 1 hour. Using foil, lift cake from the pan; remove foil from the cake. Cut into 6 rows by 4 rows.

Nutritional Info: 1 Tea Cake: Calories 130; Total Fat 8g (Saturated Fat 3.5g); Sodium 85mg; Total Carbohydrate 11g (Dietary Fiber 0g); Protein 2g. Exchanges: 1 Other Carbohydrate, 1-1/2 Fat. Carbohydrate Choices: 1.

Betty's **Kitchen Tip**

For a deeper almond flavor, toast the almonds before grinding them. Place them in a single layer on a cookie sheet with sides. Bake in a 375°F oven 5 to 8 minutes or until the almonds are golden brown.

banana split cheesecake

Prep Time: 25 Minutes
Start to Finish: 8 Hours 35 Minutes
Servings: 16

Crust
1-1/2	cups finely crushed chocolate wafer crumbs
1/4	cup butter or margarine, melted

Filling
3	packages (8 oz each) cream cheese, softened
3/4	cup granulated sugar

1	teaspoon vanilla
4	eggs
1	cup mashed very ripe bananas (2 medium)

Topping and Garnish
1	cup whipping cream
3	tablespoons powdered sugar
16	maraschino cherries, drained, patted dry

1 Heat oven to 325°F. Wrap the outside bottom and side of a 10-inch springform pan with heavy-duty foil. In a small bowl, mix the crust ingredients; press into the bottom and 1-1/2 inches up side of the pan. Bake 10 to 12 minutes or until set. Reduce oven temperature to 300°F. Cool crust 10 minutes.

2 In a large bowl, beat the cream cheese, granulated sugar and vanilla with an electric mixer on medium speed until smooth. Beat in eggs, one at a time, just until blended. Beat in bananas. Pour into the crust. Bake at 300°F 1 hour to 1 hour 10 minutes or until the edge of the cheesecake is set 2 inches from the edge of the pan but center still jiggles slightly when moved. Turn oven off; open the oven door 4 inches. Leave cheesecake in the oven 30 minutes. Run small metal spatula around edge of pan. Cool on cooling rack 30 minutes. Refrigerate 6 hours or overnight.

3 Run a small metal spatula around the edge of the pan; remove the side of the pan. In a chilled medium bowl, beat the whipping cream and powdered sugar on high speed until soft peaks form. Pipe onto the cheesecake. Garnish with maraschino cherries. Store covered in the refrigerator.

Nutritional Info: 1 Serving: Calories 350; Total Fat 25g (Saturated Fat 14g); Sodium 250mg; Total Carbohydrate 26g (Dietary Fiber 0g); Protein 5g. Exchanges: 1-1/2 Starch, 5 Fat. Carbohydrate Choices: 2.

"tie-dye" cupcakes

Prep Time: 35 Minutes
Start to Finish: 1 Hour 20 Minutes
Servings: 24 cupcakes

- -

1   box Betty Crocker® SuperMoist®
    white cake mix
Water, vegetable oil and egg whites called
for on cake mix box
Betty Crocker® gel food colors or paste food colors
(red, orange, yellow, green, blue and purple)
2   containers (1 lb each) Betty Crocker®
    Rich & Creamy white frosting

- -

1 Heat oven to 350°F (325°F for dark or nonstick pans). Place a white paper baking cup in each of 24 regular-size muffin cups. Make cake mix as directed on box for cupcakes using water, oil and egg whites.

2 Divide batter evenly among 6 medium bowls. Add a different food color to each bowl to make red, orange, yellow, green, blue and purple. Place 1 level teaspoon of each color batter into each muffin cup, layering colors in order of rainbow—red, orange, yellow, green, blue and purple. Do not stir! Each cup will be about half full. Bake 15 to 20 minutes or until a toothpick comes out clean. Cool 10 minutes. Remove to cooling racks. Cool completely.

3 Divide frosting evenly among 3 medium bowls. Tint 1 red, 1 yellow and 1 blue with food colors. Refrigerate about 30 minutes. In a large (16-inch) decorating bag fitted with #16 star tip, place spoonfuls of each color of frosting side by side, alternating colors and working up from the bag tip. Do not stir colors together. Starting at 12 o'clock on the outer edge of each cupcake and using constant pressure on the bag, pipe the frosting clockwise 3 rotations, working toward the center and ending in a small peak.

Nutritional Info: 1 Cupcake: Calories 260; Total Fat 9g (Saturated Fat 2g); Sodium 230mg; Total Carbohydrate 42g (Dietary Fiber 0g); Protein 1g. Exchanges: 3 Other Carbohydrate, 2 Fat. Carbohydrate Choices: 3.

Betty's Kitchen Tip

Be sure to use white or light-colored paper baking cups so you can see the "tie-dyed" colors of the cupcake through the paper.

key lime-coconut cream bundt cake

Prep Time: 30 Minutes
Start to Finish: 2 Hours 40 Minutes
Servings: 16

1 cup graham cracker crumbs	3/4 cup whipping cream
1/3 cup packed brown sugar	4 teaspoons grated lime peel
3 tablespoons butter, melted	1/4 cup Key lime juice
3 cups Gold Medal® all-purpose flour	1 cup flaked coconut
2-1/2 teaspoons baking powder	1 cup powdered sugar
1/2 teaspoon salt	1/2 teaspoon grated lime peel
3/4 cup butter, softened	4 to 5 teaspoons Key lime juice
1-1/2 cups granulated sugar	2 tablespoons flaked coconut, toasted
4 eggs	

1 Heat oven to 350°F. Grease a 12-cup fluted tube cake pan with shortening; lightly flour. In a small bowl, mix cracker crumbs, brown sugar and 3 tablespoons butter. In a medium bowl, mix flour, baking powder and salt; set aside.

2 In a large bowl, beat 3/4 cup butter and granulated sugar with an electric mixer on medium speed 2 minutes. Add eggs, one at a time, beating after each addition. On low speed, alternately beat in flour mixture and

whipping cream. Add 4 teaspoons lime peel and 1/4 cup lime juice; beat just until blended. Stir in 1 cup coconut. Sprinkle half of crumb mixture in the bottom of the pan. Spoon half of batter over the mixture in the pan; spread evenly. Sprinkle with remaining crumb mixture; top with remaining batter. Bake 45 to 55 minutes or until a toothpick comes out clean. Cool 15 minutes. Remove cake from pan to a cooling rack. Cool completely, about 1 hour.

3 In a small bowl, stir the powdered sugar, 1/2 teaspoon lime peel and 4 to 5 teaspoons lime juice. Spoon glaze over the top of the cake. Sprinkle with 2 tablespoons coconut. Use a serrated knife to cut the cake.

Nutritional Info: 1 Serving: Calories 410; Total Fat 18g (Saturated Fat 11g); Sodium 300mg; Total Carbohydrate 57g (Dietary Fiber 1g); Protein 5g. Exchanges: 1 Starch, 3 Other Carbohydrate, 3-1/2 Fat. Carbohydrate Choices: 4.

Betty's Kitchen Tip

Fresh-squeezed lime juice can be used in place of the Key lime juice. One lime yields about 5 teaspoons juice and 3 teaspoons grated peel.

coconut tres leches cake

Prep Time: 25 Minutes
Start to Finish: 4 Hours 5 Minutes
Servings: 15

- 1 box Betty Crocker® SuperMoist® white cake mix
- 1-1/4 cups water
- 1/3 cup vegetable oil
- 3 egg whites
- 1/2 teaspoon coconut extract, if desired
- 1 cup milk
- 2 cups whipping cream
- 1 can (14 oz) cream of coconut (not coconut milk)
- 1 cup coconut, toasted

Sliced kiwifruit, if desired

1 Heat oven to 350°F (325°F for dark or nonstick pan). Spray the bottom only of a 13x9-inch pan with cooking spray.

2 In a large bowl, beat the cake mix, water, oil and egg whites and coconut extract with an electric mixer on low speed 30 seconds. Beat on medium speed 2 minutes, scraping bowl occasionally. Pour into pan. Bake 27 to 32 minutes or until a toothpick comes out clean. Cool 5 minutes. With a long-tined fork, poke the top of the hot cake every 1/2 inch, wiping the fork occasionally to reduce sticking. In a medium bowl, mix milk, 3/4 cup of the whipping cream and the cream of coconut with a whisk until blended. Microwave on High 1 minute 30 seconds or until heated. Carefully pour the mixture over the warm cake. Cover; refrigerate 3 hours or until chilled.

3 In a small bowl, beat the remaining 1-1/4 cups whipping cream with a mixer on high speed until stiff. (Do not overbeat.) Spread over the cake; sprinkle with the coconut. Cut the cake into squares; serve with any remaining cream mixture from the pan. Garnish with kiwifruit.

Nutritional Info: 1 Serving: Calories 410; Total Fat 29g (Saturated Fat 19g); Sodium 290mg; Total Carbohydrate 34g (Dietary Fiber 1g); Protein 4g. Exchanges: 1 Starch, 1-1/2 Other Carbohydrate, 5-1/2 Fat. Carbohydrate Choices: 2.

Betty's Kitchen Tip

Add a tropical touch by topping each serving with chopped fresh mango or papaya along with the whipped cream and toasted coconut.

vanilla bean cupcakes

Prep Time: 30 Minutes
Start to Finish: 1 Hour 20 Minutes
Servings: 24 cupcakes

Cupcakes

2	vanilla beans, each cut in half lengthwise
1-1/2	cups milk
2-1/2	cups Gold Medal® all-purpose flour
3	teaspoons baking powder
1/2	teaspoon salt
3/4	cup unsalted butter, softened

1	cup granulated sugar
4	eggs

Frosting

4	cups powdered sugar
1	cup unsalted butter, softened
1/8	teaspoon salt
	Reserved 1/4 cup milk-vanilla seed mixture

1 Scrape the vanilla bean seeds into a microwavable bowl; add beans and 3/4 cup milk to the bowl. Microwave on High 1 minute or until mixture boils. Let stand 15 minutes. Remove the beans. Add the remaining milk to the warm milk mixture; stir well. Reserve 1/4 cup milk mixture.

2 Heat oven to 350°F (325°F for dark or nonstick pans). Place a paper baking cup in each of 24 regular-size muffin cups. In a medium bowl, mix the flour, baking powder and 1/2 teaspoon salt; set aside. In a large bowl, beat 3/4 cup butter with an electric mixer on medium speed 30 seconds. Gradually add the granulated sugar, beating after each addition. Add the eggs, one at a time, beating well. Beat 2 minutes longer. On low speed, alternately add the flour mixture and the milk mixture, beating just until blended. Divide the batter evenly among the muffin cups. Bake 17 to 22 minutes or until a toothpick comes out clean. Cool 5 minutes. Remove to cooling racks. Cool completely.

3 In a large bowl, beat frosting ingredients on low speed until blended well, adding 1 tablespoon reserved milk mixture at a time. Frost the cupcakes.

Nutritional Info: 1 Cupcake: Calories 300; Total Fat 15g (Saturated Fat 9g); Sodium 140mg; Total Carbohydrate 39g (Dietary Fiber 0g); Protein 3g. Exchanges: 2-1/2 Other Carbohydrate, 3 Fat. Carbohydrate Choices: 2-1/2.

Betty's Kitchen Tip

To remove seeds from a vanilla bean, cut the bean in half lengthwise. Run the blade of a knife across the inside of the bean, gathering seeds on the edge of the knife.

mojito cupcakes

Prep Time: 1 Hour
Start to Finish: 4 Hours
Servings: 24 cupcakes

Cupcakes

- 1 box Betty Crocker® SuperMoist® white cake mix
- 1 cup seltzer water or club soda
- 1/3 cup vegetable oil
- 1/4 cup rum or 1 teaspoon rum extract plus 1/4 cup water
- 3 tablespoons chopped fresh mint leaves
- 2 teaspoons grated lime peel
- 3 egg whites

Syrup

- 1/2 cup granulated sugar
- 1/4 cup butter or margarine
- 1/3 cup rum or 1 teaspoon rum extract plus 1/3 cup water

Topping

- 3 cups whipping cream

1 Heat oven to 350°F (325°F for dark or nonstick pans). Place a paper baking cup in each of 24 regular-size muffin cups. In a large bowl, beat the cake ingredients with an electric mixer on low speed 30 seconds. Beat on medium speed 2 minutes. Divide the batter evenly among the muffin cups. Bake 16 to 21 minutes or until a toothpick comes out clean. Cool 10 minutes; keep cupcakes in cupcake pans. In a 1-quart saucepan, mix syrup ingredients. Heat to boiling over high heat, stirring frequently. Reduce the heat to medium; continue to boil about 4 minutes, stirring frequently, until slightly thickened.

2 Cut a small circle out of the center of each warm cupcake; reserve the removed pieces. Slowly pour about 1 teaspoon of syrup into each cupcake hole; replace the cake circle. Brush the top of each cupcake with the remaining syrup. Cool completely in the pans. Cover; refrigerate at least 2 hours or overnight.

3 Pipe or frost each cold cupcake with whipped cream. Garnish each with a fresh mint leaf and a quartered lime slice. Store in the refrigerator.

Nutritional Info: 1 Cupcake: Calories 200; Total Fat 10g (Saturated Fat 5g); Sodium 180mg; Total Carbohydrate 23g (Dietary Fiber 0g); Protein 1g. Exchanges: 1-1/2 Other Carbohydrate, 2 Fat. Carbohydrate Choices: 1-1/2.

molten chocolate espresso cakes

Prep Time: 15 Minutes
Start to Finish: 30 Minutes
Servings: 6

EASY QUICK

Unsweetened baking cocoa
- 6 oz bittersweet chocolate, chopped
- 3/4 cup butter or margarine, cut into pieces
- 2 teaspoons instant espresso powder or instant coffee granules
- 1 teaspoon vanilla

- 1/4 teaspoon ground cinnamon
- 4 eggs
- 1-1/2 cups powdered sugar
- 1/2 cup Original Bisquick® mix

Vanilla ice cream, if desired

1 Heat oven to 450°F. Grease the bottoms and sides of 6 (6-oz) custard cups with butter; sprinkle with cocoa. Arrange on a 15x10x1-inch baking sheet.

2 In a 2-quart saucepan, melt the chocolate and 3/4 cup butter over low heat, stirring occasionally. Remove from heat. Stir in the espresso powder, vanilla and cinnamon.

3 In a large bowl, beat eggs and powdered sugar with an electric mixer on low speed, scraping the bowl occasionally, until blended. Gradually add the chocolate mixture, beating on low speed, then gradually add the Bisquick mix, beating until blended. Divide the batter evenly among the custard cups.

4 Bake 10 to 12 minutes or until the sides are set and the centers are still soft (tops will be puffed and slightly cracked). Let stand 3 minutes.

5 Serve in the custard cups, or to unmold before serving, run a small knife or a metal spatula along the sides of the cakes to loosen. Immediately place a heatproof serving plate upside down over each cup; turn the plate and cup over and remove the cup. Sprinkle with the additional powdered sugar, if desired. Serve warm with vanilla ice cream.

Nutritional Info: 1 Serving: Calories 570; Total Fat 36g (Saturated Fat 21g); Sodium 330mg; Total Carbohydrate 55g (Dietary Fiber 2g); Protein 6g. Exchanges: 1/2 Starch, 3 Other Carbohydrate, 1/2 Medium-Fat Meat, 6-1/2 Fat. Carbohydrate Choices: 3-1/2.

Betty's Kitchen Tip

When these cakes bake, the outside becomes cake-like and the center remains very creamy like a hot fudge-custard sauce. Don't worry...the center gets hot enough to fully cook the eggs.

giant ganache-topped whoopie pie

Prep Time: 25 Minutes
Start to Finish: 1 Hour 25 Minutes
Servings: 12

Cake

1-3/4	cups Betty Crocker® SuperMoist® devil's food cake mix (from 1-lb 2.25-oz box)
1/2	cup water
1/4	cup vegetable oil
2	eggs

Filling

3/4	cup butter or margarine, softened
1	jar (7 oz) marshmallow creme
1	cup powdered sugar
1	teaspoon vanilla

Ganache

1/2	cup whipping cream
4	oz semisweet baking chocolate, chopped

1 Heat oven to 350°F (325°F for dark or nonstick pans). Spray the bottoms and sides of 2 (8-inch) round cake pans with baking spray with flour. In a large bowl, beat the cake mix, water, oil and eggs with an electric mixer on low speed until moistened. Beat on medium speed 2 minutes, scraping sides of the bowl occasionally. Pour into pans. Bake 15 to 20 minutes or until a toothpick comes out clean. Cool 10 minutes. Remove cakes from the pans to cooling racks. Cool completely.

2 In a large bowl, beat the filling ingredients with an electric mixer on high speed until light and fluffy. On a serving plate, place 1 cake layer, rounded side down. Spread filling over the cake, spreading slightly over the edge. Top with the second layer, rounded side up.

3 In a 1-quart saucepan, heat the whipping cream over low heat until hot but not boiling. Remove from heat; stir in the chocolate until melted. Cool 10 minutes. Pour the ganache over the top of the cake; spread with a spatula so it just begins to flow over the edge of the cake.

Nutritional Info: 1 Serving: Calories 410; Total Fat 24g (Saturated Fat 12g); Sodium 290mg; Total Carbohydrate 47g (Dietary Fiber 1g); Protein 3g. Exchanges: 3 Other Carbohydrate, 5 Fat. Carbohydrate Choices: 3.

Betty's Kitchen Tip

A 1-inch-wide metal spatula works well for spreading glazes, fillings and frostings.

pumpkin-chocolate pound cake

Prep Time: 15 Minutes
Start to Finish: 2 Hours 25 Minutes
Servings: 16

Cake

3	cups Gold Medal® all-purpose flour
1	tablespoon pumpkin pie spice
2	teaspoons baking powder
1	teaspoon baking soda
1/2	teaspoon salt
1	cup butter or margarine, softened
1-1/3	cups packed brown sugar
1	cup granulated sugar
4	eggs
1	can (15 oz) pumpkin (not pumpkin pie mix)
2	teaspoons vanilla
1/2	cup milk
1-1/4	cups semisweet chocolate chips

Glaze

1-1/2	cups powdered sugar
2	to 3 tablespoons milk
1/2	teaspoon vanilla

1 Heat oven to 350°F. Grease a 12-cup fluted tube cake pan with shortening and lightly flour. In a medium bowl, mix the flour, pumpkin pie spice, baking powder, baking soda and salt; set aside.

2 In a large bowl, beat the butter, brown sugar and granulated sugar with an electric mixer on medium speed until creamy. Add eggs, one at a time, beating on low speed after each addition until blended. Add pumpkin and 2 teaspoons vanilla; beat on medium speed until blended. On low speed, beat in the flour mixture alternately with 1/2 cup milk until smooth. Stir in 1 cup of the chocolate chips. Spoon batter into the pan.

3 Bake 55 to 60 minutes or until a toothpick inserted in the center comes out clean. Cool 10 minutes; remove from pan to a cooling

rack. Cool completely, about 1 hour. In a medium bowl, mix all the glaze ingredients until smooth and thick. Drizzle glaze over cake. Sprinkle with remaining 1/4 cup chocolate chips.

Nutritional Info: 1 Serving: Calories 448; Total Fat 17g (Saturated Fat 10g); Sodium 233mg; Total Carbohydrate 69g (Dietary Fiber 2g); Protein 5g. Exchanges: 1 Starch, 3 Other Carbohydrate, 3 Fat. Carbohydrate Choices: 4-1/2.

Betty's Kitchen Tip

Pound cakes got their name from the fact that they were originally made with 1 pound each of flour, sugar and eggs.

mojito cheesecake

Prep Time: 30 Minutes
Start to Finish: 8 Hours 40 Minutes
Servings: 16

Crust

 2 cups crushed vanilla wafers (about 60 wafers)
 1/4 cup butter, melted

Filling

 3 packages (8 oz each) cream cheese, softened
 1 cup granulated sugar
 1/4 cup light rum

 1 tablespoon grated lime peel
 2 tablespoons fresh lime juice
 3 eggs

Topping

 1 cup whipping cream
 3 tablespoons powdered sugar
 2 teaspoons light rum
 2 tablespoons finely chopped fresh mint

Fresh mint sprig, if desired

1 Heat oven to 350°F. Wrap the outside bottom and side of a 9-inch springform pan with heavy-duty foil. Spray the inside of the pan with cooking spray.

2 In a small bowl, mix the crust ingredients; press into the bottom of the pan. Bake about 8 to 10 minutes or until set. Reduce oven temperature to 300°F. Cool the crust 10 minutes.

3 In a large bowl, beat the cream cheese, granulated sugar, 1/4 cup rum, lime peel and lime juice with an electric mixer on medium speed until fluffy. Beat in the eggs, one at a time, until blended. Pour filling over crust. Bake at 300°F 55 to 65 minutes or until the edge of the cheesecake is set 2 inches from the edge of pan but the center still jiggles slightly when moved. Turn oven off; open the oven door 4 inches. Leave cheesecake in the oven 30 minutes. Run a small metal spatula around the edge of the pan. Cool on a cooling rack 30 minutes. Refrigerate 6 hours or overnight.

4 Run a small spatula around the edge of the pan; remove the side of the pan. In a chilled bowl, beat the topping ingredients on high speed until soft peaks form. Top each serving with whipped cream topping; garnish with a mint sprig, if desired. Store covered in the refrigerator.

Nutritional Info: 1 Serving: Calories 340; Total Fat 25g (Saturated Fat 14g); Sodium 220mg; Total Carbohydrate 24g (Dietary Fiber 0g); Protein 4g. Exchanges: 1-1/2 Starch, 5 Fat. Carbohydrate Choices: 1-1/2.

upside-down apple-spice cake

Prep Time: 15 Minutes
Start to Finish: 1 Hour
Servings: 15

EASY

1/2	cup butter
2/3	cup packed light brown sugar
1	cup chopped walnuts, toasted
1-1/2	lb apples, peeled and chopped (3 large)
1	box Betty Crocker® SuperMoist® spice cake mix

Water, vegetable oil and eggs as called for on cake mix box

1 Heat oven to 350°F. In a 13x9-inch pan, melt the butter in the oven. Sprinkle the brown sugar and walnuts over the butter; stir to combine. Sprinkle the chopped apples in the pan.

2 Prepare the cake as directed on the box for a 13x9-inch pan, using water, oil and eggs. Pour the batter over the apples and walnuts in the pan.

3 Bake 35 to 40 minutes or until a toothpick inserted in the center comes out clean. Cool on a cooling rack 2 minutes; run a knife around the sides of the pan to loosen the cake. Place a heatproof serving plate upside down on the pan; turn the plate and pan over. Remove the pan. Serve the cake warm.

Nutritional Info: 1 Serving: Calories 356; Total Fat 19g (Saturated Fat 6g); Sodium 291mg; Total Carbohydrate 45g (Dietary Fiber 1g); Protein 3g. Exchanges: 1/2 Fruit, 2-1/2 Other Carbohydrate, 3 Fat. Carbohydrate Choices 3.

Betty's Kitchen Tip

When purchasing apples, check that the variety is appropriate for your recipe. Apples that are perfect for snacking aren't always the best choice for baking and vice versa.

candied nut-topped texas sheet cake

Prep Time: 20 Minutes
Start to Finish: 2 Hours
Servings: 12

Cake

1	box Betty Crocker® SuperMoist® devil's food cake mix
2	tablespoons unsweetened baking cocoa
1-1/3	cups buttermilk
1/2	cup vegetable oil
3	eggs

Frosting and Topping

1/2	cup butter
1	cup packed brown sugar
1/4	cup milk
2	cups powdered sugar
1/2	cup chocolate-covered cashews
1/2	cup coarsely chopped cashews
1/2	cup coarsely chopped candied pecans

1 Heat oven to 350°F (or 325°F for a dark or nonstick pan). Spray the bottom only of 13x9x1-inch pan with baking spray with flour.

2 In a large bowl, beat the cake ingredients with an electric mixer on low speed 30 seconds. Beat on medium speed 2 minutes, scraping the bowl occasionally. Pour into the pan. Bake 26 minutes or until a toothpick comes out clean. Cool completely, about 1 hour.

3 Meanwhile, in a 2-quart saucepan, melt the butter over medium heat. Stir in the brown sugar. Heat to boiling, stirring constantly. Reduce heat to low; boil and stir 2 minutes. Stir in the milk; return to boiling. Remove from heat. Cool to lukewarm, about 30 minutes.

4 Gradually stir powdered sugar into the brown sugar mixture. Place a saucepan of frosting in a bowl of cold water; beat with a spoon until smooth and spreadable. If frosting becomes too stiff, stir in additional milk, 1 teaspoon at a time, or heat over low heat, stirring constantly. Frost the cake. Sprinkle evenly with cashews and pecans.

Nutritional Info: 1 Serving: Calories 590; Total Fat 29g (Saturated Fat 10g); Sodium 420mg; Total Carbohydrate 74g (Dietary Fiber 2g); Protein 6g. Exchanges: 1-1/2 Starch, 3-1/2 Other Carbohydrate, 5-1/2 Fat. Carbohydrate Choices: 5.

Betty's Kitchen Tip

The original Texas sheet cake is a chocolate cake made with buttermilk. The church-supper favorite is frosted with chocolate frosting and sprinkled with chopped pecans.

brown sugar bundt cake

Prep Time: 20 Minutes
Start to Finish: 3 Hours 40 Minutes
Servings: 16

Cake

2-1/4	cups Gold Medal® all-purpose flour
1/2	teaspoon baking powder
1/2	teaspoon salt
1-1/2	cups packed light brown sugar
3/4	cup granulated sugar
1	cup butter, softened
4	eggs
2	teaspoons vanilla
3/4	cup milk

Buttery Brown Sugar Sauce

1	cup butter
1/2	cup packed light brown sugar
2	tablespoons milk
1	tablespoon light corn syrup
1	teaspoon vanilla

1 Heat oven to 350°F. Grease the bottom and side of a 12-cup fluted tube cake pan with shortening; lightly flour. In medium bowl, mix the flour, baking powder and salt; set aside.

2 In a large bowl, beat 1-1/2 cups brown sugar, the granulated sugar and butter with an electric mixer on low speed 30 seconds, scraping the bowl constantly. Beat on medium speed until light and fluffy, about 5 minutes. Add eggs, one at a time, beating well after each. Add 2 teaspoons vanilla. On low speed, alternately beat in the flour mixture and 3/4 cup milk. Pour into the pan. Bake 54 minutes to 1 hour 10 minutes or until a toothpick comes out clean. Cool 10 minutes. Remove cake from the pan to a cooling rack. Cool completely, about 2 hours.

3 In a 2-quart saucepan, heat all sauce ingredients except vanilla to boiling over medium heat, stirring constantly. Boil and stir 2 minutes. Cool to room temperature. Stir in 1 teaspoon vanilla. Serve warm sauce with the cake.

Nutritional Info: 1 Serving: Calories 450; Total Fat 25g (Saturated Fat 15g); Sodium 280mg; Total Carbohydrate 52g (Dietary Fiber 0g); Protein 4g. Exchanges: 1 Starch, 2-1/2 Other Carbohydrate, 5 Fat. Carbohydrate Choices: 3-1/2.

Betty's Kitchen Tip

If you're trying to be health-conscious, resist the temptation to use margarine instead of butter in this recipe. Butter will give you far better flavor.

pineapple upside-down cake

Prep Time: 15 Minutes
Start to Finish: 1 Hour
Servings: 8

EASY

1/4	cup butter or margarine	1-1/2	cups Original Bisquick® mix
1/4	cup packed brown sugar	1/2	cup granulated sugar
1	can (8 oz) pineapple slices, drained, slices cut in half	1/2	cup milk or water
2	tablespoons chopped pecans, if desired	2	tablespoons vegetable oil
Maraschino cherries, if desired		1	teaspoon vanilla
		1	egg

1 Heat oven to 350°F. In a 9-inch round cake pan or an 8-inch square pan, melt butter in the oven. Sprinkle brown sugar over the butter. Arrange pineapple slices in a single layer on the sugar mixture. Sprinkle with pecans. Arrange cherries, if desired, next to each pineapple slice.

2 In a large bowl, beat all of the remaining ingredients with an electric mixer on low speed 30 seconds, scraping the bowl constantly. Beat on medium speed 4 minutes, scraping the bowl occasionally. Pour batter over the pineapple.

3 Bake 30 to 35 minutes or until a toothpick inserted in the center comes out clean. Immediately place a heatproof serving plate over the pan and turn upside down; leave the pan over cake a few minutes. Remove the pan. Let cake stand at least 10 minutes before serving.

Nutritional Info: 1 Serving: Calories 290; Total Fat 13g (Saturated Fat 5g); Sodium 290mg; Total Carbohydrate 39g (Dietary Fiber 1g); Protein 3g. Exchanges: 1 Starch, 1-1/2 Other Carbohydrate, 2-1/2 Fat. Carbohydrate Choices: 2-1/2.

Betty's Kitchen Tip

For banana upside-down cake, omit pineapple, cherries and pecans. Sprinkle 2 tablespoons chopped walnuts over the brown sugar mixture in the pan. Cut 2 bananas into slices; arrange over the brown sugar mixture.

COOKIES, CANDIES & BARS

p.227

242

250

260

triple-chocolate fudge cake truffles

Prep Time: 50 Minutes
Start to Finish: 2 Hours 25 Minutes
Servings: 36 truffles

Truffles

1	box Betty Crocker® SuperMoist® triple chocolate fudge cake mix

Water, vegetable oil and eggs as called for on cake mix box

2	tablespoons Betty Crocker® Rich & Creamy triple chocolate fudge chip frosting
1/4	cup Irish cream liqueur or whipping cream

Coating

2-1/4	cups (14 oz) chopped chocolate-flavored candy coating
3-1/2	teaspoons shortening
1/4	cup white vanilla baking chips

1 Heat oven to 350°F. Spray the bottom only of a 13x9-inch pan with cooking spray. Make and bake the cake mix as directed on the box using water, oil and eggs. Cool the cake completely.

2 Crumble the cake into a large bowl. Add the frosting and liqueur; mix well. Roll the mixture into 1-1/2-inch balls; place on a cookie sheet. In a 1-quart heavy saucepan, melt the candy coating over low heat, stirring occasionally. Stir in 3 teaspoons of the shortening until smooth.

3 Place a sheet of waxed paper on the work surface. To coat each truffle, place it on a 2-pronged meat fork; hold it over the saucepan of chocolate. Spoon chocolate over the truffle, making sure to cover the cake particles completely. Let the excess chocolate drip back into the pan. Using the tip of a knife, slide the coated truffle onto the paper. Let truffles stand at room temperature until set, about 15 minutes.

4 In a small microwavable bowl, microwave baking chips and remaining 1/2 teaspoon shortening on High 30 to 60 seconds or until the mixture is smooth. Drizzle over the truffles. Let stand until set.

Nutritional Info: 1 Truffle: Calories 170; Total Fat 9g (Saturated Fat 4g); Sodium 150mg; Total Carbohydrate 20g (Dietary Fiber 0g); Protein 2g. Exchanges: 1-1/2 Other Carbohydrate, 2 Fat. Carbohydrate Choices: 1.

Betty's Kitchen Tip

Instead of the vanilla drizzle, sprinkle the truffles with candy sprinkles, colored sugar or finely chopped nuts before the coating has set up. Or, after adding the drizzle, also add a sprinkle! Use oil-based food color to change the hue of the melted vanilla coating.

hidden treasure cookies

Prep Time: 1 Hour 15 Minutes
Start to Finish: 1 Hour 45 Minutes
Servings: 48 cookies

- 1 cup butter or margarine, softened
- 1/2 cup powdered sugar
- 1 teaspoon vanilla
- 2-1/4 cups Gold Medal® all-purpose flour
- 1/2 cup finely chopped nuts
- 1/4 teaspoon salt
- 12 caramels, unwrapped, each cut into 4 pieces

Additional powdered sugar

1 Heat oven to 400°F. In a large bowl, mix butter, 1/2 cup powdered sugar and the vanilla. Stir in flour, nuts and salt until dough holds together.

2 Mold a portion of dough around each caramel piece to form a 1-inch ball. On an ungreased cookie sheets, place the balls about 1 inch apart.

3 Bake 10 to 12 minutes or until set but not brown. Roll the warm cookies in additional powdered sugar. Cool completely on a cooling rack, about 30 minutes. Roll again in powdered sugar.

Nutritional Info: 1 Cookie: Calories 90; Total Fat 5g (Saturated Fat 2g); Sodium 45mg; Total Carbohydrate 10g (Dietary Fiber 0g); Protein 0g. Exchanges: 1/2 Other Carbohydrate, 1 Fat. Carbohydrate Choices: 1/2.

Betty's Kitchen Tip

Vary the treasure in your cookies! Try candied cherries (shown above), chocolate-covered raisins, malted milk balls and gummy candies.

chewy granola drops

Prep Time: 40 Minutes
Start to Finish: 40 Minutes
Servings: 24 cookies

1 pouch (1 lb 1.5 oz) Betty Crocker® oatmeal chocolate chip cookie mix
1/2 cup butter or margarine, melted
1 egg

1 cup flaked coconut
3/4 cup dried cranberries
1 can (6 oz) honey-roasted almonds (1-1/4 cups), coarsely chopped

1 Heat oven to 375°F. In a large bowl, stir the cookie mix, melted butter and egg until a soft dough forms. Stir in the coconut, cranberries and almonds.

2 Onto an ungreased cookie sheet, drop the dough by tablespoonfuls 2 inches apart. Press with fingers to slightly flatten.

3 Bake 11 to 12 minutes or until the edges are golden brown. Cool 2 minutes; remove from cookie sheets to a cooling rack. Store the cooled cookies covered at room temperature.

Nutritional Info: 1 Cookie: Calories 200; Total Fat 11g (Saturated Fat 5g); Sodium 115mg; Total Carbohydrate 23g (Dietary Fiber 2g); Protein 2g. Exchanges: 1/2 Starch, 1 Other Carbohydrate, 2 Fat. Carbohydrate Choices: 1-1/2.

Betty's Kitchen Tip

Use two tableware spoons to drop dough onto the cookie sheet. Scoop dough with one spoon and push it onto the cookie sheet with the other. A cookie scoop would do the job, too.

mexican spice cookies

Prep Time: 25 Minutes
Start to Finish: 1 Hour 30 Minutes
Servings: 30 cookies

- 2 tablespoons sugar
- 1-1/4 teaspoon ground cinnamon
- 1 pouch (1 lb 1.5 oz) Betty Crocker® sugar cookie mix
- 2 tablespoons Gold Medal® all purpose flour
- 1/3 cup butter or margarine, softened
- 1 egg
- 1/2 teaspoon anise seed

1 Heat oven to 375°F. In a small bowl, mix the sugar and 3/4 teaspoon of the cinnamon; set aside.

2 In a medium bowl, stir cookie mix, flour, butter, egg, anise seed, and remaining 1/2 teaspoon cinnamon until soft dough forms. Roll dough into 30 (1-inch) balls. Roll in cinnamon-sugar. On an ungreased cookie sheets, place balls about 1 inch apart.

3 Bake 9 to 12 minutes or until set and light golden brown around the edges. Cool 1 minute; remove from the cookie sheet to a cooling rack.

Nutritional Info: 1 Cookie: Calories 90; Total Fat 4g (Saturated Fat 1.5g); Sodium 65mg; Total Carbohydrate 14g (Dietary Fiber 0g); Protein 1g. Exchanges: 1/2 Starch, 1/2 Other Carbohydrate, 1/2 Fat. Carbohydrate Choices: 1.

Betty's Kitchen Tip

Anise seed comes from the anise plant, a member of the parsley family. The greenish-brown seed has a sweet black licorice flavor.

peanut butter-pecan chocolate chip-granola cookies

Prep Time: 1 Hour 30 Minutes
Start to Finish: 1 Hour 30 Minutes
Servings: 60 cookies

Amber Parsons
Parkersburg, WV
Better with Bisquick® Recipe Contest

1 cup butter, softened	1 teaspoon vanilla
1 cup creamy peanut butter	2 cups Original Bisquick® mix
3/4 cup granulated sugar	1-3/4 cups granola cereal
3/4 cup packed brown sugar	1 cup milk chocolate chips
2 eggs	1 cup coarsely chopped pecans

1 Heat oven to 350°F. In a large bowl, mix butter, peanut butter, granulated sugar, brown sugar, eggs and vanilla with a spoon. Stir in the remaining ingredients.

2 On an ungreased cookie sheets, drop the dough by rounded tablespoonfuls about 2 inches apart.

3 Bake 9 to 11 minutes or until the edges are light golden brown (do not overbake). Cool 3 minutes; remove from cookie sheets to cooling racks.

Nutritional Info: 1 Cookie: Calories 140; Total Fat 8g (Saturated Fat 3.5g); Sodium 95mg; Total Carbohydrate 13g (Dietary Fiber 0g); Protein 2g. Exchanges: 1/2 Starch, 1/2 Other Carbohydrate, 1-1/2 Fat. Carbohydrate Choices: 1.

Betty's Kitchen Tip

Any granola cereal will work in this recipe, so use your favorite!

chewy oatmeal snack bars

Prep Time: 15 Minutes
Start to Finish: 2 Hours 15 Minutes
Servings: 24 bars

EASY

- 1/2 cup butter or margarine
- 2/3 cup firmly packed brown sugar
- 2/3 cup maple-flavored syrup
- 2/3 cup crunchy peanut butter
- 1 teaspoon vanilla
- 3 cups quick-cooking oats
- 1 cup wheat germ
- 1 cup graham cracker crumbs
- 1 cup cherry- or orange-flavored sweetened dried cranberries

1 Grease the bottom and sides of a 13x9-inch pan with shortening. In a 2-quart saucepan, melt butter over medium heat. Stir in the brown sugar and syrup; heat to boiling. Boil and stir 1 minute; remove from heat. Stir in the peanut butter and vanilla until the mixture is blended.

2 Stir in the remaining ingredients, mixing well. Press evenly into the pan. Cover; refrigerate about 2 hours or until firm. Cut into 6 rows by 4 rows. Store covered in the refrigerator.

Nutritional Info: 1 Bar: Calories 220; Total Fat 9g (Saturated Fat 3.5g); Sodium 85mg; Total Carbohydrate 30g (Dietary Fiber 2g); Protein 4g. Exchanges: 1-1/2 Starch, 1/2 Other Carbohydrate, 1-1/2 Fat. Carbohydrate Choices: 2.

Betty's Kitchen Tip

Honey can be used instead of the maple-flavored syrup, and old-fashioned oats can be used instead of the quick-cooking oats.

apple spice oatmeal cookies

Prep Time: 45 Minutes
Start to Finish: 45 Minutes
Servings: 36 cookies

Cookies

1/2	cup butter or margarine, softened
1/4	cup shortening
3/4	cup packed brown sugar
1/2	cup granulated sugar
2	eggs
1	teaspoon vanilla
2	cups old-fashioned oats
1	teaspoon ground cinnamon
1/2	teaspoon ground nutmeg
1	teaspoon baking soda
1-1/2	cups Gold Medal® all-purpose flour
2	small apples, peeled and chopped (2 cups)
1	cup coarsely chopped walnuts

Glaze

2	cup powdered sugar
2	tablespoons butter or margarine, melted
1	teaspoon vanilla
1/4	cup half-and-half or milk

1 Heat oven to 350°F. In a large bowl beat 1/2 cup butter, shortening, brown sugar and granulated sugar with an electric mixer on medium speed until thoroughly mixed. Beat in the eggs and 1 teaspoon vanilla until well blended. Beat in the oats, cinnamon, nutmeg, baking soda and flour, scraping the side and bottom of the bowl once, just until blended. Stir in the apples and walnuts.

2 Onto an ungreased cookie sheet, drop the dough by rounded tablespoonfuls (scant 1/4 cup) about 2 inches apart. Bake 13 to 17 minutes or until edges are golden brown and the centers are set. Cool 2 minutes; remove from the cookie sheet to a cooling rack.

3 Meanwhile in a small bowl, stir all the glaze ingredients until smooth and thin enough to drizzle. With a spoon, drizzle about 1 teaspoon glaze onto each warm cookie. Cool completely, about 10 minutes.

Nutritional Info: 1 Cookie: Calories 170; Total Fat 8g (Saturated Fat 3g); Sodium 65mg; Total Carbohydrate 22g (Dietary Fiber 1g); Protein 2g. Exchanges: 1 Starch. Carbohydrate Choices: 1.

Betty's Kitchen Tip

Pack up these soft, spiced oatmeal cookies for a much appreciated lunch-box surprise.

dulce-frosted chipotle brownies

Prep Time: 20 Minutes
Start to Finish: 2 Hours 5 Minutes
Servings: 16 brownies

- 1 box Betty Crocker® chocolate chunk premium brownie mix
- Water, vegetable oil and eggs as called for on brownie mix box
- 1 teaspoon ground cinnamon
- 1/2 to 3/4 teaspoon chipotle chile pepper powder
- 2 cups powdered sugar
- 1/4 cup dulce de leche (from 13.4-oz can)
- 2 tablespoon butter or margarine, softened
- 2 tablespoons milk
- 1 teaspoon vanilla

1. Heat oven to 350°F (325°F for a dark or nonstick pan). Grease or spray the bottom of an 8-inch square pan with shortening or cooking spray.

2. Make the brownie mix as directed on the box, using water, oil and eggs. Stir in the cinnamon and chile pepper powder until well blended. Spread batter in pan.

3. Bake 39 to 42 minutes or until a toothpick inserted 2 inches from the pan edge comes out almost clean. Cool completely in the pan on a cooling rack, about 1 hour.

4. In a medium bowl, beat the powdered sugar, dulce de leche, butter, milk and vanilla with an electric mixture on low speed until smooth and creamy. Frost brownies. Cut into 4 rows by 4 rows.

Nutritional Info: 1 Brownie: Calories 340; Total Fat 13g (Saturated Fat 4g); Sodium 220mg; Total Carbohydrate 53g (Dietary Fiber 2g); Protein 4g. Exchanges: 1 Starch, 2-1/2 Other Carbohydrate, 2-1/2 Fat. Carbohydrate Choices: 3-1/2.

Betty's Kitchen Tip

For a party-worthy presentation, cut these rich brownies into bite-sized squares and serve in decorative papers. Display them on a pretty tray.

cranberry bars

Prep Time: 25 Minutes
Start to Finish: 1 Hour 45 Minutes
Servings: 36 bars

Crust

2	cups Gold Medal® all-purpose flour
1/2	cup powdered sugar
1	cup cold butter

Filling

6	cups fresh or frozen (do not thaw) cranberries

3/4	cup cranberry juice
1-1/3	cups granulated sugar
3	eggs, slightly beaten
1/3	cup powdered sugar, if desired

1 Heat oven to 350°F. Line the bottom and sides of a 13x9-inch pan with foil, leaving the foil overhanging at two opposite sides of the pan.

2 In a medium bowl, mix flour and 1/2 cup powdered sugar. Cut in the butter, using a pastry blender (or pulling two table knives through the ingredients in opposite directions), until mixture is crumbly. Press in the bottom of pan. Bake 25 minutes or until edges are lightly browned.

3 Meanwhile, in a 3-quart saucepan, stir the cranberries, 1/2 cup of the cranberry juice and the granulated sugar. Heat to boiling over medium-high heat. Cook 10 minutes, stirring frequently, until the cranberries begin to burst. Remove from heat; stir in eggs and remaining 1/4 cup cranberry juice with a whisk. Pour over the partially baked crust.

4 Bake 20 minutes or until the crust is golden and filling is set. Cool completely in the pan on a cooling rack, about 1 hour. Use foil to lift bars out of the pan. Cut into 9 rows by 4 rows. Sprinkle the bars with 1/3 cup powdered sugar.

Nutritional Info: 1 Bar: Calories 128; Total Fat 6g (Saturated Fat 3g); Sodium 52mg; Total Carbohydrate 18g (Dietary Fiber 1g); Protein 1g. Exchanges: 1 Other Carbohydrate, 1 Fat. Carbohydrate Choices: 1.

Betty's Kitchen Tip

Stock up on cranberries while they're abundant in stores. Just toss them in the freezer and use as you need; they'll be good for about a year.

mocha pecan balls

Prep Time: 55 Minutes
Start to Finish: 1 Hour 15 Minutes
Servings: 48 cookies

- 1 roll (16.5 oz) refrigerated sugar cookies
- 1/4 cup unsweetened baking cocoa
- 1 tablespoon instant espresso coffee powder or granules
- 1 cup finely chopped pecans
- 48 milk chocolate candy drops or pieces, unwrapped
- 3/4 cup powdered sugar

1. Heat oven to 375°F. Break up the cookie dough into a large bowl. Add cocoa, coffee powder and pecans; mix well.

2. Shape the dough into 48 (1-inch) balls; wrap each around 1 milk chocolate candy. Place balls 2 inches apart on ungreased cookie sheets.

3. Bake 8 to 10 minutes or until set. Immediately remove from cookie sheets. Cool 5 minutes or until slightly cooled.

4. Roll cookies in powdered sugar. Cool completely, about 15 minutes. Roll again in powdered sugar. Store tightly covered at room temperature.

Nutritional Info: 1 Cookie: Calories 95; Total Fat 5g (Saturated Fat 1g); Sodium 40mg; Total Carbohydrate 12g (Dietary Fiber 0g); Protein 1g. Exchanges: 1 Other Carbohydrate, 1 Fat. Carbohydrate Choices: 1.

Betty's Kitchen Tip

If the dough is too soft to handle, cover and refrigerate about 1 hour or until firm.

browned butter pumpkin bars

Prep Time: 20 Minutes
Start to Finish: 2 Hours 5 Minutes
Servings: 48 bars

Bars

2	cups Gold Medal® all-purpose flour
1-1/2	cups granulated sugar
2	teaspoons baking powder
1	teaspoon baking soda
1/4	teaspoon salt
2	teaspoons pumpkin pie spice
2	teaspoons grated orange peel
1/2	cup orange juice
1/2	cup vegetable oil
1	cup canned pumpkin (not pumpkin pie mix)
2	eggs

Frosting

1/3	cup butter (do not use margarine)
2	cups powdered sugar
1/2	teaspoon vanilla
2	to 4 tablespoons milk

Orange peel strips, if desired

1 Heat oven to 350°F. Grease the bottom and sides of a 15x10x1-inch pan with shortening; lightly flour or spray with baking spray with flour.

2 In a large bowl, beat the bar ingredients with an electric mixer on low speed, scraping the bowl occasionally, until moistened. Beat on medium speed 2 minutes, scraping the bowl occasionally. Spread into the pan.

3 Bake 23 to 27 minutes or until a toothpick inserted in the center comes out clean. Cool completely, about 1 hour.

4 In a 2-quart saucepan, heat the butter over medium heat, stirring constantly, until light golden brown. Remove from the heat. Stir in powdered sugar, vanilla and enough milk until mixture is smooth and spreadable. Immediately spread frosting over the bars. Refrigerate about 15 minutes or until set.

5 For bars, cut into 8 rows by 6 rows. If desired, garnish each bar with an orange peel strip.

Nutritional Info: 1 Bar: Calories 100; Total Fat 4g (Saturated Fat 1g); Sodium 70mg; Total Carbohydrate 16g (Dietary Fiber 0g); Protein 1g. Exchanges: 1 Other Carbohydrate, 1 Fat. Carbohydrate Choices: 1.

Betty's Kitchen Tip

Pumpkin pie spice is a blend of spices used to flavor pumpkin. If you want to make your own, mix 1/4 teaspoon ground ginger, 1/4 teaspoon ground nutmeg, 1-1/2 teaspoons ground cinnamon and 1/8 teaspoon ground cloves.

caramel-toffee chunk brownies

Prep Time: 15 Minutes
Start to Finish: 3 Hours
Servings: 32 brownies

EASY

3	cups Gold Medal® all-purpose flour
1-1/2	teaspoons baking powder
1/4	teaspoon baking soda
1/2	teaspoon salt
2	cups packed brown sugar
1	cup butter, melted
3	eggs
3	teaspoons vanilla
8	bars (1.4 oz each) chocolate-covered English toffee candy, chopped
3/4	cup quick-cooking oats

1 Heat oven to 350°F. Spray a 13x9-inch pan with cooking spray.

2 In a medium bowl, mix flour, baking powder, baking soda and salt. In a large bowl, mix brown sugar, butter, eggs and vanilla with a wooden spoon until blended. Add the flour mixture; stir until blended. Stir in candy and oats. Spread into the pan.

3 Bake 40 to 45 minutes or until a toothpick inserted in the center comes out clean. Cool completely in the pan on a cooling rack, about 2 hours. Cut bars into 8 rows by 4 rows.

Nutritional Info: 1 Brownie: Calories 218; Total Fat 10g (Saturated Fat 5g); Sodium 163mg; Total Carbohydrate 30g (Dietary Fiber 1g); Protein 2g. Exchanges: 1/2 Starch, 1-1/2 Other Carbohydrate, 2 Fat. Carbohydrate Choices: 2.

Betty's Kitchen Tip

For a trendy—and flavorful—finish, sprinkle the tops of these brownies with coarse sea salt.

chocolate-glazed malt cookies

Prep Time: 40 Minutes
Start to Finish: 1 Hour 5 Minutes
Servings: 30 cookies

Cookies

2	cups Gold Medal® all-purpose flour
3/4	cup unsweetened baking cocoa
3/4	cup malted milk powder
1	teaspoon baking soda
1	cup butter, softened
2/3	cup granulated sugar
2/3	cup packed brown sugar
2	eggs
1	teaspoon vanilla

Glaze

1/4	cup butter, softened
1/2	cup packed brown sugar
1/4	cup milk
3/4	cup malted milk powder
1/4	cup unsweetened baking cocoa

Chopped chocolate-covered malted milk balls, if desired

1 Heat oven to 350°F. In a medium bowl, mix flour, 3/4 cup cocoa, 3/4 cup malted milk powder and the baking soda; set aside. In a large bowl, beat 1 cup butter, the granulated sugar and 2/3 cup brown sugar with an electric mixer on medium speed 5 minutes or until light and fluffy. Add eggs, one at a time, beating until blended. Beat in the vanilla. Beat in the flour mixture just until blended. Onto an ungreased cookie sheet, drop dough by rounded tablespoonfuls 2 inches apart.

2 Bake 9 to 11 minutes or until the cookies are puffed and the edges are set but the centers are still soft. Cool 5 minutes; remove from the cookie sheet to a cooling rack. Cool completely.

3 In a 2-quart saucepan, heat 1/4 cup butter, 1/2 cup brown sugar and the milk over medium heat 2 minutes, stirring occasionally, until smooth. Remove from heat. Add 3/4 cup malted milk powder and 1/4 cup cocoa; stir until smooth. Spread glaze on the tops of the cookies. Sprinkle with malted milk ball pieces, if desired.

Nutritional Info: 1 Cookie: Calories 231; Total Fat 9g (Saturated Fat 5g); Sodium 150mg; Total Carbohydrate 36g (Dietary Fiber 2g); Protein 3g. Exchanges: 1-1/2 Fat. Carbohydrate Choices: 2-1/2.

Betty's Kitchen Tip

Chocolate and cocoa are made from liquefied, ground, roasted and shelled cocoa beans—also called cacao—processed in different ways.

easy monster cookies

Prep Time: 1 Hour
Start to Finish: 1 Hour
Servings: 18 cookies

- 1 pouch (1 lb 1.5 oz) Betty Crocker® chocolate chip cookie mix
- 1 pouch (1 lb 1.5 oz) Betty Crocker® peanut butter cookie mix
- 1-1/2 cups quick-cooking oats
- 1 cup butter or margarine, softened
- 3 eggs
- 2 cups candy-coated milk chocolate candies

1 Heat oven to 375°F. In a large bowl, stir all the ingredients except candies until a soft dough forms. Stir in the candies.

2 Onto ungreased cookie sheets, drop dough by about 1/4 cupfuls about 3 inches apart.

3 Bake 12 to 13 minutes or until light golden brown. Cool 2 minutes; remove from the cookie sheets to cooling racks. Store the cooled cookies in a covered container at room temperature.

Nutritional Info: 1 Cookie: Calories 480; Total Fat 23g (Saturated Fat 12g); Sodium 340mg; Total Carbohydrate 61g (Dietary Fiber 1g); Protein 6g. Exchanges: 2 Starch, 2 Other Carbohydrate, 4-1/2 Fat. Carbohydrate Choices: 4.

Betty's Kitchen Tip

To make 3 dozen smaller cookies, for each cookie, drop dough by 2 heaping tablespoonfuls about 2 inches apart onto ungreased cookie sheets. Bake 10 to 12 minutes.

orange-spice drops

Prep Time: 1 Hour
Start to Finish: 2 Hours
Servings: 36 cookies

- 1 pouch (1 lb 1.5 oz) Betty Crocker® sugar cookie mix
- 1/3 cup mascarpone cheese or 1 package (3 oz) cream cheese
- 1/4 cup butter or margarine, softened
- 1 tablespoon grated orange peel
- 1 tablespoon fresh orange juice
- 1/4 teaspoon pumpkin pie spice
- 1 egg
- 1 cup finely chopped pecans
- 2 cups white candy melts, coating wafers or white vanilla baking chips (12 oz)

Edible orange glitter, if desired

---

1 Heat oven to 375°F. In a large bowl, beat cookie mix, cheese and butter on low speed until well mixed. Add orange peel, orange juice, pumpkin pie spice and egg; beat until thoroughly mixed.

2 Using a small cookie scoop, shape the dough into 1-inch balls. Roll balls in the pecans. On an ungreased cookie sheet, place the balls 2 inches apart.

3 Bake 11 to 13 minutes or until the edges are light golden brown. Cool 5 minutes. Remove from the cookie sheet to a cooling rack. Cool completely.

4 In a small microwavable bowl, microwave the candy melts uncovered on High 1 to 2 minutes, stirring every 30 seconds, until the candy is melted and can be stirred smooth. Dip each cookie halfway into the melted candy, letting the excess drip off. Place on waxed paper until almost set. Sprinkle the dipped half of each cookie with edible glitter. Let the cookies stand until candy coating is completely set, about 1 hour. Store between sheets of waxed paper in a tightly covered container.

Nutritional Info: 1 Cookie: Calories 150; Total Fat 8g (Saturated Fat 3.5g); Sodium 65mg; Total Carbohydrate 18g (Dietary Fiber 0g); Protein 2g. Exchanges: 1 Starch, 1-1/2 Fat. Carbohydrate Choices: 1.

Betty's Kitchen Tip

Be sure to store crisp cookies separately from softer ones. The specific texture of each type of cookie will last longer.

gingersnap cream sandwiches

Prep Time: 1 Hour 10 Minutes
Start to Finish: 1 Hour 20 Minutes
Servings: 28 sandwich cookies

. . . .

Cookies
1	pouch (1 lb 1.5 oz) Betty Crocker® sugar cookie mix
1/2	cup butter, softened
1	egg, slightly beaten

Filling
1/2	cup butter, softened
2	cups powdered sugar
1	teaspoon vanilla
1/2	cup finely chopped crystallized ginger

. . . .

1 Heat oven to 375°F. In a medium bowl, beat the cookie ingredients with an electric mixer on medium speed 30 seconds or until the mixture looks like coarse crumbs. Mix with hands until a soft dough forms.

2 On a lightly floured surface, roll the dough to 1/4-inch thickness. (If the dough is too sticky to roll out, cover and refrigerate 15 minutes.) Cut with a floured 1-3/4-inch fluted cookie cutter. On ungreased cookie sheets, place the cutouts 2 inches apart.

3 Bake 8 to 9 minutes or until the edges are set. Cool 1 minute; remove from cookie sheets to cooling racks. Cool completely, about 10 minutes.

4 In a large bowl, beat 1/2 cup butter, the powdered sugar and vanilla with an electric mixer on medium speed until light and fluffy. For each sandwich cookie, spread slightly less than 1 tablespoon filling on the bottom of a cookie. Top with the second cookie, bottom side down; gently press together. Sprinkle crystallized ginger on edges of the filling.

Nutritional Info: 1 Sandwich Cookie: Calories 179; Total Fat 8g (Saturated Fat 5g); Sodium 187mg; Total Carbohydrate 25g (Dietary Fiber 0g); Protein 1g. Exchanges: 1/2 Starch, 1 Other Carbohydrate, 1-1/2 Fat. Carbohydrate Choices: 1-1/2.

Betty's Kitchen Tip

You can make these cookies in stages. Once the cookies are baked, cover them tightly and make the filling and assemble them within a few days.

ultimate fudge mocha brownies

Prep Time: 20 Minutes
Start to Finish: 2 Hours 25 Minutes
Servings: 32 brownies

Brownies

1/2	cup semisweet chocolate chips
1/2	cup butter or margarine
1	cup packed dark brown sugar
2	eggs
2	tablespoons coffee-flavored liqueur
1	teaspoon vanilla
3/4	cup Gold Medal® all-purpose flour
2	tablespoons unsweetened baking cocoa
1/2	teaspoon salt

Frosting

1/3	cup butter or margarine, softened
2	cups powdered sugar
2	tablespoons coffee-flavored liqueur

Glaze

1/2	cup whipping cream
1	tablespoon light corn syrup
1	cup semisweet chocolate chips (6 oz)

1 Heat oven to 350°F. Line 8-inch square pan with foil; spray foil with cooking spray.

2 In a 3-quart saucepan, melt 1/2 cup chocolate chips and 1/2 cup butter over low heat, stirring constantly; remove from heat. Cool completely. Stir in brown sugar, eggs, 2 tablespoons liqueur and the vanilla with whisk. Stir in flour, cocoa and salt. Spread evenly in the pan. Bake 20 minutes or until the center is set. Cool completely.

3 In a medium bowl, combine the frosting ingredients with an electric mixer on medium speed until smooth and spreadable. Frost the brownies. Refrigerate at least 15 minutes.

4 In a small microwavable bowl, microwave glaze ingredients on High 1 minute; stir. Microwave 15 seconds longer; stir until melted and smooth. Pour glaze over the frosting; spread to cover. Refrigerate until set. With a wet knife, cut into 8 rows by 4 rows. Store covered in refrigerator.

Nutritional Info: 1 Brownie: Calories 173; Total Fat 9g (Saturated Fat 5g); Sodium 87mg; Total Carbohydrate 23g (Dietary Fiber 1g); Protein 1g. Exchanges: 1-1/2 Other Carbohydrate, 1-1/2 Fat. Carbohydrate Choices: 1-1/2.

Betty's Kitchen Tip

For easier cutting, cool brownies and bars completely and use a plastic knife. Or, look for nonstick knives that make cutting a cinch.

mocha-caramel cookies

Prep Time: 35 Minutes
Start to Finish: 35 Minutes
Servings: 24 cookies

- 1 cup Gold Medal® all-purpose flour
- 1/2 cup unsweetened baking cocoa
- 4 teaspoons instant espresso coffee powder or granules
- 1/2 teaspoon baking soda
- 1/2 teaspoon salt
- 1/2 cup butter or margarine, softened
- 1-1/3 cups bittersweet chocolate chips
- 1-1/2 cups sugar
- 2 eggs
- 1 teaspoon vanilla
- 1 bag (11 oz) caramel baking bits

1 Heat oven to 325°F. In a medium bowl, mix the flour, cocoa, coffee powder, baking soda and salt; set aside.

2 In a large microwavable bowl, microwave the butter and 2/3 cup of the chocolate chips uncovered on High about 1 minute, stirring once, until melted. Add the sugar, eggs and vanilla; stir until blended. Add the flour mixture, mixing just until blended (the dough will be thick). Fold in the remaining 2/3 cup chocolate chips and the baking bits.

3 Onto an ungreased cookie sheet, drop the dough by 2 tablespoonfuls 2 inches apart. Bake 15 minutes or until the edges are set and tiny cracks form on the surface. Cool 5 minutes; remove to a cooling rack.

 **Kitchen Tip**

Try using these big, chewy cookies for making extra-special ice cream sandwiches.

Nutritional Info: 1 Cookie: Calories 220; Total Fat 12g (Saturated Fat 7g); Sodium 125mg; Total Carbohydrate 30g (Dietary Fiber 1g); Protein 3g. Exchanges: 2 Other Carbohydrate, 2 Fat. Carbohydrate Choices: 2.

double-layer peppermint fudge

Prep Time: 30 Minutes
Start to Finish: 1 Hour 30 Minutes
Servings: 117 candies

LOW FAT

Fudge Layer

- 1 bag (12 oz) semisweet chocolate chips (2 cups)
- 1 container (1 lb) Betty Crocker® Rich & Creamy chocolate frosting

Peppermint Layer

- 1 bag (12 oz) white vanilla baking chips (2 cups)

- 1 container (1 lb) Betty Crocker® Rich & Creamy vanilla frosting
- 2 drops red food color
- 1/2 cup finely crushed hard peppermint candies
- 2 milk chocolate candy bars (1.55 oz each), chopped

1 Line a 13x9-inch pan with foil, leaving the foil overhanging at 2 opposite sides of the pan; lightly grease the foil with butter.

2 In a 3-quart saucepan, heat chocolate chips over very low heat, stirring constantly, until melted and smooth. Remove from the heat. Stir in the chocolate frosting. Spread in the pan. Refrigerate 20 minutes.

3 Meanwhile, in another 3-quart saucepan, heat the white chips over very low heat, stirring constantly, until mixture is melted and smooth. Remove from heat. Stir in the vanilla frosting and food color. Fold in the crushed peppermint candies. Spread carefully over the chilled chocolate layer. Sprinkle the chopped candy bars over the top; press in lightly. Refrigerate until set.

4 Use the foil to lift fudge out of pan. Cut into 13 rows by 9 rows.

Nutritional Info: 1 Candy: Calories 70; Total Fat 3g (Saturated Fat 2g); Sodium 20mg; Total Carbohydrate 10g (Dietary Fiber 0g); Protein 0g. Exchanges: 1/2 Other Carbohydrate, 1 Fat. Carbohydrate Choices: 1/2.

Betty's Kitchen Tip

You can make and freeze this fudge ahead of time for gift giving. Then, thaw and place individual fudge pieces in small paper or foil cups and arrange in festive gift boxes.

chocolate meringue cookies

Prep Time: 1 Hour 25 Minutes
Start to Finish: 1 Hour 55 Minutes
Servings: 36 cookies

1-2/3 cups Gold Medal® all-purpose flour	2 cups sugar
1/2 cup sifted unsweetened baking cocoa	1 whole egg
1 teaspoon baking powder	1/4 teaspoon almond extract
1/2 teaspoon baking soda	4 egg whites
1/4 teaspoon salt	1 cup finely chopped almonds
1 cup butter, softened	1/2 cup semisweet chocolate chunks

1 In a small bowl, mix flour, cocoa, baking powder, baking soda and salt; set aside. In a large bowl, beat butter and 1 cup of the sugar with an electric mixer on high speed until light and fluffy. Add the whole egg and almond extract, beating until blended. On low speed, beat in the flour mixture until blended. Cover; refrigerate at least 30 minutes.

2 Heat oven to 350°F. Line a large cookie sheet with cooking parchment paper. In a large bowl, beat egg whites with an electric mixer on high speed until foamy. Add remaining 1 cup sugar, 1 tablespoon at a time, beating until stiff peaks form and sugar is dissolved. Fold in almonds.

3 Roll dough by 2 heaping teaspoonfuls into balls. On a cookie sheet, place balls 2 inches apart. Press the balls with palm of hand to flatten slightly. In the center of each flattened cookie, place 2 chocolate chunks. Spoon 2 heaping tablespoonfuls meringue over each cookie, covering chocolate chunks completely.

4 Bake 15 to 18 minutes or until meringue is set. Cool 1 minute; remove from the cookie sheet to a cooling rack. Store in an airtight container up to 1 week.

Nutritional Info: 1 Cookie: Calories 142; Total Fat 7g (Saturated Fat 4g); Sodium 99mg; Total Carbohydrate 18g (Dietary Fiber 1g); Protein 2g. Exchanges: 1 Other Carbohydrate, 1-1/2 Fat. Carbohydrate Choices: 1.

Betty's Kitchen Tip

Shiny, smooth-surfaced or textured aluminum cookie sheets provide the best baking results.

molasses chewies

Prep Time: 30 Minutes
Start to Finish: 30 Minutes
Servings: 30 cookies

2	cups Gold Medal® all-purpose flour
2	teaspoons baking soda
2	teaspoons pumpkin pie spice
1/2	teaspoon salt
3/4	cup butter or margarine, softened
1	cup granulated sugar
1/4	cup molasses
1	egg
1/3	cup turbinado sugar (raw sugar) or coarse sugar

1 Heat oven to 350°F. Spray a cookie sheet with cooking spray.

2 In a medium bowl, mix the flour, baking soda, pumpkin pie spice and salt, set aside. In a large bowl, beat the butter and granulated sugar with an electric mixer on medium speed until light and fluffy. Add molasses and egg, beating until combined. On low speed, beat in the flour mixture until blended.

3 Shape the dough into 1-inch balls; roll in turbinado sugar. On a cookie sheet, place the balls 2 inches apart.

4 Bake 12 minutes or until the edges are set. Cool 5 minutes; remove from the cookie sheet to a cooling rack.

Nutritional Info: 1 Cookie: Calories 120; Total Fat 5g (Saturated Fat 3g); Sodium 167mg; Total Carbohydrate 18g (Dietary Fiber 0g); Protein 1g. Exchanges: 1 Other Carbohydrate, 1 Fat. Carbohydrate Choices: 1.

Betty's Kitchen Tip

Rolling the dough in turbinado sugar gives the cookies a "crackled" effect and also imparts an extra bit of sweetness and crunch.

toasted coconut cheesecake bars

Prep Time: 10 Minutes
Start to Finish: 3 Hours
Servings: 15 bars

EASY

1   box (1 lb 1 oz) Betty Crocker® dark chocolate Premium brownie mix
Water, vegetable oil and eggs as called for on brownie mix box
3   packages (8 oz each) cream cheese, softened
3/4   cup sugar

1   teaspoon almond extract
3   eggs
1-1/2   cups flaked coconut, toasted
4   oz bittersweet baking chocolate, chopped
Additional toasted coconut, if desired

1 Heat oven to 350°F. Line the bottom and sides of a 13x9-inch pan with foil, leaving the foil overhanging at 2 opposite sides of the pan; spray foil with cooking spray.

2 Make the brownies as directed on the box, using water, oil and eggs. Spread in the pan. In a large bowl, beat the cream cheese, sugar and almond extract with an electric mixer on medium speed until light and fluffy. Beat in the eggs, one at a time, just until blended. Fold in 1-1/2 cups coconut. Drop the mixture by tablespoonfuls over brownie batter in the pan.

3 Bake 50 minutes or until the cream cheese filling is light brown. Cool completely in the pan on a cooling rack, about 2 hours. Use the foil to lift bars out of pan. Cut into 5 rows by 3 rows.

4 In a small resealable freezer plastic bag, place the bittersweet chocolate; seal bag. Microwave on High about 1 minute or until softened. Gently squeeze the bag until chocolate is smooth; cut off a tiny corner of the bag. Squeeze the bag to drizzle chocolate over the bars. Sprinkle with additional coconut. Store the bars covered in the refrigerator.

Nutritional Info: 1 Bar: Calories 587; Total Fat 36g (Saturated Fat 18g); Sodium 377mg; Total Carbohydrate 59g (Dietary Fiber 1g); Protein 8g. Exchanges: 1/2 Starch, 3-1/2 Other Carbohydrate, 7 Fat. Carbohydrate Choices: 4.

Betty's Kitchen Tip

Lining a pan with heavy-duty foil has multiple benefits. Bars come out of the pan easily, plus it stays clean, so you can re-line it and make another batch in no time!

sweet 'n salty pretzel brownies

Prep Time: 15 Minutes
Start to Finish: 2 Hours 10 Minutes
Servings: 24 brownies

EASY

1-1/2 cups crushed pretzels

1/4 cup sugar

1/2 cup butter or margarine, melted

1 box (1 lb 2.4 oz) Betty Crocker® Original Supreme Premium brownie mix

1/4 cup water

1/4 cup vegetable oil

2 eggs

1 container (1 lb) Betty Crocker® Rich & Creamy vanilla frosting

1 cup coarsely chopped pretzels

1 cup coarsely chopped mixed nuts

1 Heat oven to 350°F. In a medium bowl, mix the crushed pretzels, sugar and butter. Press in an ungreased 13x9-inch pan. Bake 8 minutes. Cool 20 minutes.

2 In a medium bowl, stir the brownie mix, contents of chocolate syrup pouch (from the brownie mix box), water, oil and eggs until blended. Carefully spread the batter over the cooled crust.

3 Bake 19 to 22 minutes or until a toothpick comes out almost clean. Cool completely on a cooling rack, about 1 hour.

4 Frost the cooled brownies with vanilla frosting. Sprinkle with the chopped pretzels and nuts. Cut the brownies into 4 rows by 6 rows.

Nutritional Info: 1 Brownie: Calories 300; Total Fat 13g (Saturated Fat 4g); Sodium 310mg; Total Carbohydrate 42g (Dietary Fiber 1g); Protein 3g. Exchanges: 1-1/2 Starch, 1-1/2 Other Carbohydrate, 2 Fat. Carbohydrate Choices: 3.

Betty's Kitchen Tip

Peanuts or walnuts can be used instead of the mixed nuts if you prefer.

cinnamon roll cookies

Prep Time: 25 Minutes
Start to Finish: 1 Hour 10 Minutes
Servings: 20 cookies

- 1   pouch (1 lb 1.5 oz) Betty Crocker® sugar cookie mix
- 1/2   cup butter or margarine, softened
- 1/4   cup Gold Medal® all-purpose flour
- 1   egg

- 1   tablespoon butter, melted
- 1/4   cup granulated sugar
- 1   tablespoon ground cinnamon
- 3/4   cup powdered sugar
- 1   tablespoon milk

1. In a medium bowl, stir the cookie mix, softened butter, flour and egg until dough forms. On a floured surface, roll the dough to about 1/4-inch thickness. Brush with melted butter.

2. In a small bowl, mix the granulated sugar and cinnamon; sprinkle evenly over the dough. Roll up the dough jelly-roll fashion, starting at the long side. Wrap the roll in plastic wrap. Freeze 30 minutes or until firm.

3. Heat oven to 375°F. Cut the dough into 3/4-inch slices. On an ungreased cookie sheet, place the slices 2 inches apart.

4. Bake 11 to 12 minutes or until the edges are light golden brown. Cool 2 minutes; remove from the cookie sheet to a cooling rack. Cool completely, about 15 minutes.

5. In a small bowl, mix the powdered sugar and milk until smooth. Drizzle over the cooled cookies.

Nutritional Info: 1 Cookie: Calories 190; Total Fat 8g (Saturated Fat 4g); Sodium 107mg; Total Carbohydrate 28g (Dietary Fiber 0g); Protein 1g. Exchanges: 2 Other Carbohydrate, 1/2 Fat. Carbohydrate Choices: 2.

Betty's Kitchen Tip

Cinnamon Roll Cookies make a creative addition to any brunch spread. They're a fun play on the breakfast classic.

key lime bars

Prep Time: 15 Minutes
Start to Finish: 4 Hours 20 Minutes
Servings: 36 bars

EASY

- 1-1/2 cups graham cracker crumbs
- 1/3 cup butter or margarine, melted
- 3 tablespoons sugar
- 1 package (8 oz) cream cheese, softened
- 1 can (14 oz) sweetened condensed milk (not evaporated)
- 1/4 cup Key lime juice or regular lime juice
- 1 tablespoon grated lime peel

Additional lime peel, if desired

1 Heat oven to 350°F. Grease the bottom and sides of a 9-inch square pan with shortening or cooking spray.

2 In a small bowl, mix the cracker crumbs, butter and sugar thoroughly with a fork. Press evenly in the bottom of the pan. Refrigerate while preparing the cream cheese mixture.

3 In a small bowl, beat the cream cheese with an electric mixer on medium speed until light and fluffy. Gradually beat in the condensed milk until smooth. Beat in lime juice and lime peel. Spread over the crust.

4 Bake about 35 minutes or until the center is set. Cool 30 minutes. Cover loosely; refrigerate at least 3 hours or until chilled. Cut into 6 rows by 6 rows. Garnish with additional lime peel. Store bars covered in the refrigerator.

Nutritional Info: 1 Bar: Calories 90; Total Fat 5g (Saturated Fat 3g); Sodium 70mg; Total Carbohydrate 10g (Dietary Fiber 0g); Protein 1g. Exchanges: 1/2 Other Carbohydrate, 1 Fat. Carbohydrate Choices: 1/2.

Betty's Kitchen Tip

Melting butter and softening cream cheese is easy when you use the microwave. Microwave butter 1 minute on High in a microwavable bowl to melt, and unwrapped cream cheese 15 seconds on High to soften.

red velvet thumbprints

Prep Time: 45 Minutes
Start to Finish: 1 Hour 15 Minutes
Servings: 42 cookies

---

1 cup butter, softened	2-1/2 cups Gold Medal® all-purpose flour
1 cup sugar	3 tablespoons unsweetened baking cocoa
1 egg	1/4 teaspoon salt
4 teaspoons red food color	1 bag (11 oz) white vanilla baking chips (about 2 cups)
1 teaspoon vanilla	

---

1 Heat oven to 350°F. Line a cookie sheet with cooking parchment paper.

2 In a large bowl, beat butter and sugar with an electric mixer on medium speed about 2 minutes or until creamy. Stir in the egg, food color and vanilla until well blended. On low speed, beat in the flour, cocoa and salt until blended.

3 Shape the dough into 1-inch balls. On cookie sheets, place the balls 2 inches apart. Press thumb into the center of each cookie to make an indentation, but do not press all the way to the cookie sheet.

4 Bake 12 minutes or until set. Cool 2 minutes; quickly remake indentations with the end of a wooden spoon, if needed. Remove from the cookie sheet to a cooling rack. Cool completely, about 10 minutes.

5 In a small microwavable bowl, microwave white baking chips uncovered on High 30 to 50 seconds, stirring once, until softened and chips can be stirred smooth. Spoon melted chips into a resealable food-storage plastic bag; seal bag. Cut off a tiny corner of the bag. Twist the bag above the melted chips. Squeeze the bag to fill each thumbprint cookie. Let stand until set.

Nutritional Info: 1 Cookie: Calories 130; Total Fat 7g (Saturated Fat 4.5g); Sodium 70mg; Total Carbohydrate 15g (Dietary Fiber 0g); Protein 1g. Exchanges: 1/2 Starch, 1/2 Other Carbohydrate, 1-1/2 Fat. Carbohydrate Choices: 1.

Betty's Kitchen Tip

Use any shade of food color you wish to best fit the occasion, whether you're celebrating a holiday, birthday, sporting event or just because.

chocolate billionaires

Prep Time: 40 Minutes
Start to Finish: 50 Minutes
Servings: 50 candies

- 1 bag (14 oz) caramels, unwrapped
- 3 tablespoons water
- 1-1/2 cups chopped pecans, toasted
- 1-1/4 cups crisp rice cereal
- 3 cups semisweet chocolate chips (18 oz)
- 2 teaspoons shortening

1 Line two cookie sheets with waxed paper; spray the paper with cooking spray. In a 4-quart heavy saucepan, heat caramels and water over low heat, stirring constantly, until melted and smooth. Remove from heat. Stir in the pecans and cereal until coated. Roll the mixture into 1-inch balls; place on cookie sheets.

2 In a 3-quart heavy saucepan, heat the chocolate chips and shortening over low heat, stirring constantly, until melted and smooth. Remove from heat. Dip caramel-cereal balls into the melted chocolate, coating completely. Return to the cookie sheets. Refrigerate 10 minutes or just until set. Store candies tightly covered at room temperature.

Nutritional Info: 1 Candy: Calories 124; Total Fat 7g (Saturated Fat 3g); Sodium 25mg; Total Carbohydrate 16g (Dietary Fiber 1g); Protein 2g. Exchanges: 1 Other Carbohydrate, 1 Fat. Carbohydrate Choices: 1.

Betty's Kitchen Tip

Experiment with different cereals for this recipe, including peanut butter or chocolate puffs.

double mint brownies

Prep Time: 10 Minutes
Start to Finish: 3 Hours 5 Minutes
Servings: 48 brownies

EASY

- 1 box (1 lb 2.3 oz) Betty Crocker® fudge brownie mix
- Water, vegetable oil and eggs as called for on brownie mix box
- 1/2 cup unsalted butter, softened
- 1 box (1 lb) powdered sugar (4 cups)

- 5 tablespoons whipping cream
- 2 teaspoons peppermint extract
- 6 drops green food color, if desired
- 1 cup thin rectangular crème de menthe chocolate candies, unwrapped and shaved (about 34 candies)

1 Heat oven to 350°F. Line the bottom and sides of a 13x9-inch pan with foil, leaving the foil overhanging at two opposite sides of the pan; spray foil with cooking spray.

2 Make the brownies as directed on the box for fudge-like brownies, using water, oil and eggs. Spread batter in the pan.

3 Bake 25 minutes or until a toothpick inserted 2 inches from the edge of the pan comes out clean. Cool completely on a cooling rack, about 30 minutes.

4 In a large bowl, beat the butter, powdered sugar, 1/4 cup of the whipping cream and the peppermint extract with an electric mixer on medium speed until smooth. If the frosting is too thick, stir in remaining 1 tablespoon whipping cream. Stir in the food color. Frost the brownies. Refrigerate at least 2 hours. Use the foil to lift brownies out of the pan. Cut into 8 rows by 6 rows. Top with shaved candies.

Nutritional Info: 1 Brownie: Calories 149; Total Fat 8g (Saturated Fat 3g); Sodium 37mg; Total Carbohydrate 20g (Dietary Fiber 0g); Protein 1g. Exchanges: 1-1/2 Other Carbohydrate, 1 Fat. Carbohydrate Choices: 1-1/2.

Betty's Kitchen Tip

Use shortening or cooking spray to grease baking pans but only when the recipe says doing so is needed.

hazelnut cappuccino crinkles

Prep Time: 30 Minutes
Start to Finish: 30 Minutes
Servings: 30 cookies

QUICK

1	pouch (1 lb 1.5 oz) Betty Crocker® double chocolate chunk cookie mix
3	tablespoons vegetable oil
2	tablespoons hazelnut-flavored syrup
2	teaspoons instant coffee granules or crystals
1	egg
1/2	cup powdered sugar
30	chocolate-covered coffee beans

1 Heat oven to 375°F. In a large bowl, stir cookie mix, oil, syrup, coffee granules and egg until a soft dough forms.

2 Shape the dough into 1-inch balls; roll each in powdered sugar. On an ungreased cookie sheet, place the balls 2 inches apart.

3 Bake about 9 minutes or until set. Immediately press 1 coffee bean into the top of each cookie. Cool 1 minute; remove from the cookie sheet to a cooling rack.

Nutritional Info: 1 Cookie: Calories 100; Total Fat 4g (Saturated Fat 1g); Sodium 65mg; Total Carbohydrate 16g (Dietary Fiber 0g); Protein 0g. Exchanges: 1 Other Carbohydrate, 1/2 Fat. Carbohydrate Choices: 1.

Betty's Kitchen Tip

Find hazelnut-flavored syrup in the coffee section of your grocery store. Gift a coffee lover with a large mug full of Hazelnut Cappuccino Crinkles wrapped and tied with ribbon.

fruitcake-filled icebox cookies

Prep Time: 25 Minutes
Start to Finish: 3 Hours 25 Minutes
Servings: 60 cookies

1 cup butter, softened	2-1/4 cups Gold Medal® all-purpose flour
1 cup superfine sugar	1/2 teaspoon salt
1 egg	1 loaf (16 oz) fruitcake
2 teaspoons rum extract or vanilla	1-1/2 cups finely chopped pecans or walnuts

1. In a large bowl, beat butter and sugar with an electric mixer on medium speed until light and fluffy. Beat in the egg and rum extract. On medium-low speed, beat in the flour and salt until blended. Cover; refrigerate at least 1 hour.

2. Cut the fruitcake lengthwise in half. Shape each portion into a 10-1/2-inch log on cooking parchment paper. Divide the cookie dough in half. On a lightly floured surface, roll each portion of dough into an 11x9-inch rectangle. Place 1 fruitcake log on the long edge of 1 dough rectangle; roll up jelly-roll fashion, starting from the long side. Coat outside of roll generously with nuts. Repeat with the second portion of fruitcake and dough. Wrap tightly in plastic wrap; refrigerate 2 hours or until firm.

3. Heat oven to 350°F. Unwrap the dough; cut into 1/4-inch slices. On ungreased cookie sheets, place slices 3 inches apart. Bake about 12 minutes or until lightly golden. Remove from cookie sheets to cooling racks.

Nutritional Info: 1 Cookie: Calories 102; Total Fat 6g (Saturated Fat 2g); Sodium 72mg; Total Carbohydrate 12g (Dietary Fiber 1g); Protein 1g. Exchanges: 1 Other Carbohydrate, 1 Fat. Carbohydrate Choices: 1.

Betty's Kitchen Tip

Don't have superfine sugar on hand? Make your own by processing granulated sugar in a food processor 1 to 2 minutes.

tropical macaroons

Prep Time: 50 Minutes
Start to Finish: 50 Minutes
Servings: 24 cookies

- 3 egg whites
- 2/3 cup sugar
- 3 cups flaked coconut
- 1 cup finely chopped tropical trio dried fruit
- 1/2 cup finely chopped macadamia nuts, lightly toasted
- 3 tablespoons finely chopped crystallized ginger

1 Heat oven to 325°F. Line cookie sheets with cooking parchment paper.

2 In a large bowl, beat the egg whites with an electric mixer until foamy. Add the sugar, 1 tablespoon at a time, beating 2 to 4 minutes until stiff peaks form and sugar is dissolved. Fold in the coconut, dried fruit, macadamia nuts and ginger. Onto cookie sheets, drop the mixture by rounded tablespoonfuls 2 inches apart.

3 Bake 18 minutes or until set and lightly browned. Cool 1 minute; remove from cookie sheets to cooling racks.

Nutritional Info: 1 Cookie: Calories 126; Total Fat 6g (Saturated Fat 3g); Sodium 46mg; Total Carbohydrate 18g (Dietary Fiber 2g); Protein 1g. Exchanges: 1 Other Carbohydrate, 1 Fat. Carbohydrate Choices: 1.

Betty's Kitchen Tip

For added tropical flavor and color, substitute 1/2 cup chopped dried papaya or mango in place of the crystallized ginger.

frosted maple cookies

Prep Time: 50 Minutes
Start to Finish: 1 Hour 20 Minutes
Servings: 72 cookies

Cookies

2/3	cup shortening
2/3	cup butter, softened
2	cups granulated sugar
2	eggs
2	teaspoons maple flavor
3-1/2	cups Gold Medal® all-purpose flour
2	teaspoons baking powder
1/2	teaspoon salt

Frosting

1/2	cup butter, softened
2	cups powdered sugar
1	teaspoon maple flavor
2	tablespoons milk

Maple or brown sugar

1 Heat oven to 350°F. Line cookie sheets with cooking parchment paper.

2 In a large bowl, beat shortening, 2/3 cup butter and 1-1/2 cups of the granulated sugar with an electric mixer on medium speed until creamy. Beat in the eggs and 2 teaspoons maple flavor. On low speed, beat in flour, baking powder and salt just until combined.

3 Shape the dough into 1-inch balls. Roll the balls in remaining 1/2 cup granulated sugar. On cookie sheets, place the balls 2 inches apart.

4 Bake 10 to 12 minutes or until set and bottoms are lightly browned. Remove from cookie sheets to cooling racks; cool completely, about 20 minutes.

5 In a medium bowl, beat frosting ingredients with an electric mixer on medium speed until smooth. Spread 1 teaspoon frosting on top of each cookie. Sprinkle with maple or brown sugar.

Nutritional Info: 1 Cookie: Calories 102; Total Fat 5g (Saturated Fat 2g); Sodium 57mg; Total Carbohydrate 14g (Dietary Fiber 0g); Protein 1g. Exchanges: 1 Other Carbohydrate, 1 Fat. Carbohydrate Choices: 1.

Betty's Kitchen Tip

You can find maple sugar at specialty food shops and on the Internet.

raspberry-orange thumbprints

Prep Time: 50 Minutes
Start to Finish: 2 Hours
Servings: 36 cookies

- -

1	cup butter, softened
3/4	cup granulated sugar
1	egg
1	teaspoon grated orange peel
1/2	teaspoon vanilla
2	cups Gold Medal® all-purpose flour
1/2	teaspoon salt

Powdered sugar, if desired

1/4	cup raspberry jam (or other favorite flavor)

- -

1 In a large bowl, beat the butter with an electric mixer on medium speed until creamy; add the granulated sugar, beating until blended. Add the egg, orange peel and vanilla; beat until blended. On low speed, beat in the flour and salt until blended. Wrap the dough in plastic wrap. Refrigerate 1 hour.

2 Heat oven to 350°F. Line a cookie sheet with cooking parchment paper. Shape the dough into 1-inch balls. On the cookie sheet, place the balls 2 inches apart. Press thumb into the center of each cookie to make an indentation, but do not press all the way to the cookie sheet.

3 Bake 12 to 15 minutes or until light golden brown. Quickly remake indentations with the end of a wooden spoon, if necessary. Immediately remove from the cookie sheet to a cooling rack; cool completely. Sprinkle with powdered sugar. Fill each thumbprint with about 1/4 teaspoon of jam.

Nutritional Info: 1 Cookie: Calories 95; Total Fat 5g (Saturated Fat 3g); Sodium 80mg; Total Carbohydrate 11g (Dietary Fiber 0g); Protein 1g. Exchanges: 1/2 Other Carbohydrate, 1 Fat. Carbohydrate Choices: 1/2.

Betty's Kitchen Tip

Raspberry-Orange Thumbprints should be stored in a container with a loosely fitting lid, such as a cookie tin.

warm toasted
marshmallow s'mores bars

Prep Time: 20 Minutes
Start to Finish: 55 Minutes
Servings: 24 bars

1   pouch (1 lb 1.5 oz) Betty Crocker®
    sugar cookie mix
1   cup graham cracker crumbs

1   cup butter or margarine, melted
3   cups milk chocolate chips (18 oz)
4-1/2   cups miniature marshmallows

1 Heat oven to 375°F. In a large bowl, stir together the cookie mix and cracker crumbs. Stir in the butter until a soft dough forms. Press into an ungreased 13x9-inch pan.

2 Bake 18 to 20 minutes or until set. Immediately sprinkle the chocolate chips over the baked layer. Let stand 3 to 5 minutes or until the chocolate begins to melt. Spread the chocolate evenly over the baked layer.

3 Set oven control to broil. Sprinkle the marshmallows over the melted chocolate. Broil with the top 5 to 6 inches from the heat 20 to 30 seconds or until the marshmallows are toasted. (Watch closely; the marshmallows will brown quickly.) Cool 10 minutes. Cut into 6 rows by 4 rows. Serve warm. Store any remaining bars tightly covered.

Nutritional Info: 1 Bar: Calories 310; Total Fat 16g (Saturated Fat 9g); Sodium 160mg; Total Carbohydrate 39g (Dietary Fiber 1g); Protein 3g. Exchanges: 1 Starch, 1-1/2 Other Carbohydrate, 3 Fat. Carbohydrate Choices: 2-1/2.

Betty's Kitchen Tip

To reheat, place individual bars on a microwavable plate. Microwave uncovered on High about 15 seconds or until warm.

frosting cereal bars

Prep Time: 10 Minutes
Start to Finish: 40 Minutes
Servings: 24 bars

EASY

- 1 container (1 lb) Betty Crocker® Rich & Creamy milk chocolate frosting
- 1/4 cup butter, cut into pieces
- 1 bag (11.5 oz) milk chocolate chips (2 cups)
- 5 cups Cocoa Puffs® cereal
- 1 cup dry-roasted peanuts
- 1/2 cup miniature candy-coated chocolate candies

1 Spray the bottom only of a 13x9-inch pan with cooking spray.

2 Spoon frosting into a large microwavable bowl; add the butter. Microwave uncovered on High 1 minute 30 seconds. Stir well; microwave 1 minute longer or until melted and hot. Sprinkle the chocolate chips over the hot mixture. Do not stir. Microwave on High 30 seconds. Let stand 2 to 3 minutes or until the chips are melted. Stir to blend. Stir in the cereal and peanuts.

3 Spoon the mixture into the pan. Sprinkle candies over the cereal mixture; pat lightly to evenly spread the mixture in the pan and to press the candies into the mixture. Refrigerate 30 minutes or until chilled and set. Cut into 6 rows by 4 rows.

Nutritional Info: 1 Bar: Calories 240; Total Fat 13g (Saturated Fat 6g); Sodium 160mg; Total Carbohydrate 29g (Dietary Fiber 1g); Protein 3g. Exchanges: 1/2 Starch, 1-1/2 Other Carbohydrate, 2-1/2 Fat. Carbohydrate Choices: 2.

Betty's Kitchen Tip

For peanut butter bars, substitute 1 bag (10 ounces) peanut butter chips and 1/2 cup creamy peanut butter for the chocolate chips, stirring in the peanut butter after the chips are melted. Use lightly salted cocktail peanuts for the dry-roasted peanuts. Be sure to store the bars tightly covered so they stay crisp.

best lemon bars

Prep Time: 15 Minutes
Start to Finish: 2 Hours 50 Minutes
Servings: 24 bars

EASY

Crust

- 1 pouch (1 lb 1.5 oz) Betty Crocker® sugar cookie mix
- 2 tablespoons Gold Medal® all-purpose flour
- 1/2 cup cold butter

Filling

- 4 egg yolks
- 1 can (14 oz) sweetened condensed milk (not evaporated)
- 1 tablespoon Gold Medal® all-purpose flour
- Grated peel of 1 lemon (about 2 teaspoons)
- 1/3 cup fresh lemon juice
- 1 tablespoon powdered sugar

1 Heat oven to 350°F. Spray the bottom only of a 13x9-inch pan with cooking spray.

2 In a large bowl, stir the cookie mix and 2 tablespoons flour. Cut in the butter, using a pastry blender (or pulling two table knives through the ingredients in opposite directions), until the mixture looks like fine crumbs. Press the mixture into the bottom of the pan. Bake 13 to 15 minutes or until the edges are lightly browned.

3 Meanwhile, in a medium bowl, mix the egg yolks, condensed milk, 1 tablespoon flour, the lemon peel and lemon juice with a whisk. Pour over the hot crust. Bake 18 to 20 minutes longer or until the filling is set. Cool on a cooling rack 1 hour. Cover; refrigerate bars until thoroughly chilled, about 1 hour.

4 Sprinkle the bars with powdered sugar. Cut into 6 rows by 4 rows. Store tightly covered in the refrigerator.

Nutritional Info: 1 Bar: Calories 190; Total Fat 8g (Saturated Fat 4g); Sodium 110mg; Total Carbohydrate 26g (Dietary Fiber 0g); Protein 2g. Exchanges: 1/2 Starch, 1 Other Carbohydrate, 1-1/2 Fat. Carbohydrate Choices: 2.

Betty's Kitchen Tip

If desired, garnish each bar with a few fresh blueberries for a sweet-tart topper. Bars can be frozen, tightly wrapped, up to 3 months.

fig-walnut gingerbread bars

Prep Time: 15 Minutes
Start to Finish: 3 Hours
Servings: 16 bars

1	pouch (1 lb 1.5 oz) Betty Crocker® gingerbread cookie mix
1/2	cup butter, softened
1	egg
1	jar (11.5 oz) fig preserves
1/2	cup chopped dried Calimyrna figs
2	tablespoons packed brown sugar
1/2	cup chopped walnuts, toasted

Powdered sugar, if desired

1 Heat oven to 350°F. Line an 8 inch square pan with foil, leaving the foil overhanging at two opposite sides of the pan; spray the foil with cooking spray.

2 In a large bowl, stir cookie mix, butter and egg until soft dough forms. Reserve 2/3 cup dough. Press the remaining dough into the bottom of the pan. Bake 15 minutes.

3 In a small bowl, mix the preserves, chopped figs and brown sugar. Spread over the partially baked cookie crust. Stir the walnuts into the reserved dough; crumble over the filling.

4 Bake 30 to 32 minutes or until golden. Cool completely in the pan on a cooling rack, about 2 hours. Use foil to lift bars out of the pan. Cut into 4 rows by 4 rows. Sprinkle the bars with powdered sugar.

Nutritional Info: 1 Bar: Calories 275; Total Fat 11g (Saturated Fat 5g); Sodium 269mg; Total Carbohydrate 41g (Dietary Fiber 1g); Protein 3g. Exchanges: 1/2 Starch, 2 Other Carbohydrate, 2 Fat. Carbohydrate Choices: 2-1/2.

Betty's Kitchen Tip

Gingerbread cookie mix brings a wonderful holiday spice flavor to these gooey fig bars.

cappuccino pistachio shortbread

Prep Time: 30 Minutes
Start to Finish: 1 Hour
Servings: 32 cookies

3	tablespoons instant cappuccino coffee mix	1-3/4	cups Gold Medal® all-purpose flour
1	tablespoon water	3/4	cup chopped pistachio nuts
3/4	cup butter or margarine, softened	1/3	cup white baking chips
1/2	cup powdered sugar	1	teaspoon shortening

1 Heat oven to 350°F. In a medium bowl, stir coffee mix in water until dissolved. Stir in the butter and powdered sugar. Stir in the flour and 1/2 cup of the nuts, using hands if necessary, until a stiff dough forms.

2 Divide dough in half. Shape each half into a ball. On a lightly floured surface, pat each ball into a 6-inch round, about 1/2 inch thick. Cut each round into 16 wedges. On an ungreased cookie sheet, arrange the wedges about 1/2 inch apart with pointed ends toward the center.

3 Bake 12 to 15 minutes or until golden brown. Immediately remove from the cookie sheet to a cooling rack. Cool completely, about 30 minutes.

4 Place the remaining 1/4 cup nuts in a small bowl. In a small microwavable bowl, microwave the white baking chips and shortening uncovered on Medium (50%) 3 to 4 minutes, stirring after 2 minutes, until the mixture can be stirred smooth and is thin enough to drizzle. Dip an edge of each cookie into the melted mixture, then into nuts. Place on waxed paper; let stand until set.

Nutritional Info: 1 Cookie: Calories 105; Total Fat 7g (Saturated Fat 3g); Sodium 45mg; Total Carbohydrate 10g (Dietary Fiber 0g); Protein 2g. Exchanges: 1/2 Other Carbohydrate, 1-1/2 Fat. Carbohydrate Choices: 1/2.

Betty's Kitchen Tip

Pistachio nuts not only add texture but also lend a hint of green color to this shortbread treat.

DOWN-HOME DESSERTS

p. 270

271

281

280

brown sugar-sweet potato tarts

Prep Time: 30 Minutes
Start to Finish: 1 Hour 45 Minutes
Servings: 8 tarts

Pastry

2-2/3	cups Gold Medal® all-purpose flour
1	teaspoon salt
1	cup shortening
7	to 8 tablespoons cold water

Filling

1	can (23 oz) sweet potatoes, drained, 2 tablespoons syrup reserved

3/4	cup packed brown sugar
3	eggs, beaten
1-1/2	teaspoons pumpkin pie spice
1/2	teaspoon salt
1	cup evaporated milk

Topping

Whipped cream, if desired

1 Heat oven to 425°F. In a large bowl, mix flour and 1 teaspoon salt. Cut in the shortening, using a pastry blender, until pieces are the size of small peas. Sprinkle with cold water, 1 tablespoon at a time, tossing with a fork until all the flour is moistened and the pastry almost leaves the side of the bowl.

2 Divide the pastry in half. Roll each half into a 13-inch round; cut each into 4 (5-inch) rounds. In each of 8 (4-1/2-inch) foil tart pans, fit a pastry round into the bottom and just up to top edge. Place on a large cookie sheet. Bake 3 to 4 minutes or until dry; cool. Cut the pastry scraps into small leaf shapes. Place the cutouts on another cookie sheet; sprinkle with granulated sugar, if desired. Bake 6 to 7 minutes or until golden brown; cool.

3 In a food processor, place the sweet potatoes and 2 tablespoons reserved syrup. Cover; process until smooth. Spoon into a large bowl. Add the brown sugar, eggs, pumpkin pie spice and 1/2 teaspoon salt. Beat until smooth. Stir in the milk. Pour mixture into partially baked tart shells. Reduce oven temperature to 375°F. Bake 25 to 35 minutes or until a knife inserted in the center comes out clean. Cool completely, about 30 minutes. Remove from the pans. Garnish with pastry leaves and whipped cream.

Nutritional Info: 1 Tart: Calories 620; Total Fat 30g (Saturated Fat 8g); Sodium 540mg; Total Carbohydrate 78g (Dietary Fiber 4g); Protein 10g. Exchanges: 3 Starch, 2 Other Carbohydrate, 6 Fat. Carbohydrate Choices: 5.

praline pumpkin dessert

Prep Time: 20 Minutes
Start to Finish: 1 Hour 20 Minutes
Servings: 12

- 1   can (15 oz) pumpkin (not pumpkin pie mix)
- 1   can (12 oz) evaporated milk
- 3   eggs
- 1   cup sugar
- 4   teaspoons pumpkin pie spice
- 1   box Betty Crocker® SuperMoist® golden vanilla cake mix
- 1-1/2   cups chopped pecans or walnuts
- 3/4   cup butter or margarine, melted

Whipping cream, if desired
Additional pumpkin pie spice, if desired

1 Heat oven to 350°F. Grease the bottom and sides of a 13x9-inch pan with shortening or cooking spray. In a medium bowl, beat the pumpkin, milk, eggs, sugar and 4 teaspoons pumpkin pie spice with a wire whisk until smooth. Pour into the pan.

2 Sprinkle dry cake mix over the pumpkin mixture. Sprinkle with pecans. Pour the melted butter evenly over top of dessert.

3 Bake 50 to 60 minutes or until a knife inserted in the center comes out clean. Cool slightly and serve warm or chilled with a dollop of whipped cream sprinkled with pumpkin pie spice. Store covered in the refrigerator.

Nutritional Info: 1 Serving: Calories 350; Total Fat 24g (Saturated Fat 9g); Sodium 160mg; Total Carbohydrate 28g (Dietary Fiber 2g); Protein 5g. Exchanges: 1-1/2 Starch, 1/2 Other Carbohydrate, 4-1/2 Fat. Carbohydrate Choices: 2.

Betty's Kitchen Tip

Use canned pumpkin, not pumpkin pie mix, for this dessert. Pumpkin pie mix contains sugar and spices, not just pumpkin.

apple-ginger-cranberry crisp

Prep Time: 15 Minutes
Start to Finish: 1 Hour 25 Minutes
Servings: 12

EASY

Filling

4	medium tart cooking apples, peeled and sliced (about 4-1/2 cups)
2	Gala apples, peeled and sliced (about 2 cups)
2	cups fresh or frozen (do not thaw) cranberries
1	cup packed brown sugar
3	tablespoons Gold Medal® all-purpose flour
3	tablespoons cold butter, cut into 6 pieces
2	tablespoons lemon juice
2	teaspoons grated gingerroot
1-1/2	teaspoons ground cinnamon

Topping

1	cup Gold Medal® all-purpose flour
1/2	cup quick-cooking or old-fashioned oats
1/2	cup packed brown sugar
3	tablespoons finely chopped crystallized ginger
1/2	cup cold butter or margarine, cut into 8 pieces
1/4	cup chopped walnuts

Vanilla ice cream, if desired

1 In a large bowl, mix all of the filling ingredients. Let stand 30 minutes.

2 Heat oven to 400°F. Spray a 13x9-inch pan with cooking spray. Spoon the apple mixture into the pan.

3 In a medium bowl, mix 1 cup flour, oats, 1/2 cup brown sugar and the ginger. Cut in 1/2 cup butter, using a pastry blender (or pulling two table knives through the ingredients in opposite directions), until the mixture is crumbly. Stir in the walnuts. Sprinkle evenly over the apples.

4 Bake 40 minutes or until the apples are tender when pierced with a fork and the topping is golden brown. Serve with ice cream.

Nutritional Info: 1 Serving: Calories 297; Total Fat 13g (Saturated Fat 7g); Sodium 8mg; Total Carbohydrate 46g (Dietary Fiber 3g); Protein 3g. Exchanges: 1/2 Starch, 1 Fruit, 1 Other Carbohydrate, 2-1/2 Fat. Carbohydrate Choices: 3.

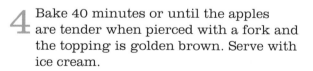

Betty's Kitchen Tip

Serve fruit crisps within 24 hours of baking for the best flavor and quality. They make tasty breakfast items as leftovers, too!

banana split cake parfaits

Prep Time: 25 Minutes
Start to Finish: 2 Hours 15 Minutes
Servings: 12

- 1 box Betty Crocker® SuperMoist® yellow cake mix
- 1 box (4-serving size) banana instant pudding and pie filling mix
- 3/4 cup vegetable oil
- 3/4 cup buttermilk
- 1 teaspoon vanilla
- 4 eggs
- 2 ripe bananas, mashed
- 1-1/2 quarts vanilla ice cream
- 1 box (10 oz) frozen sweetened sliced strawberries, thawed
- 3/4 cup hot fudge topping
- 3/4 cup frozen (thawed) whipped topping
- 12 maraschino cherries with stems

1. Heat oven to 350°F (325°F for dark or nonstick pan). Spray the bottom only of a 13x9-inch pan with baking spray with flour. In a large bowl, beat the cake mix, pudding mix, oil, buttermilk, vanilla, eggs and bananas with an electric mixture on low speed 30 seconds. Beat on medium speed 2 minutes. Pour into the pan.

2. Bake 50 to 55 minutes or until deep golden brown and a toothpick inserted in the center comes out clean. Cool completely, about 1 hour.

3. Cut the cake in half lengthwise, then cut it crosswise 11 times to make a total of 24 slices. Place 2 cake slices in each of 12 banana split dishes or parfait glasses. Top each serving with 2 small scoops of ice cream. Spoon the strawberries over one scoop. Drizzle the hot fudge topping over the other scoop. Garnish each serving with whipped topping, fudge topping and a maraschino cherry.

Nutritional Info: 1 Serving: Calories 610; Total Fat 27g (Saturated Fat 10g); Sodium 560mg; Total Carbohydrate 83g (Dietary Fiber 2g); Protein 7g. Exchanges: 2 Starch, 3-1/2 Other Carbohydrate, 5 Fat. Carbohydrate Choices: 5-1/2.

Betty's Kitchen Tip

Banana splits usually have three toppings: strawberry, chocolate and pineapple. If your family likes pineapple, spoon a little pineapple topping over the ice cream. If you don't have parfait dishes or long banana split ones, just cut cake into squares and use round dessert bowls.

blueberry-peach cobbler with walnut biscuits

Prep Time: 30 Minutes
Start to Finish: 1 Hour 40 Minutes
Servings: 6

Fruit Mixture

8	medium fresh peaches (about 2 lb), peeled, each cut into 6 wedges
1	cup fresh blueberries
1	tablespoon cornstarch
1/2	cup granulated sugar
1	tablespoon lemon juice
1/4	teaspoon ground cinnamon

Dash salt

Biscuit Topping

1	cup Original Bisquick® mix
1/4	teaspoon ground nutmeg
2	tablespoons milk
2	tablespoons butter or margarine, softened
2	tablespoons granulated sugar
2/3	cup chopped walnuts
2	teaspoons milk, if desired
1	tablespoon coarse sugar

1 Heat oven to 400°F. In a medium bowl, stir all fruit mixture ingredients; let stand 10 minutes to allow the sugar to pull juices from the peaches.

2 Transfer the fruit mixture to an ungreased 8-inch square (2-quart) glass baking dish. Bake uncovered about 10 minutes or until the fruit is bubbling. Remove from oven; stir. Bake 10 to 12 minutes longer or until bubbly around the edges (fruit must be hot in the middle so the biscuit topping bakes completely).

3 Meanwhile, in a medium bowl, stir biscuit topping ingredients except 2 teaspoons milk and coarse sugar until a firm dough forms. Drop the dough by 6 spoonfuls onto the warm fruit mixture. Brush the dough with 2 teaspoons milk; sprinkle with coarse sugar.

4 Bake 25 to 30 minutes or until the biscuits are deep golden brown and the center of the biscuits are no longer doughy on the bottom. Cool 10 minutes on a cooling rack. Serve warm.

Nutritional Info: 1 Serving: Calories 410; Total Fat 15g (Saturated Fat 4g); Sodium 300mg; Total Carbohydrate 62g (Dietary Fiber 5g); Protein 5g. Exchanges: 1-1/2 Starch, 1-1/2 Fruit, 1 Other Carbohydrate, 3 Fat. Carbohydrate Choices: 4.

mini apple crostatas

Prep Time: 15 Minutes
Start to Finish: 35 Minutes
Servings: 4

EASY

- 1 Pillsbury® refrigerated pie crust, softened as directed on box
- 2 tablespoons sugar
- 1/4 teaspoon ground cinnamon
- 1 large baking apple, peeled, cored and thinly sliced (about 2 cups)
- 8 teaspoons caramel topping

1 Heat oven to 425°F. Line a cookie sheet with cooking parchment paper. Unroll the crust on a work surface. Roll out slightly; cut into 4 (5-inch) rounds. Place the rounds on the cookie sheet.

2 In a medium bowl, mix the sugar and cinnamon. Add the apple slices; toss to coat with the sugar mixture. Divide the apple slices evenly onto the center of each round. Fold 1/2-inch of crust over the filling, pinching slightly so that the crust lies flat over the apples.

3 Bake 18 to 20 minutes or until the crust is golden brown and the apples are tender. Drizzle 2 teaspoons caramel topping over each crostata. Serve warm with ice cream, if desired.

Nutritional Info: 1 Serving: Calories 360; Total Fat 15g (Saturated Fat 6g); Sodium 300mg; Total Carbohydrate 52g (Dietary Fiber 2g); Protein 4g. Exchanges: 2 Starch, 1-1/2 Other Carbohydrate, 2-1/2 Fat. Carbohydrate Choices: 3-1/2.

Betty's Kitchen Tip

Soft dollops of fresh whipped cream make a tasty topper with the caramel.

chocolate-dipped pecan wedges

Prep Time: 25 Minutes
Start to Finish: 3 Hours 25 Minutes
Servings: 36 cookies

Crust

2	cups Gold Medal® all-purpose flour
1/2	cup granulated sugar
1/4	teaspoon salt
3/4	cup cold butter or margarine, cut into small pieces
1	egg

Filling

1	cup packed brown sugar
1/2	cup granulated sugar
1	cup butter (do not use margarine)
1/2	cup honey
4	cups coarsely chopped pecans
1/4	cup whipping cream
1	teaspoon grated orange peel

Glaze

1	bag (12 oz) semisweet chocolate chips (2 cups)
4	teaspoons shortening

Kosher salt, if desired

1 Heat oven to 375°F. Line the bottom and sides of a 13x9-inch pan with foil; grease foil with shortening. In a food processor, place the flour, 1/2 cup granulated sugar, salt and 3/4 cup butter. Process until it reaches the consistency of coarse crumbs. Add egg; process until dough forms a ball. Press into the pan.

2 Bake 15 minutes, until edges are lightly golden. Cool on a cooling rack. Reduce oven temperature to 325°F. In a 3-quart saucepan, cook the brown sugar, 1/2 cup granulated sugar, 1 cup butter and the honey over medium heat until the butter melts. Increase heat to high; boil 1 minute. Remove from heat; stir in the pecans, whipping cream and orange peel. Pour over the crust.

3 Bake 40 to 45 minutes or until the filling is set at least 2 inches from the edge of the pan but the center still jiggles slightly. Cool completely. Cut into 6 rows by 3 rows; cut each cookie in half diagonally.

4 In a small microwavable bowl, microwave the chocolate chips and shortening 1 to 2 minutes or until smooth. Dip the tip of each triangle into the glaze. Sprinkle with kosher salt.

Nutritional Info: 1 Cookie: Calories 305; Total Fat 22g (Saturated Fat 9g); Sodium 101mg; Total Carbohydrate 29g (Dietary Fiber 2g); Protein 3g. Exchanges: 1/2 Starch, 1-1/2 Other Carbohydrate, 4 Fat. Carbohydrate Choices: 2.

caramel-pear crumble

Prep Time: 20 Minutes
Start to Finish: 1 Hour 5 Minutes
Servings: 8

6	slightly ripe medium Bartlett pears (about 3 lb), peeled and sliced (about 6 cups)
1	cup caramel bits
1/4	cup packed brown sugar
2	tablespoons Gold Medal® all-purpose flour
1	teaspoon ground cinnamon
1/2	pouch (1 lb 1.5 oz) Betty Crocker® oatmeal cookie mix (about 1-1/2 cups)
1/4	cup cold butter or margarine, cut into pieces
1/4	cup caramel topping

1 Heat oven to 375°F. Spray the bottom and sides of an 8-inch square (2-quart) glass baking dish with cooking spray.

2 In a large bowl, mix pears, caramel bits, brown sugar, flour and cinnamon until evenly coated. Spread in the dish. In the same bowl, place the cookie mix. Cut in the butter, using a pastry blender (or pulling two table knives through the mix in opposite directions), until the mixture looks like coarse crumbs. Crumble over the pears.

3 Bake 45 minutes or until the pears are tender and crumb topping is golden brown. Drizzle with caramel.

Nutritional Info: 1 Serving: Calories 342; Total Fat 9g (Saturated Fat 4g); Sodium 188mg; Total Carbohydrate 69g (Dietary Fiber 5g); Protein 3g. Exchanges: 1-1/2 Fruit, 2-1/2 Other Carbohydrate, 1 Fat. Carbohydrate Choices: 4.

Betty's Kitchen Tip

Use the leftover 1/2 pouch cookie mix as a streusel for muffins. Cut in 1/4 cup cold butter and sprinkle on batter before baking.

pear-apple-granola crisp

Prep Time: 10 Minutes
Start to Finish: 1 Hour 10 Minutes
Servings: 8

EASY

- 2 lb Bosc pears, peeled and coarsely chopped (4 cups)
- 2 lb Pink Lady apples or other firm apples, peeled and coarsely chopped (4 cups)
- 1/2 cup sugar
- 2 tablespoons Gold Medal® all-purpose flour
- 2 tablespoons lemon juice
- 1 teaspoon ground cinnamon

- 1/2 teaspoon ground nutmeg
- 1 cup chopped pitted dates
- 4 oz chèvre (goat) cheese, crumbled (1 cup)
- 2 cups Cascadian Farm® organic fruit & nut granola
- 1/2 cup butter or margarine, melted
- 3 tablespoons honey

1 Heat oven to 375°F. Spray the bottom and sides of a 13x9-inch (3-quart) glass baking dish with cooking spray.

2 In a large bowl, stir pears, apples, sugar, flour, lemon juice, cinnamon and nutmeg. Fold in the dates and cheese. Spread in the baking dish. In the same bowl, mix the granola and butter; sprinkle over the fruit mixture. Drizzle with honey.

3 Bake 50 to 60 minutes or until apples are tender and topping is golden brown, covering with foil after 20 minutes to prevent excessive browning. Serve warm.

Nutritional Info: 1 Serving: Calories 432; Total Fat 17g (Saturated Fat 10g); Sodium 168mg; Total Carbohydrate 71g (Dietary Fiber 7g); Protein 5g. Exchanges: 1 Starch, 1-1/2 Other Carbohydrate, 3 Fat. Carbohydrate Choices: 4-1/2.

Betty's Kitchen Tip

Omit the goat cheese, if desired. The crisp is great with or without the hint of cheese.

cherry-raspberry chocolate cobbler

Prep Time: 10 Minutes
Start to Finish: 40 Minutes
Servings: 8

EASY

Jeanne Holt
Mendota Heights, MN
Better with Bisquick® Recipe Contest

- 1   can (21 oz) cherry pie filling
- 1/2   teaspoon almond extract
- 2   cups fresh raspberries
- 3/4   cup chocolate ice cream
- 1/2   cup bittersweet chocolate chips
- 1   cup Original Bisquick® mix
- 3   tablespoons sliced almonds

1. Heat oven to 375°F. In a medium bowl, combine the pie filling and extract; fold in the raspberries. Spread in an ungreased 8-inch square pan. Bake for 15 minutes.

2. Meanwhile, in a medium microwavable bowl, microwave the ice cream and chocolate chips on High about 1 minute 30 seconds, stirring every 30 seconds, until smooth. Add the Bisquick mix; mix well. Let stand until fruit is done baking.

3. Drop the dough into 8 mounds (about 3 tablespoons each) on hot fruit. Sprinkle each mound with almonds. Bake 15 to 18 minutes longer or until the chocolate topping is just set. Serve warm.

Nutritional Info: 1 Serving: Calories 260; Total Fat 8g (Saturated Fat 3.5g); Sodium 200mg; Total Carbohydrate 44g (Dietary Fiber 4g); Protein 3g. Exchanges: 1 Starch, 1/2 Fruit, 1-1/2 Other Carbohydrate, 1-1/2 Fat. Carbohydrate Choices: 3.

Betty's Kitchen Tip

Bittersweet chocolate chips are not as sweet as the common semisweet type. Find them near the other chocolate chips at the grocery store.

red velvet whoopie pies

Prep Time: 50 Minutes
Start to Finish: 1 Hour 5 Minutes
Servings: 14

Cookies

2	tablespoons butter, softened
1/2	cup granulated sugar
1-1/2	cups Original Bisquick® mix
2	tablespoons unsweetened baking cocoa
1	egg
1/3	cup milk

1	teaspoon vanilla
2	teaspoons red food color

Filling

4	oz (half of 8-oz package) cream cheese, softened
1/4	cup butter, softened
1/2	teaspoon vanilla
1-1/4	cups powdered sugar

1 Heat oven to 350°F. Line 2 large cookie sheets with cooking parchment paper.

2 In a medium bowl, beat 2 tablespoons butter and the granulated sugar with an electric mixer on low speed until mixture is light and fluffy. Add the remaining cookie ingredients. Beat on medium speed 4 minutes, scraping the bowl occasionally, until smooth. Onto the cookie sheets, drop 28 slightly rounded tablespoonfuls of dough at least 2 inches apart.

3 Bake 8 to 10 minutes or until the tops spring back when lightly touched. Cool 2 minutes. Remove from the cookie sheets to cooling racks; cool completely.

4 In a medium bowl, beat the cream cheese, 1/4 cup butter and 1/2 teaspoon vanilla with an electric mixer on low speed until well combined. Slowly add the powdered sugar, beating on low speed until blended. Increase the mixer speed to medium; beat 1 minute.

5 For each whoopie pie, spread 1 generous tablespoon of filling on the bottom of a cookie; place the second cookie, bottom side down, on the filling. Store in the refrigerator. Sprinkle with additional powdered sugar, if desired.

Nutritional Info: 1 Serving: Calories 210; Total Fat 10g (Saturated Fat 5g); Sodium 230mg; Total Carbohydrate 27g (Dietary Fiber 0g); Protein 2g. Exchanges: 1 Starch, 1 Other Carbohydrate, 2 Fat. Carbohydrate Choices: 2.

Betty's Kitchen Tip

If you're a coconut lover, try adding 2 tablespoons toasted coconut to the filling.

almond streusel apple pie

Prep Time: 15 Minutes
Start to Finish: 2 Hours 5 Minutes
Servings: 8

EASY

Pastry

1	Pillsbury® refrigerated pie crust, softened as directed on box

Filling

1/2	cup granulated sugar
2	tablespoons Gold Medal® all-purpose flour
1/2	teaspoon ground cinnamon
1/8	teaspoon salt
1/4	teaspoon almond extract
7	cups thinly sliced peeled apples (about 7 medium)

Streusel

1/2	cup Gold Medal® all-purpose flour
1/2	cup packed brown sugar
1/4	cup firm butter or margarine, cut into pieces
1/2	cup sliced almonds

1 Heat oven to 425°F. Place the pie crust in a 9-inch glass pie plate as directed on the box for One-Crust Filled pie.

2 In a large bowl, mix all filling ingredients except the apples. Stir in the apples until coated. Spoon into crust-lined pie plate.

3 In a small bowl, mix all the streusel ingredients except almonds with a pastry blender or fork until crumbly. Sprinkle over the apples.

4 Bake 35 to 45 minutes, covering entire surface of the pie with foil for the last 15 to 20 minutes to prevent overbrowning, until apples are tender and juice is bubbly. Sprinkle with the almonds. Bake uncovered 2 to 3 minutes longer or until the almonds are toasted. Cool completely, about 1 hour.

Nutritional Info: 1 Serving: Calories 430; Total Fat 19g (Saturated Fat 6g); Sodium 230mg; Total Carbohydrate 61g (Dietary Fiber 3g); Protein 4g. Exchanges: 1 Starch, 2 Fruit, 1 Other Carbohydrate, 4 Fat. Carbohydrate Choices: 4.

Betty's Kitchen Tip

Use tart, firm apples, layering them so there isn't too much space in between. Because apples shrink during baking, a pie may have a gap between the apples and the crust.

pumpkin meringue pie

Prep Time: 25 Minutes
Start to Finish: 5 Hours 50 Minutes
Servings: 8

1	Pillsbury® refrigerated pie crust, softened as directed on box		3/4	teaspoon ground ginger
3	whole eggs		1/4	teaspoon salt
3/4	cup packed brown sugar		1/4	teaspoon ground cloves
1	can (15 oz) pumpkin (not pumpkin pie mix)		1	teaspoon vanilla
1	cup half-and-half		6	egg whites
1	teaspoon ground cinnamon		1/2	teaspoon cream of tartar
			1	cup granulated sugar

1 Heat oven to 425°F. Place the pie crust in a 9-inch glass pie plate as directed on the box for One-Crust Filled Pie. Prick the bottom and side of pastry thoroughly with a fork. Bake 12 to 15 minutes or until light golden brown; cool on a cooling rack.

2 Reduce oven temperature to 350°F. In a medium bowl, beat eggs with a wire whisk. Stir in the brown sugar and pumpkin until well blended. Stir in the half-and-half, cinnamon, ginger, salt, cloves and vanilla until blended. Pour into partially baked crust. Bake 45 to 50 minutes or until golden brown and the center is almost set.

3 In a large bowl, beat egg whites and cream of tartar with an electric mixer on medium speed until soft peaks form. Gradually add granulated sugar, 2 tablespoons at a time, beating on high speed until stiff, glossy peaks form. Spread meringue over the hot filling to the edge of the crust. Bake 15 to 17 minutes or until the meringue is light brown. Cool the pie away from drafts about 4 hours. Store in the refrigerator.

Nutritional Info: 1 Serving: Calories 350; Total Fat 12g (Saturated Fat 6g); Sodium 289mg; Total Carbohydrate 56g (Dietary Fiber 2g); Protein 8g. Exchanges: 1 Starch, 2 Other Carbohydrate, 1/2 Medium-Fat Meat, 1-1/2 Fat. Carbohydrate Choices: 4.

Betty's Kitchen Tip

For best results, make meringue on a cool, dry day. Humidity causes it to become sticky and spongy because the sugar absorbs moisture.

browned butter pecan pie

Prep Time: 30 Minutes
Start to Finish: 5 Hours 25 Minutes
Servings: 8

- 1/2 cup butter (do not use margarine)
- 1 cup sugar
- 1 cup light corn syrup
- 1 teaspoon vanilla bean paste or vanilla
- 1/4 teaspoon salt
- 4 eggs, beaten
- 1 Pillsbury® refrigerated pie crust, softened as directed on box
- 1-1/4 cups pecan halves

1 In a 2-quart saucepan, melt the butter over medium heat, stirring frequently. Cook 2 to 5 minutes, stirring often, until the butter stops foaming and browned bits form at the bottom of the pan. Stir in the sugar and corn syrup. Cook over low heat 15 to 18 minutes, stirring frequently, until the sugar is dissolved. Cool 1 hour. Add the vanilla bean paste, salt and eggs; beat with a wire whisk until mixture is well blended.

2 Heat oven to 325°F. Place the pie crust in a 9-inch glass pie plate as directed on the box for One-Crust Filled Pie. Pour the filling into a crust-lined plate. Arrange the pecan halves in concentric circles on top of the filling. With a fork, gently press the pecans into the filling to glaze, keeping the pecans in circular pattern.

3 Bake 50 to 55 minutes or until the filling is set and the crust is golden brown. Cover the crust edge with strips of foil after 40 minutes to prevent excessive browning. Cool completely on a cooling rack, 3 to 4 hours, before slicing.

Nutritional Info: 1 Serving: Calories 588; Total Fat 32g (Saturated Fat 12g); Sodium 327mg; Total Carbohydrate 74g (Dietary Fiber 2g); Protein 5g. Exchanges: 1 Starch, 4 Other Carbohydrate, 5-1/2 Fat. Carbohydrate Choices: 5.

Betty's Kitchen Tip

Choose a pie plate that is glass or aluminum with an anodized (dull) finish. Shiny pans can cause crusts to become soggy because they reflect too much heat.

german chocolate pie

Prep Time: 20 Minutes
Start to Finish: 5 Hours 10 Minutes
Servings: 10

1   Pillsbury® refrigerated pie crust, softened as directed on box
1   package (4 oz) sweet baking chocolate, chopped
1/4   cup butter or margarine
1   can (12 oz) evaporated milk
1-1/2   cups sugar
2   tablespoons cornstarch

1/8   teaspoon salt
4   egg yolks
1/2   teaspoon vanilla
1/4   teaspoon almond extract
1   cup flaked coconut
1   cup chopped pecans

1   Heat oven to 375°F. Place pie crust in a 9-inch glass pie plate as directed on the box for One-Crust Filled Pie. In a 1-quart saucepan, heat the chocolate and butter over medium-low heat until melted and the mixture can be stirred smooth. Remove from heat; gradually stir in the milk.

2   In a medium bowl, mix the sugar, cornstarch and salt. In a small bowl, mix the egg yolks, vanilla and almond extract. Gradually add the chocolate mixture to the egg mixture, stirring with a wire whisk. Add the chocolate-egg yolk mixture to the cornstarch mixture, whisking slowly. Pour the filling into the crust-lined plate.

3   In a small bowl, mix the coconut and pecans; sprinkle over the filling.

4   Bake 45 to 50 minutes or until it is puffed up and almost set. Cool completely on a cooling rack, about 4 hours.

Nutritional Info: 1 Serving: Calories 483; Total Fat 27g (Saturated Fat 12g); Sodium 240mg; Total Carbohydrate 58g (Dietary Fiber 3g); Protein 6g. Exchanges: 1 Starch, 3 Other Carbohydrate, 4-1/2 Fat. Carbohydrate Choices: 4.

Betty's Kitchen Tip

The pie may be slightly soft when just out of the oven, but it will set up nicely for slicing once cooled. Dress up each piece with whipped cream, toasted coconut and chocolate shavings.

easy french apple dessert squares

Prep Time: 25 Minutes
Start to Finish: 1 Hour 50 Minutes
Servings: 15

Streusel

1	cup Original Bisquick® mix
1/2	cup packed brown sugar
1/4	cup cold butter or margarine
3/4	cup chopped nuts

Fruit Mixture

6	cups sliced peeled tart apples (6 medium)
2	teaspoons ground cinnamon
1/2	teaspoon ground nutmeg
1	cup Original Bisquick® mix
1	cup granulated sugar
1	cup milk
2	tablespoons butter or margarine, melted
4	eggs, beaten

1. Heat oven to 350°F. Spray a 13x9-inch pan with cooking spray.

2. In a medium bowl, mix 1 cup Bisquick mix and the brown sugar. Cut in 1/4 cup butter, using the pastry blender (or pulling two table knives through the ingredients in opposite directions), until crumbly. Stir in the nuts; set aside.

3. In a large bowl, mix the apples, cinnamon and nutmeg; spoon into the pan. In a medium bowl, stir remaining ingredients until well blended. Pour the mixture over the apples. Sprinkle with streusel.

4. Bake 45 to 55 minutes or until a knife inserted in the center comes out clean and the top is golden brown. Cool 30 minutes or until set before cutting into squares. Store in the refrigerator.

Betty's Kitchen Tip

Top each Easy French Apple Dessert Square with a slice of Cheddar cheese or a generous scoop of vanilla ice cream.

Nutritional Info: 1 Serving: Calories 290; Total Fat 12g (Saturated Fat 5g); Sodium 280mg; Total Carbohydrate 39g (Dietary Fiber 2g); Protein 4g. Exchanges: 1 Starch, 1-1/2 Other Carbohydrate, 2-1/2 Fat. Carbohydrate Choices: 2-1/2.

frozen cherry-chocolate chip cake

Prep Time: 25 Minutes
Start to Finish: 4 Hours 55 Minutes
Servings: 16

1	box Betty Crocker® SuperMoist® white cake mix
1	box (4-serving size) white chocolate instant pudding and pie filling mix
1	cup water
1/3	cup vegetable oil
4	egg whites

6	cups cherry-chocolate chip ice cream
1	cup whipping cream
1	package (6 oz) white chocolate baking bars, chopped
1/4	cup hot fudge topping, warmed

Fresh mint springs, if desired

1 Heat oven to 350°F (325°F for dark or nonstick pan). Spray the bottom only of a 13x9-inch pan with baking spray with flour.

2 In a large bowl, beat cake mix, dry pudding mix, water, oil and egg whites with an electric mixer on low speed 30 seconds. Beat on medium speed 2 minutes (batter will be very thick). Pour into the pan. Bake 29 to 35 minutes or until a toothpick comes out clean. Cool completely.

3 Meanwhile, place ice cream in the refrigerator to soften. Cut the cake into 1- to 1-1/2-inch squares with a serrated knife. In a very large bowl, stir the ice cream until very soft. Add the cake squares; stir until the cake is coated (cake pieces will break up). Spoon the mixture back into the pan. Smooth the top. Freeze about 3 hours or until firm.

4 In a 1-quart saucepan, heat the whipping cream until hot but not boiling. Stir in the chopped white chocolate until melted and smooth. Pour into small bowl. Refrigerate 1 hour 30 minutes to 2 hours or until cold. Beat the chilled white chocolate mixture on high speed until soft peaks form (do not overbeat). Spread over the ice cream cake. Drizzle hot fudge topping over the cake. Serve immediately, or cover and freeze until serving time.

Nutritional Info: 1 Serving: Calories 410; Total Fat 20g (Saturated Fat 10g); Sodium 400mg; Total Carbohydrate 53g (Dietary Fiber 0g); Protein 5g. Exchanges: 1 Starch, 2-1/2 Other Carbohydrate, 4 Fat. Carbohydrate Choices: 3-1/2.

Betty's Kitchen Tip

For clean-edged slices, don't take this cake out of the freezer until immediately before serving. Use a serrated knife when cutting it.

strawberry s'more ice cream cake

Prep Time: 35 Minutes
Start to Finish: 8 Hours 5 Minutes
Servings: 12

Crust

1-1/2	cups graham cracker crumbs
3	tablespoons sugar
1/4	cup butter or margarine, melted

Filling

8	cups (1/2-gallon carton) strawberry ice cream, slightly softened
1	jar (16 oz) hot fudge topping

Topping

2	cups miniature marshmallows (from 10.5-oz bag)

1. Heat oven to 350°F. In a medium bowl, mix graham cracker crumbs and sugar. Stir in the melted butter. Firmly press into the bottom of an ungreased 13x9-inch pan. Bake 10 minutes or until the crust in browned. Cool 15 minutes.

2. Spoon half of ice cream over the cooled crust, spreading evenly. In a small microwavable bowl, reserve 1/3 cup hot fudge topping; cover and set aside. Microwave the remaining topping in an uncovered jar on High 1 minute or until softened. Stir the topping; spoon and spread it over the ice cream. Spoon and spread the remaining ice cream over the topping. Freeze cake until firm, 4 hours or overnight.

3. Set oven control to broil. Top the dessert evenly with marshmallows. Broil 1 to 2 minutes or until the marshmallows are lightly browned. Freeze the cake about 3 hours. Before serving, microwave the reserved 1/3 cup hot fudge topping uncovered on High 10 seconds. Stir; drizzle topping over dessert. Let stand 5 minutes before serving.

Nutritional Info: 1 Serving: Calories 430; Total Fat 18g (Saturated Fat 10g); Sodium 300mg; Total Carbohydrate 63g (Dietary Fiber 2g); Protein 6g. Exchanges: 2 Starch, 2 Other Carbohydrate, 3-1/2 Fat. Carbohydrate Choices: 4.

Betty's Kitchen Tip

Create a different ice cream dessert by substituting your favorite ice cream and/or ice cream topping. About 20 graham cracker squares will yield 1-1/2 cups crushed crumbs. Crush the crackers in a resealable plastic bag with a rolling pin, or use a food processor and pulse crackers until crumbs form.

salted turtle tartlets

Prep Time: 30 Minutes
Start to Finish: 3 Hours
Servings: 30 tartlets

- 1 box Pillsbury® refrigerated pie crusts, softened as directed on box
- 1 cup sugar
- 1/4 cup light corn syrup
- 1/3 cup water
- 2/3 cup whipping cream

- 3/4 teaspoon vanilla
- 1/4 cup unsalted butter, cut into pieces
- 1/2 cup pecan halves, toasted and chopped
- 4 oz bittersweet chocolate, chopped
- 1 teaspoon coarse sea salt

1 Heat oven to 450°F. Remove crusts from the pouches; unroll onto a work surface. With a 2-1/2-inch round cookie cutter, cut 15 rounds from each crust; discard scraps. Fit the rounds into ungreased mini muffin cups, pressing in gently. Prick with a fork. Bake 10 to 12 minutes or until the edges are light golden brown. Cool on a cooling rack about 15 minutes. Remove from muffin cups to a cookie sheet.

2 In a heavy 1-quart saucepan, combine the sugar, corn syrup and water. Cook over medium-high heat 10 minutes, gently swirling occasionally, until the mixture turns dark golden brown. Add 1/3 cup of the whipping cream and the vanilla; stir until bubbling stops. Remove from heat. Stir in the butter until smooth. Divide the caramel evenly among the mini muffin cups. (You'll have about 1/3 cup caramel left over. Store it in the refrigerator.) Sprinkle pecans evenly over the caramel. Let stand 15 minutes.

3 Place the chocolate in a heatproof bowl. In a 1-quart saucepan, heat the remaining 1/3 cup whipping cream to simmering; pour over chocolate. Let stand 2 minutes. Stir until smooth. Spoon the chocolate over the tartlets. Cool 5 minutes. Sprinkle with sea salt. Let stand 2 hours or until set.

Nutritional Info: 1 Tartlet: Calories 156; Total Fat 10g (Saturated Fat 5g); Sodium 119mg; Total Carbohydrate 18g (Dietary Fiber 0g); Protein 1g. Exchanges: 1/2 Starch, 1/2 Other Carbohydrate, 2 Fat. Carbohydrate Choices: 1.

Betty's Kitchen Tip

Keep this recipe in mind when you're planning a party. These decadent treats serve a crowd and are the ideal size for mingling.

SPECIAL-OCCASION SWEETS

p. 288

306

289

312

spring chicks cake pops

Prep Time: 30 Minutes
Start to Finish: 2 Hours 30 Minutes
Servings: 48 cake pops

1 box Betty Crocker® SuperMoist® cake mix (any flavor)	48 paper lollipop sticks
Water, vegetable oil and eggs as called for on cake mix box	Block of white plastic foam
1 cup Betty Crocker® Rich & Creamy frosting (any non-chip, no-nut flavor)	48 orange heart sprinkles
	96 yellow heart sprinkles
3 bags (14 oz each) yellow candy melts	96 orange wildflower sprinkles
	96 blue or green mini confetti sprinkles

1 Make and bake the cake mix in a 13x9-inch pan as directed on the box, using water, oil and eggs. Cool cake completely. Crumble the cake into a bowl. Add the frosting; mix well. Roll into 1-inch balls; place on a waxed paper-lined cookie sheet. Freeze until firm. Keep refrigerated.

2 In a microwavable bowl, microwave one bag of candy melts uncovered on Medium (50%) 1 minute, then in 15-second intervals, until melted; stir until smooth. Remove several cake balls from the refrigerator at a time. Dip the tip of one lollipop stick about 1/2 inch into the melted candy and insert the stick into 1 cake ball no more than halfway. Dip into the melted candy to cover; tap off any excess. (Reheat candy in the microwave or add vegetable oil if too thick to coat.) Poke the opposite end of the stick into a foam block. Allow coating to set. Repeat with remaining candy and cake balls.

3 With a toothpick, dot a small amount of leftover melted candy on a cake pop for the beak; attach one orange heart sprinkle, pointed side out. With the same technique, attach two yellow sprinkles for wings, pointed side out, on the sides of the pop; attach two orange wildflower sprinkles at the bottom of the pop for feet; and attach two blue sprinkles for eyes.

Nutritional Info: 1 Cake Pop: Calories 220; Total Fat 11g (Saturated Fat 6g); Sodium 110mg; Total Carbohydrate 27g (Dietary Fiber 0g); Protein 2g. Exchanges: 2 Other Carbohydrate, 2 Fat. Carbohydrate Choices: 2.

Betty's Kitchen Tip

You don't have to make all the cake pops at once. Cut the cake into thirds. One piece will make about 16 cake pops and you can freeze the rest of the cake for another time. Use 1/3 cup frosting and one bag of the candy melts.

marshmallow birthday cupcakes

Prep Time: 25 Minutes
Start to Finish: 1 Hour 25 Minutes
Servings: 24 cupcakes

Cupcakes

1   box Betty Crocker® SuperMoist® white cake mix

Water, vegetable oil and egg whites as called for on cake mix box

Frosting and Decorations

2   containers (1 lb each) Betty Crocker® Rich & Creamy white frosting

24   large marshmallows

Betty Crocker® Decorating Decors colored sugar or candy sprinkles

Betty Crocker® white or colored birthday candles

1   Heat oven to 350°F (325°F for dark or nonstick pans). Place a paper baking cup in each of 24 regular-size muffin cups. Make and bake the cake mix as directed on the box for cupcakes, using water, oil and egg whites. Cool completely, about 30 minutes.

2   Frost the cooled cupcakes. For each cupcake, cut 1 marshmallow with a dampened kitchen scissors into slices; sprinkle with colored sugar. Arrange slices on the cupcakes in flower shapes. Place a candle in the center of each flower.

Nutritional Info: 1 Frosted Cupcake (Undecorated): Calories 300; Total Fat 9g (Saturated Fat 2g); Sodium 240mg; Total Carbohydrate 52g (Dietary Fiber 0g); Protein 1g. Exchanges: 3-1/2 Other Carbohydrate, 2 Fat. Carbohydrate Choices: 3-1/2.

Betty's Kitchen Tip

Check out party-supply or cake-decorating stores for fun birthday candles. Lots of new and unique shapes are available. Use edible glitter in place of the colored sugar or candy sprinkles. It adds sparkle to cake decorations.

raspberry-fudge fantasy torte

Prep Time: 35 Minutes
Start to Finish: 2 Hours 30 Minutes
Servings: 12 to 16

Cake

2/3	cup miniature semisweet chocolate chips
1	box Betty Crocker® SuperMoist® chocolate fudge cake mix
1	cup water
1/2	cup butter or margarine, softened
3	eggs

Filling and Topping

3	cups whipping cream
1/3	cup powdered sugar
1-1/2	cups fresh raspberries
1/3	cup seedless raspberry preserves
1-1/2	cups miniature semisweet chocolate chips

1. Heat oven to 350°F. Grease bottoms and sides of 2 (8- or 9-inch) round cake pans with shortening; lightly flour. In a small bowl, toss 2/3 cup chocolate chips with 1 tablespoon of the cake mix. In a large bowl, beat the remaining cake mix, water, butter and eggs with an electric mixer on low speed 1 minute, scraping the bowl constantly. Stir in the coated chocolate chips. Pour into pans. Bake as directed on the box for 8- or 9-inch rounds. Cool 10 minutes. Remove from pans to cooling racks. Cool completely, about 1 hour.

2. In a chilled large bowl, beat the whipping cream and powdered sugar with an electric mixer on high speed until soft peaks form. In a medium bowl, gently stir together 1 cup of the raspberries and the preserves. Fold in 1-1/2 cups of the whipped cream.

3. Cut each cake layer horizontally to make two layers. On a serving plate, place one layer, cut-side up. Spread with about 3/4 cup raspberry-cream mixture. Repeat with the second and third layers. Top with the remaining layer. Frost the side and top of the cake with the remaining whipped cream. Arrange the remaining 1/2 cup raspberries on top of the cake. Press 1-1/2 cups chocolate chips into the side of the cake.

Nutritional Info: 1 Serving: Calories 640; Total Fat 41g (Saturated Fat 25g); Sodium 420mg; Total Carbohydrate 61g (Dietary Fiber 3g); Protein 6g. Exchanges: 2 Starch, 2 Other Carbohydrate, 8 Fat. Carbohydrate Choices: 4.

Betty's Kitchen Tip

Add the raspberries to the top of this cake immediately before serving. If you place them on the frosting too soon, some of their color may "bleed" into the frosting.

white chocolate truffles

Prep Time: 25 Minutes
Start to Finish: 2 Hours 50 Minutes
Servings: 18 truffles

- -

12	oz white chocolate baking bars or squares, chopped
2	tablespoons whipping cream
1	tablespoon dark rum
1	cup flaked coconut

- -

1 In a 2-quart heavy saucepan, heat 8 oz white chocolate, the whipping cream and rum over low heat, stirring constantly, until chocolate is softened and the mixture can be stirred smooth. Remove from heat; transfer to a small bowl. Place plastic wrap on the surface of the mixture. Refrigerate about 2 hours until mixture is firm enough to hold its shape.

2 Line a cookie sheet with waxed paper. Scoop rounded teaspoonfuls of the white chocolate mixture onto a cookie sheet; roll the mixture lightly to shape into 1-inch balls. Freeze 15 minutes.

3 Heat oven to 350°F. Bake coconut in a shallow pan 5 to 7 minutes, stirring occasionally, until golden brown.

4 In a small microwavable bowl, microwave the remaining 4 oz white chocolate uncovered on High 45 to 60 seconds, stirring once, until softened and chocolate can be stirred smooth. Place the coconut in a resealable food-storage plastic bag or between sheets of waxed paper; crush slightly with a rolling pin.

5 In a shallow dish, place coconut. Dip each truffle into melted white chocolate; coat immediately with the coconut. Return to the cookie sheet; refrigerate 10 minutes or until firm. Store covered in the refrigerator.

Nutritional Info: 1 Truffle: Calories 130; Total Fat 7g (Saturated Fat 6g); Sodium 13mg; Total Carbohydrate 16g (Dietary Fiber 0g); Protein 0g. Exchanges: 1 Other Carbohydrate, 1-1/2 Fat. Carbohydrate Choices: 1.

Betty's Kitchen Tip

Replace the coconut with any embellishment you choose. Chopped dried cranberries, crushed nuts or sprinkles would all be delicious.

bride and groom shower cakes

Prep Time: 40 Minutes
Start to Finish: 3 Hours 25 Minutes
Servings: 16

1   box Betty Crocker® SuperMoist®
    cake mix (any flavor)
Water, vegetable oil and eggs as called for
on cake mix box
1   can (8.4 oz) Betty Crocker®
    Cupcake Icing cloud white
1   can (8.4 oz) Betty Crocker®
    Cupcake Icing petal pink

1   can (6.4 oz) Betty Crocker® Easy
    Flow black decorating icing
1   can (6.4 oz) Betty Crocker® Easy
    Flow red decorating icing
1   can (6.4 oz) Betty Crocker® Easy
    Flow white decorating icing
White decorating decors

1 Heat oven to 350°F. Grease the bottom of 2 (8-inch) heart-shaped foil pans with shortening or cooking spray. Make and bake the cake mix for 8-inch pans, as directed on the box, using water, oil and eggs. Cool 10 minutes. Pour into pans. Run a knife around sides of the pans to loosen cakes; remove cakes from the pans to cooling racks. Cool cakes completely, about 1 hour.

2 For the bride cake, place 1 cake layer on a serving plate. Frost the cake with white cupcake icing. Using pink icing, frost the upper portion of heart cake in a V-shape for skin. Using a writing tip and white cupcake icing, pipe a lace design on the dress and V-shaped edge of the dress. Use decorating decors to make the necklace.

3 For the groom cake, place remaining cake layer on a serving plate. Frost with black decorating icing, leaving a V-shape at the top of the cake. Using white decorating icing, frost a V-shape for the shirt. Using black decorating icing, pipe on black buttons and lapels. Using red decorating icing, pipe a red bow tie onto the shirt.

Nutritional Info: 1 Serving: Calories 310; Total Fat 11g (Saturated Fat 6g); Sodium 220mg; Total Carbohydrate 49g (Dietary Fiber 0g); Protein 2g. Exchanges: 3-1/2 Other Carbohydrate, 2 Fat. Carbohydrate Choices: 3.

Betty's Kitchen Tip

For a girls-only shower, decorate one cake for the bride. Then, instead of a groom theme, decorate the other cake similar to the bride cake but use icing colors of the bridesmaids' dresses.

strawberry mousse dessert cups

Prep Time: 25 Minutes
Start to Finish: 1 Hour 25 Minutes
Servings: 24

LOW FAT

1/2	teaspoon unflavored gelatin
1	tablespoon whipping cream
1	cup sliced fresh strawberries
1/2	cup powdered sugar
1/2	cup whipping cream
1/2	teaspoon vanilla
24	miniature dessert or cordial chocolate cups

Additional sliced fresh strawberries, if desired

1 In a small bowl, sprinkle the gelatin over 1 tablespoon whipping cream, set aside to soften the gelatin.

2 In a food processor, process 1 cup strawberries and the powdered sugar until smooth.

3 In a 1-quart saucepan, cook the strawberry mixture and softened gelatin over medium heat, beating with a whisk occasionally, until the mixture comes to a simmer and the gelatin is dissolved. Remove from heat; cool 30 minutes.

4 In a small bowl, beat 1/2 cup whipping cream and vanilla with an electric mixer on high speed until stiff peaks form. On low speed, beat strawberry mixture into whipped cream until blended.

5 Spoon strawberry mousse into a decorating bag fitted with a small star tip. Pipe the mousse into chocolate cups. Refrigerate until set, about 30 minutes, or up to 2 hours before serving. Garnish each cup with additional strawberries.

Betty's Kitchen Tip

If premade chocolate cups are unavailable, you can make your own by painting the inside of mini paper cups with tempered chocolate or confectionery chocolate (this kind does not require tempering but is sweeter).

Nutritional Info: 1 Serving: Calories 50; Total Fat 3g (Saturated Fat 2g); Sodium 0mg; Total Carbohydrate 6g (Dietary Fiber 0g); Protein 0g. Exchanges: 1/2 Other Carbohydrate, 1/2 Fat. Carbohydrate Choices: 1/2.

school days applesauce cupcakes

Prep Time: 40 Minutes
Start to Finish: 2 Hours 10 Minutes
Servings: 24 cupcakes

Cupcakes
1	box Betty Crocker® SuperMoist® yellow cake mix
1/2	teaspoon ground cinnamon
3/4	cup apple cider or juice
1/3	cup unsweetened applesauce
3	eggs

Frosting
1/2	cup butter or margarine
1	cup packed brown sugar
1/4	cup milk
2	cups powdered sugar

Decoration
1/2	cup Betty Crocker® Whipped fluffy white frosting (from 12-oz container)

48 miniature chocolate candy bars (from 12-oz bag), unwrapped

1 Heat oven to 350°F (325°F for dark or nonstick pans). Place a paper baking cup in each of 24 regular-size muffin cups. In a large bowl, beat cupcake ingredients with an electric mixer on low speed 30 seconds. Beat on medium speed about 2 minutes. Divide the batter evenly among muffin cups. Bake 18 to 23 minutes or until a toothpick comes out clean. Cool 10 minutes. Remove cupcakes to cooling racks. Cool completely.

2 In a 2-quart saucepan, melt the butter over medium heat. Stir in brown sugar; heat to boiling, stirring constantly. Stir in the milk; return to a boil. Remove from heat. Beat in the powdered sugar with an electric mixer on low speed until smooth. Frost the cupcakes. (If the frosting becomes thick, stir in 1/2 teaspoon milk.)

3 For each cupcake, pipe a computer keyboard and screen onto two chocolate candy bars. Pipe the frosting on one long edge of the keyboard; use the frosting to adhere the screen to the keyboard. Pipe a small amount of frosting on the bottom of the computer; place on the cupcake.

Nutritional Info: 1 Cupcake: Calories 300; Total Fat 11g (Saturated Fat 6g); Sodium 190mg; Total Carbohydrate 48g (Dietary Fiber 1g); Protein 2g. Exchanges: 1/2 Starch, 2-1/2 Other Carbohydrate, 2 Fat. Carbohydrate Choices: 3.

Betty's Kitchen Tip

To use these creative cupcakes as place cards for a party, pipe the initials of each guest on the "computer screen" before attaching the "screens" to the cupcakes.

espresso-ganache tartlets

Prep Time: 20 Minutes
Start to Finish: 50 Minutes
Servings: 45 tartlets

6	tablespoons whipping cream
4-1/2	teaspoons instant espresso coffee powder or granules
3	tablespoons sugar
2	tablespoons unsalted butter
8	oz bittersweet baking chocolate, chopped
1/4	teaspoon vanilla
3	packages (1.9 oz each) frozen mini phyllo (filo) shells or 45 foil candy cups (about 1-1/4 inch)
45	dark chocolate-covered espresso beans

1 In a 2-quart saucepan, heat whipping cream, coffee powder, sugar and butter over medium-high heat, stirring frequently, until sugar is dissolved. Remove from heat. Add chocolate; stir until the mixture is smooth. Stir in vanilla.

2 Divide the mixture evenly among filo shells or candy cups. Top each with one chocolate-covered espresso bean. Refrigerate 30 minutes or until ganache is firm. Store in the refrigerator. Serve at room temperature.

Nutritional Info: 1 Tartlet: Calories 68; Total Fat 4g (Saturated Fat 2g); Sodium 17mg; Total Carbohydrate 7g (Dietary Fiber 0g); Protein 1g. Exchanges: 1/2 Other Carbohydrate, 1 Fat. Carbohydrate Choices: 1/2.

Betty's Kitchen Tip

If espresso beans aren't your garnish of choice, use a sprinkle of chocolate shavings instead.

easter chicks cupcakes

Prep Time: 30 Minutes
Start to Finish: 1 Hour 35 Minutes
Servings: 24 cupcakes

Cupcakes
1   box Betty Crocker® SuperMoist® yellow or devil's food cake mix

Water, vegetable oil and eggs as called for on cake mix box

Frosting and Decorations
2-1/2   cups shredded coconut

Yellow liquid food color
1   (1-lb) container Betty Crocker® Rich & Creamy vanilla frosting
48   brown miniature candy-coated chocolate candies
24   small orange gumdrops

1 Heat oven to 350°F (325°F for dark or nonstick pans). Place a paper baking cup in each of 24 regular-size muffin cups.

2 Make and bake the cake mix as directed on the box for 24 cupcakes. Cool 10 minutes. Remove cupcakes from the pans to cooling racks. Cool completely, about 30 minutes.

3 Meanwhile, place the coconut in a resealable food-storage plastic bag. Add about 8 drops yellow liquid food color; seal the bag and shake to mix. Set aside.

4 Frost the cooled cupcakes with vanilla frosting. Top with yellow coconut. For eyes, add brown candies. Cut gumdrops to look like beaks; place on the cupcakes.

Nutritional Info: 1 Frosted Cupcake (Undecorated): Calories 260; Total Fat 11g (Saturated Fat 5g); Sodium 210mg; Total Carbohydrate 38g (Dietary Fiber 0g); Protein 1g. Exchanges: 2-1/2 Other Carbohydrate, 2 Fat. Carbohydrate Choices: 2-1/2.

Betty's Kitchen Tip

If you have only one pan and a recipe calls for more cupcakes than your pan will make, just cover and refrigerate the rest of the batter while baking the first batch. Cool the pan about 15 minutes, then bake the rest of the batter, adding 1 to 2 minutes to the bake time.

christmas ball cookies

Prep Time: 50 Minutes
Start to Finish: 1 Hour 50 Minutes
Servings: 24 sandwich cookies

- -

1-1/4	cups butter, softened
1-1/2	cups powdered sugar
1/8	teaspoon salt
1/2	teaspoon almond extract
2	cups Gold Medal® all-purpose flour

Red, green and white sanding sugar

| 1 | tablespoon milk |

- -

1 In a large bowl, beat 1 cup of the butter, 1/2 cup of the powdered sugar and the salt with an electric mixer on medium speed about 2 minutes or until creamy. Beat in 1/4 teaspoon of the almond extract. On low speed, beat in the flour just until combined. Cover; refrigerate 30 minutes.

2 Heat oven to 350°F. Line cookie sheets with cooking parchment paper. Shape the dough into 48 (3/4-inch) balls. Roll 16 balls in each color of sanding sugar, coating completely. On the cookie sheets, place the balls 1 inch apart.

3 Bake 15 minutes or until set and the bottoms are light golden brown. Remove from the cookie sheets to cooling racks. Cool completely, about 30 minutes.

4 In a small bowl, beat remaining 1/4 cup butter, 1 cup powdered sugar, 1/4 teaspoon almond extract and milk with an electric mixer on medium speed until smooth. For each sandwich cookie, spread about 1/2 teaspoon filling on the bottom of one cookie; top with second cookie, bottom side down, to form ball.

***Betty's* Kitchen Tip**

Speed up the recipe and omit the filling. Simply serve them as colorful sugar cookies, and you'll have twice as many to go around!

Nutritional Info: 1 Sandwich Cookie: Calories 161; Total Fat 10g (Saturated Fat 6g); Sodium 97mg; Total Carbohydrate 18g (Dietary Fiber 0g); Protein 1g. Exchanges: 1/2 Starch, 1/2 Other Carbohydrate, 2 Fat. Carbohydrate Choices: 1.

slumber party cake

Prep Time: 30 Minutes
Start to Finish: 2 Hours 20 Minutes
Servings: 12

Cake

1 box Betty Crocker® SuperMoist® white cake mix

Water, vegetable oil and eggs as called for on cake mix box

Frosting and Decorations

1 can (8.4 oz) Betty Crocker® Cupcake Icing buttercup yellow

5 large marshmallows, flattened

5 creme-filled peanut butter sandwich cookies

1 can (8.4 oz) Betty Crocker® Cupcake Icing meadow green

Betty Crocker® Easy Flow decorating icing (any colors)

1 container Betty Crocker® Decorating Decors confetti

1 Heat oven to 350°F (325°F for dark or nonstick pan). Grease the bottom only of a 13x9-inch pan with shortening or cooking spray. Make and bake the cake mix as directed on the box for a 13x9-inch pan, using water, oil and egg whites. Cool 10 minutes. Run the knife around the side of the pan to loosen. Place a cooling rack upside down over the pan; turn the rack and the pan over. Remove the pan. Cool the cake completely, about 1 hour.

2 Starting at the short side of the cake, frost one-third of the cake with yellow Cupcake Icing to be the sheet. Place the flattened marshmallows on the sheet for pillows; place the cookies on top of the pillows for faces.

3 Frost the remaining cake and a portion of the sandwich cookies with green Cupcake Icing to be the blanket, leaving the top portion of the cookie unfrosted for faces. Pipe hair and faces onto the cookies, using Easy Flow decorating icing. Using star tip, outline blanket with Easy Flow decorating icing. Sprinkle with confetti decors. Store loosely covered at room temperature.

Nutritional Info: 1 Serving: Calories 340; Total Fat 12g (Saturated Fat 5g); Sodium 340mg; Total Carbohydrate 56g (Dietary Fiber 0g); Protein 3g. Exchanges: 3-1/2 Other Carbohydrate, 2-1/2 Fat. Carbohydrate Choices: 4.

Betty's Kitchen Tip

If you'd prefer, substitute 1 container (1 lb) Betty Crocker® Rich & Creamy vanilla frosting for the Cupcake Icings. Spoon about one-third of the frosting into a bowl and tint with yellow food color. Place remaining frosting in another bowl and tint with green food color.

double almond wedding cupcakes

Prep Time: 30 Minutes
Start to Finish: 1 Hour 30 Minutes
Servings: 18 cupcakes

. . . .

Cupcakes

- 1 box Betty Crocker® SuperMoist® white cake mix

Water, vegetable oil and egg whites as called for on cake mix box

- 1 tablespoon almond extract

Frosting

- 1-1/4 cups butter, softened
- 2-1/2 cups powdered sugar
- 2 tablespoons whipping cream
- 2 teaspoons almond extract

Garnish

Jordan almonds, if desired

. . . .

1 Heat oven to 350°F (325°F for dark or nonstick pans). Place a paper baking cup in each of 18 regular-size muffin cups. Make the cake mix as directed on the box, using water, oil and egg whites and adding 1 tablespoon almond extract. Divide the batter evenly among the muffin cups, filling each about three-quarters full.

2 Bake 18 to 20 minutes or until a toothpick inserted in the center of a cupcake comes out clean. Cool 10 minutes. Remove the cupcakes from pans to cooling racks. Cool completely, about 30 minutes.

3 In a medium bowl, beat the butter and powdered sugar with an electric mixer on low speed until blended. Add the whipping cream and 2 teaspoons almond extract; beat on high speed until well blended. Fit a #46 tip in a decorating bag and fill with frosting. Use the tip, with smooth side facing down, to generously pipe frosting in a circular motion.

Nutritional Info: 1 Cupcake: Calories 340; Total Fat 18g (Saturated Fat 10g); Sodium 300mg; Total Carbohydrate 40g (Dietary Fiber 0g); Protein 2g. Exchanges: 2-1/2 Other Carbohydrate, 4 Fat. Carbohydrate Choices: 2-1/2.

Betty's Kitchen Tip

Wrap each cupcake in a laser-cut cupcake wrap or other decorative paper. Tint frosting with water-based food color to coordinate with the wedding colors if you desire.

plum-cardamom linzer cookies

Prep Time: 50 Minutes
Start to Finish: 2 Hours 10 Minutes
Servings: 12 cookies

3/4 cup slivered almonds, toasted, ground	1/4 teaspoon salt
2-1/2 cups Gold Medal® all-purpose flour	1-1/4 cups butter, softened
1 teaspoon grated lemon peel	1 cup powdered sugar, sifted
1/2 teaspoon baking powder	1 cup plum jam or jelly
1/2 teaspoon ground cardamom	3 tablespoons powdered sugar

1 In a medium bowl, mix the ground almonds, flour, lemon peel, baking powder, cardamom and salt with a whisk; set aside. In a large bowl, beat the butter with an electric mixer on medium speed until creamy. Gradually add 1 cup powdered sugar; beat until light and fluffy. On low speed, beat in the flour mixture just until blended. Divide the dough in half. Cover with plastic wrap; refrigerate 1 hour or until firm.

2 Heat oven to 350°F. Line a cookie sheet with cooking parchment paper or lightly grease with shortening or cooking spray.

3 On a lightly floured surface, roll each portion of dough to 1/8-inch thickness. Cut with a floured 2-1/2-inch fluted round or scalloped cookie cutter. Cut the centers out of half of the cookies with 1-1/4-inch fluted round cookie cutter. On the cookie sheets, place the solid cookies, hollow cookies and cutout centers 1 inch apart.

4 Bake 9 to 11 minutes or until the edges are light golden. Remove from the cookie sheets to cooling racks; cool completely. Spread each solid cookie with 2 teaspoons jam. Top each with a hollow cookie. Spoon a little more jam into the opening of each, if desired. Sift 3 tablespoons powdered sugar over sandwich cookies and cutouts.

Nutritional Info: 1 Cookie: Calories 417; Total Fat 23g (Saturated Fat 12g); Sodium 237mg; Total Carbohydrate 51g (Dietary Fiber 2g); Protein 4g. Exchanges: 3-1/2 Other Carbohydrate, 4 Fat. Carbohydrate Choices: 3-1/2.

Betty's Kitchen Tip

Keep dough from getting sticky as you work by dividing it and rolling it out in batches. Once you've cut out the cookies, repeat the process.

christmas truffles

Prep Time: 1 Hour 25 Minutes
Start to Finish: 3 Hours
Servings: 80 truffles

• •

1   box Betty Crocker® SuperMoist®
    German chocolate cake mix
Water, vegetable oil and eggs as called
for on cake mix box
1   bottle (1 oz) red food color
1   tablespoon unsweetened baking cocoa
1   cup Betty Crocker® Rich & Creamy cream
    cheese frosting (from 1-lb container)
3   bags (14 oz each) white or green candy
    melts or coating wafers
Red sugar

• •

1   Heat oven to 350°F. Spray a 13x9-inch pan
    with baking spray with flour. In a large
    bowl, beat the cake mix, water, oil, eggs,
    food color and cocoa with an electric mixer
    on low speed 30 seconds. Beat on medium
    speed 2 minutes. Pour into the pan.

2   Bake 40 to 45 minutes or until a
    toothpick inserted near the center comes
    out clean. Cool completely in the pan on
    a cooling rack.

3   Line cookie sheets with waxed paper.
    Remove the cake from the pan and crumble
    into large bowl; stir in the frosting. Roll
    the mixture into 1-1/4-inch balls; place on
    the cookie sheets.

4   Melt the candy melts as directed on the
    package. Dip each cake ball into the melted
    coating, tapping off the excess and taking
    care not to get crumbs in the coating.
    Return to cookie sheets. Decorate with
    sugar before the coating sets.

Nutritional Info: 1 Truffle: Calories 133; Total Fat 6g (Saturated
Fat 4g); Sodium 75mg; Total Carbohydrate 18g (Dietary Fiber 0g);
Protein 2g. Exchanges: 1 Other Carbohydrate, 1 Fat. Carbohydrate
Choices: 1.

Betty's Kitchen Tip

Chilling the dough balls before you dip them
into the melted coating will help them set
somewhat quickly, so top with sugar right away.

chocolate tiramisu cake

Prep Time: 25 Minutes
Start to Finish: 1 Hour 35 Minutes
Servings: 8

Cake

1   box Betty Crocker® SuperMoist®
    German chocolate cake mix

Water, vegetable oil and eggs as called
for on cake mix box

Soaking Syrup

1/4   cup granulated sugar

1   teaspoon instant coffee granules or crystals

1/4   cup water

1/4   cup coffee-flavored liqueur

Filling

1   cup whipping cream

1   container (8 oz) mascarpone cheese
    or 1 package (8 oz) cream cheese, softened

2   tablespoons powdered sugar

2   teaspoons vanilla

Garnish

Unsweetened baking cocoa

1 Heat oven to 350°F. Grease the bottoms and sides of 2 (9-inch) round cake pans with shortening or cooking spray. Make and bake the cake as directed on the box. Cool 10 minutes. Remove from pans to cooling racks. Cool completely.

2 In a 1-quart saucepan, mix the granulated sugar, coffee granules and water. Heat to boiling over medium heat. Boil and stir 1 minute. Remove from heat. Stir in the liqueur. Cool completely. Brush the flat side of each cake layer with soaking syrup

until it has been absorbed. Place cakes in the freezer 5 minutes.

3 In a chilled small bowl, beat the whipping cream with an electric mixer on high speed until stiff peaks form. In another small bowl, beat the mascarpone cheese, powdered sugar and vanilla with an electric mixer on low speed until blended. Fold whipped cream into the mascarpone mixture until smooth. Place one cake layer, bottom side up, on a serving plate. Spread on half of the mascarpone mixture. Top with the second cake layer, bottom side up. Spread with the remaining mascarpone mixture. Store in the refrigerator. Sprinkle with cocoa before serving.

Nutritional Info: 1 Serving: Calories 640; Total Fat 38g (Saturated Fat 16g); Sodium 540mg; Total Carbohydrate 67g (Dietary Fiber 2g); Protein 7g. Exchanges: 1-1/2 Starch, 3 Other Carbohydrate, 7-1/2 Fat. Carbohydrate Choices: 4-1/2.

Betty's Kitchen Tip

If you'd prefer not to use coffee liqueur in the Soaking Syrup, increase the amount of water to 1/2 cup and increase the instant coffee measurement to 2-1/2 teaspoons.

raspberry-swirl cheesecake bars

Prep Time: 15 Minutes
Start to Finish: 2 Hours 10 Minutes
Servings: 20 bars

EASY

24	thin chocolate wafer cookies, crushed (1-1/2 cups crumbs)
6	tablespoons butter or margarine, melted
2	packages (8 oz each) cream cheese, softened
1/2	cup sugar
2	eggs
2	tablespoons Gold Medal® all-purpose flour
1/2	teaspoon almond extract
1/3	cup seedless red raspberry jam
20	fresh raspberries

1 Heat oven to 325°F. Line an 8-inch square pan with foil, leaving 1 inch of the foil overhanging at two opposite sides of the pan; spray the foil with cooking spray.

2 In a medium bowl, mix cookie crumbs and butter. Press into the pan. Bake 12 minutes. Cool 15 minutes.

3 Meanwhile, in another medium bowl, beat cream cheese and sugar with an electric mixer on medium speed until smooth. Add the eggs, one at a time, beating just until blended. Beat in the flour and almond extract. Pour over the cooled crust. Drop jam by teaspoonfuls over the batter; swirl the jam through the batter with a knife for a marbled design.

4 Bake 30 to 40 minutes or until set. Cool completely on a cooling rack, about 1 hour. Use the foil to lift bars out of the pan. Cut into 5 rows by 4 rows; top each bar with a raspberry. Store in the refrigerator.

Nutritional Info: 1 Bar: Calories 189; Total Fat 13g (Saturated Fat 7g); Sodium 168mg; Total Carbohydrate 16g (Dietary Fiber 0g); Protein 3g. Exchanges: 1 Other Carbohydrate, 2-1/2 Fat. Carbohydrate Choices: 1.

Betty's Kitchen Tip

For another popular flavor combo, use orange marmalade instead of raspberry jam, and top with a halved kumquat rather than a berry.

lemon cake with raspberry mousse

Prep Time: 20 Minutes
Start to Finish: 2 Hours 10 Minutes
Servings: 16

1	box Betty Crocker® SuperMoist® lemon cake mix	
1	cup buttermilk	
1/2	cup vegetable oil	
1	teaspoon grated lemon peel	

3	eggs	
2	cups raspberry pie filling (from 21-oz can)	
1-1/2	cups whipping cream	

Fresh raspberries, if desired

Mint leaves, if desired

1 Heat oven to 350°F (325°F for dark or nonstick pans). Grease or spray two 8- or 9-inch round cake pans. In a large bowl, beat the cake mix, buttermilk, oil, lemon peel and eggs with an electric mixer on low speed 30 seconds. Beat on medium speed 2 minutes, scraping the bowl occasionally. Pour batter into the pans.

2 Bake as directed on the box. Cool 10 minutes. Run a knife around the side of pans to loosen the cakes; remove from the pans to cooling racks. Cool completely, about 1 hour.

3 On a serving plate, place one cake layer, rounded side down, Spread 3/4 cup of the pie filling over cake layer to within 1/4 inch of edge. Top with the second layer, rounded side up. In a chilled medium bowl, beat the whipping cream with an electric mixer on high speed until soft peaks form. Beat in the remaining 1-1/4 cups pie filling on low speed just until blended. Frost the side and top of the cake with raspberry mousse. Garnish with fresh raspberries and mint leaves. Store in the refrigerator.

Nutritional Info: 1 Serving: Calories 310; Total Fat 17g (Saturated Fat 7g); Sodium 230mg; Total Carbohydrate 35g (Dietary Fiber 1g); Protein 3g. Exchanges: 1/2 Starch, 2 Other Carbohydrate, 3-1/2 Fat. Carbohydrate Choices: 2.

Betty's Kitchen Tip

For a smooth mousse, strain the raspberry seeds out of the pie filling: Place the filling in a mesh strainer or sieve over a bowl and use the back of a spoon to press the filling through the sieve.

bourbon-chestnut bonbons

Prep Time: 30 Minutes
Start to Finish: 6 Hours 30 Minutes
Servings: 80 bonbons

- 12 oz fine-quality bittersweet chocolate, chopped
- 1/2 cup whipping cream
- 2 cups sweetened chestnut spread (from 17.5-oz can)
- 1/4 cup bourbon
- 1/2 cup sifted unsweetened baking cocoa
- 12 oz semisweet baking chocolate, chopped

1. In a medium bowl, place the bittersweet chocolate. In a 1-quart saucepan, heat the whipping cream to simmering. Remove from heat and pour over the chocolate; let stand 2 minutes. Stir until the chocolate is melted. Stir in the chestnut spread and bourbon until well blended. Cover; chill 4 hours or until firm.

2. Line cookie sheets with cooking parchment or waxed paper. Shape teaspoonfuls of the chocolate mixture into balls. Place on the cookie sheets; freeze 1 hour or until firm.

3. In a glass pie plate, place the cocoa. In a medium microwavable bowl, microwave semisweet chocolate uncovered on High 1 to 2 minutes, stirring once, until the chocolate can be stirred smooth. Using hands, drop frozen bonbons in the melted chocolate and roll with hands to coat completely. Gently drop the coated balls in cocoa, shaking the pie plate to coat. Return balls to the cookie sheets. Refrigerate 1 hour or until coating is firm. Store in the refrigerator or freezer.

Nutritional Info: 1 Bonbon: Calories 75; Total Fat 4g (Saturated Fat 2g); Sodium 0mg; Total Carbohydrate 9g (Dietary Fiber 0g); Protein 1g. Exchanges: 1/2 Other Carbohydrate, 1 Fat. Carbohydrate Choices: 1/2.

Betty's Kitchen Tip

A perfect bite to treat a big crowd, wonderful bourbon-chestnut bonbons are made even more rich thanks to bittersweet chocolate.

stars and stripes cupcakes

Prep Time: 45 Minutes
Start to Finish: 1 Hour 45 Minutes
Servings: 8 cupcakes

- -

3/4 cup Gold Medal® all-purpose flour

3/4 teaspoon baking powder

1/4 teaspoon salt

1/4 cup butter, softened

1/3 cup granulated sugar

1/2 cup sour cream

2 eggs

3/4 teaspoon almond extract

1 jar (6 oz) maraschino cherries, drained, finely chopped and patted dry

1 cup powdered sugar

1 tablespoon light corn syrup

2 teaspoons water

1/4 teaspoon almond extract

1 tube (4.25 oz) Betty Crocker® red decorating icing

8 blue candy stars

- -

1 Heat oven to 350°F (325°F for dark or nonstick pan). Place a red paper baking cup in each of 8 regular-size muffin cups.

2 In a small bowl, mix the flour, baking powder and salt. In a medium bowl, beat butter and granulated sugar with electric mixer on high speed until creamy. Beat the sour cream, eggs and 1/2 teaspoon of the almond extract. On low speed, beat into the flour mixture just until blended. Stir in the cherries. Divide the batter evenly among the muffin cups.

3 Bake 20 to 25 minutes or until a toothpick comes out clean. Cool 5 minutes. Remove to a cooling rack. Cool completely.

4 Meanwhile, in a small bowl, mix the powdered sugar, corn syrup, water and remaining 1/4 teaspoon almond extract until smooth. Spoon glaze over the cupcakes. Let stand 10 minutes.

5 Place the tube of red icing in a 4-cup measuring cup filled with warm water; let stand 5 minutes. Place one blue candy star on each glazed cupcake as shown. Remove the tube of red icing from the water; wipe it dry. Squeeze the tube several times to mix and soften the icing. Using the red icing with a writing tip, pipe wavy stripes on cupcakes to resemble flags.

Nutritional Info: 1 Cupcake: Calories 320; Total Fat 12g (Saturated Fat 8g); Sodium 190mg; Total Carbohydrate 50g (Dietary Fiber 0g); Protein 3g. Exchanges: 3-1/2 Other Carbohydrate, 2-1/2 Fat. Carbohydrate Choices: 3.

Betty's Kitchen Tip

Look for red paper baking cups at kitchen specialty stores or wherever cake decorating supplies are sold.

tiramisu cupcakes

Prep Time: 35 Minutes
Start to Finish: 1 Hour 55 Minutes
Servings: 24 cupcakes

1	box Betty Crocker® SuperMoist® White cake mix
1	cup water
1/3	cup vegetable oil
1/4	cup brandy
3	egg whites
3	tablespoons instant espresso coffee granules or powder

1/3	cup boiling water
2	tablespoons corn syrup
1	package (8 oz) cream cheese, softened
1/2	cup powdered sugar
2	cups whipping cream

Unsweetened baking cocoa
Chocolate-covered espresso beans, if desired

1 Heat oven to 350°F (325°F for dark or nonstick pans). Place a paper baking cup in each of 24 regular-size muffin cups. In a large bowl, beat the cake mix, water, oil, brandy and egg whites with an electric mixer on low speed 30 seconds. Beat on medium speed 2 minutes. Divide batter evenly among the muffin cups. Bake 16 to 21 minutes or until a toothpick comes out clean. Meanwhile, in a small bowl, stir the espresso granules and boiling water.

Stir in the corn syrup. Cool 10 minutes. Pierce the top of each warm cupcake with a large-tined fork. Slowly spoon 1 teaspoon espresso mixture over the top of each cupcake, allowing it to soak into the holes. Cool completely. Remove cupcakes from the pans.

2 In a medium bowl, beat the cream cheese and powdered sugar with an electric mixer on low speed until mixed. Beat on high speed until smooth. On high speed, gradually beat in the whipping cream until stiff peaks form, about 2 minutes. Dollop whipped cream onto the cupcakes. Sprinkle with cocoa and top with espresso beans, if desired.

Nutritional Info: 1 Cupcake: Calories 220; Total Fat 13g (Saturated Fat 7g); Sodium 200mg; Total Carbohydrate 23g (Dietary Fiber 0g); Protein 2g. Exchanges: 1-1/2 Other Carbohydrate, 2-1/2 Fat. Carbohydrate Choices: 1-1/2.

Betty's Kitchen Tip

For a sweeter espresso syrup, add extra corn syrup to taste. To easily sprinkle baking cocoa over cupcakes, place the cocoa in a fine strainer and tap gently over the cupcakes.

chocolate-espresso cupcakes

Prep Time: 15 Minutes
Start to Finish: 1 Hour 10 Minutes
Servings: 12 cupcakes

EASY

1	cup Gold Medal® all-purpose flour
1/2	cup unsweetened baking cocoa
1/2	teaspoon baking soda
1/4	teaspoon salt
2	egg whites
1	whole egg
1	cup granulated sugar
1/4	cup canola or vegetable oil
1/2	cup light chocolate soy milk
2	teaspoons instant espresso coffee powder or granules
1-1/2	teaspoons vanilla

Powdered sugar and chocolate-covered coffee beans, if desired

1 Heat oven to 375°F. Place a paper baking cup in each of 12 regular-size muffin cups.

2 In a medium bowl, mix the flour, cocoa, baking soda and salt; set aside. In another medium bowl, beat the egg whites, whole egg, granulated sugar and oil with an electric mixer on medium-high speed 1 to 2 minutes or until well mixed. On low speed, alternately add flour mixture and soy milk, beating after each addition, until well blended. Add the espresso powder and vanilla; beat on low speed 30 seconds. Divide the batter evenly among the muffin cups, filling each one with about 3 tablespoons batter.

3 Bake 15 to 20 minutes or until a toothpick comes out clean. Cool 5 minutes; remove from the pan to a cooling rack. Cool completely, about 30 minutes. Just before serving, sift powdered sugar over the cupcakes. Garnish with coffee beans.

Nutritional Info: 1 Cupcake: Calories 170; Total Fat 6g (Saturated Fat 1g); Sodium 125mg; Total Carbohydrate 27g (Dietary Fiber 1g); Protein 3g. Exchanges: 1/2 Starch, 1-1/2 Other Carbohydrate, 1 Fat. Carbohydrate Choices: 2.

Betty's Kitchen Tip

For Raspberry-Chocolate Cupcakes, omit the vanilla and espresso powder. Add 2 teaspoons raspberry extract with the soy milk. Serve with fresh raspberries on top.

white hot chocolate cupcakes

Prep Time: 15 Minutes
Start to Finish: 1 Hour
Servings: 24 cupcakes

EASY

14 oz white chocolate baking bars or squares, chopped
1 box Betty Crocker® SuperMoist® white cake mix

Water, vegetable oil and eggs as called for on cake mix box
12 large marshmallows, cut in half crosswise
Unsweetened baking cocoa

1 Heat oven to 350°F. Place a paper baking cup in each of 24 regular-size muffin cups. Microwave 4 oz of the white chocolate on High 30 to 60 seconds, stirring once, until chocolate can be stirred smooth; set aside.

2 Make the cake mix as directed on the box, using water, oil and eggs. Stir in melted white chocolate. Divide the batter evenly among muffin cups. Bake as directed. Cool 5 minutes; remove from pans to cooling racks. Cool completely.

3 Microwave the remaining 10 oz white chocolate on High 1 minute 30 seconds, stirring after 30 seconds, until chocolate can be stirred smooth. Dip the tops of the cupcakes in melted chocolate. Arrange the dipped cupcakes on a cookie sheet. Refrigerate until set, about 10 minutes.

4 Set the oven control to broil. Line a cookie sheet with cooking parchment paper. Place the marshmallows, cut sides down, on the cookie sheet. Broil 1 to 2 minutes or until golden brown. Let stand 2 to 3 minutes. With a metal spatula, slide a toasted marshmallow half onto each cupcake. Sprinkle with cocoa.

Nutritional Info: 1 Cupcake: Calories 235; Total Fat 10g (Saturated Fat 4.5g); Sodium 161mg; Total Carbohydrate 33g (Dietary Fiber 0g); Protein 3g. Exchanges: 1 Starch, 1 Other Carbohydrate, 1-1/2 Fat. Carbohydrate Choices: 2.

Betty's Kitchen Tip

Keep the marshmallows from being a mess by spraying the spatula with a bit of cooking spray.

chocolate snowballs

Prep Time: 1 Hour
Start to Finish: 1 Hour 20 Minutes
Servings: 60 cookies

- 1 pouch (1 lb 1.5 oz) Betty Crocker® sugar cookie mix

Egg and butter called for on cookie mix package

- 1/4 cup Gold Medal® all-purpose flour
- 1/4 cup unsweetened baking cocoa
- 1/2 cup finely chopped almonds
- 1 teaspoon almond extract
- 60 Hershey's® Kisses® Brand milk chocolates, unwrapped
- 3/4 cup powdered sugar

1 Heat oven to 375°F. In a large bowl, stir the cookie mix, egg, butter, flour, cocoa, almonds and extract with a spoon until a soft dough forms.

2 Shape the dough into 60 (3/4-inch) balls; wrap each around 1 milk chocolate candy. On ungreased cookie sheets, place balls about 2 inches apart.

3 Bake 8 to 10 minutes. Immediately remove from cookie sheets to cooling racks. Cool slightly, about 5 minutes. Roll the cookies in powdered sugar. Cool completely, about 15 minutes. Roll again in powdered sugar.

Nutritional Info: 1 Cookie: Calories 90; Total Fat 4.5g (Saturated Fat 2g); Sodium 35mg; Total Carbohydrate 12g (Dietary Fiber 0g); Protein 1g. Exchanges: 1 Other Carbohydrate, 1 Fat. Carbohydrate Choices: 1.

HERSHEY'S® KISSES® trademark and trade dress and the conical figure plume device are used under license.

Betty's Kitchen Tip

Keep powdered sugar from getting everywhere by storing different flavors and varieties of cookies in separate containers.

chocolate mousse duo

Prep Time: 45 Minutes
Start to Finish: 1 Hour 45 Minutes
Servings: 12

1/2 cup milk chocolate chips
4 tablespoons milk
4 tablespoons unsalted butter

1/2 cup dark chocolate chips
1-1/2 cups whipping cream
Additional milk or dark chocolate chips, if desired

1 In a small microwavable bowl, microwave milk chocolate chips, 2 tablespoons of the milk and 2 tablespoons of the butter uncovered on High 50 to 60 seconds, stirring until smooth. Cool to room temperature, about 20 minutes.

2 In another small microwavable bowl, microwave the dark chocolate chips, the remaining 2 tablespoons milk and 2 tablespoons butter uncovered on High 30 to 40 seconds, stirring until smooth. Cool 10 minutes.

3 Meanwhile, in a chilled medium bowl, beat whipping cream with an electric mixer on high speed until stiff peaks form. Reserve 1/2 cup whipped cream for the garnish.

4 Fold 1 cup of the remaining whipped cream into the dark chocolate mixture. Fold remaining 1 cup whipped cream into the milk chocolate mixture. Divide and layer the chocolate mixtures evenly among 12 shot glasses. Tap each with reserved whipped cream. Refrigerate at least 1 hour. Sprinkle with chocolate chips.

Nutritional Info: 1 Serving: Calories 200; Total Fat 17g (Saturated Fat 11g); Sodium 20mg; Total Carbohydrate 10g (Dietary Fiber 0g); Protein 1g. Exchanges: 1/2 Other Carbohydrate, 3-1/2 Fat. Carbohydrate Choices: 1/2.

Betty's Kitchen Tip

To fill the glasses neatly, place the mousses in pastry bags without a decorating tip or in resealable plastic bags with one bottom corner cut off each. Then, pipe in the mousse.

vanilla-raspberry panna cotta

Prep Time: 25 Minutes
Start to Finish: 2 Hours 35 Minutes
Servings: 8

- 1 tablespoon cold water
- 1 teaspoon unflavored gelatin
- 2/3 cup whipping cream
- 2/3 cup milk
- 1/3 cup sugar
- 1/2 teaspoon vanilla
- 1-1/3 cups fresh raspberries
- 2 tablespoons honey

Fresh mint sprigs

1. In a small bowl, sprinkle the gelatin over cold water; set aside to soften the gelatin.

2. In a 2-quart heavy saucepan, heat the whipping cream, milk, sugar and vanilla over medium heat to a simmer, stirring frequently until the sugar is dissolved. Remove from heat. With a whisk, stir in the softened gelatin until completely dissolved. Cool to room temperature, about 15 minutes.

3. Place 2 raspberries in the bottom of each of 8 shot glasses. Divide the cream mixture evenly among the glasses. Refrigerate until set, about 2 hours.

4. Just before serving, top each panna cotta with the remaining raspberries and drizzle with 3/4 teaspoon honey. Garnish with mint.

Nutritional Info: 1 Serving: Calories 130; Total Fat 7g (Saturated Fat 4g); Sodium 15mg; Total Carbohydrate 17g (Dietary Fiber 1g); Protein 1g. Exchanges: 1 Other Carbohydrate, 1-1/2 Fat. Carbohydrate Choices: 1.

Betty's Kitchen Tip

Steep the cream mixture with fresh herbs, such as chamomile or lemon verbena, for a different flavor. Strain before dividing into the glasses.

salted caramel shortbread cookies

Prep Time: 1 Hour 20 Minutes
Start to Finish: 2 Hours 45 Minutes
Servings: 36 cookies

Cookies

1-1/2	cups unsalted butter, softened
3/4	cup sugar
1	teaspoon vanilla
3-1/2	cups Gold Medal® all-purpose flour

Topping

1	bag (14 oz) caramels, unwrapped
2	tablespoons milk
4	oz semisweet chocolate, chopped
1	tablespoon butter
1	teaspoons coarse (kosher or sea) salt

1 Heat oven to 350°F. In a large bowl, beat 1-1/2 cups butter with an electric mixer on high speed until creamy. Beat in the sugar and vanilla. On low speed, beat in the flour until blended. Divide dough in half. Between two sheets of waxed paper, roll one portion of dough 1/4 inch thick. Cut with 2-1/2-inch round cookie cutter. On an ungreased cookie sheet, place the cutouts about 2 inches apart. Repeat with the second portion of dough.

2 Bake 12 to 14 minutes or until set and just barely light golden (do not overbake). Remove from the cookie sheets to cooling racks; cool completely.

3 In a medium microwavable bowl, microwave caramels and milk uncovered on High 2 minutes 30 seconds, stirring every 30 seconds, until melted and smooth. Frost each cookie with about 1 rounded teaspoon caramel mixture.

4 In a small microwavable bowl, melt the chocolate and 1 tablespoon butter uncovered on High 1 minute 30 seconds, stirring every 30 seconds, until melted and smooth. Drizzle chocolate over the caramel on each cookie. Sprinkle generously with salt. Let stand until set.

Nutritional Info: 1 Cookie: Calories 190; Total Fat 10g (Saturated Fat 6g); Sodium 150mg; Total Carbohydrate 24g (Dietary Fiber 0g); Protein 2g. Exchanges: 1 Starch, 1/2 Other Carbohydrate, 2 Fat. Carbohydrate Choices: 1-1/2.

Betty's Kitchen Tip

For a quick and easy way to drizzle chocolate, spoon melted chocolate into a small resealable food-storage plastic bag. Cut off a tiny corner of the bag and squeeze the bag to drizzle the chocolate evenly over the cookies. If desired, substitute 1 can (13.4 ounces) dulce de leche (caramelized sweetened condensed milk) for caramels and milk. Spread each cookie with dulce de leche and proceed as directed.

GIFTS FROM THE KITCHEN

p.323

314   327   315

triple-nut toffee

Prep Time: 40 Minutes
Start to Finish: 1 Hour 10 Minutes
Servings: 36 pieces

- 1/3   cup chopped pecans
- 1/3   cup slivered almonds
- 1/3   cup cashew halves and pieces
- 1/2   packed brown sugar

- 1/2   cup granulated sugar
- 1   cup butter or margarine
- 1/4   cup water
- 1/2   cup semisweet chocolate chips

1 Heat oven to 350°F. Line a 15x10x1-inch pan with foil. Spread nuts in the pan. Bake uncovered for 6 to 10 minutes, stirring occasionally, until light brown. Pour into a small bowl; set aside. Set the foil-lined pan aside, as well.

2 Meanwhile, in a heavy 2-quart saucepan, cook the brown sugar, granulated sugar, butter and water over medium-high heat 4 to 6 minutes, stirring constantly with a wooden spoon, until the mixture comes to a full boil. Boil 20 to 25 minutes, stirring frequently, until a candy thermometer reaches 300°F or a small amount of the mixture dropped into a cup of very cold water spreads into hard, brittle threads. (Watch carefully so the mixture does not burn.) Immediately remove from the heat.

3 Stir in 1/2 cup of the nuts; immediately pour toffee into the same foil-lined pan. Quickly spread the mixture to a 1/4-inch thickness with a rubber spatula. Sprinkle with chocolate chips; let stand about 1 minute or until the chips are completely softened. Spread the softened chocolate evenly over the toffee. Sprinkle with the remaining nuts.

4 Refrigerate about 30 minutes or until the chocolate is firm. Break into pieces. Store in a tightly covered container.

Nutritional Info: 1 Piece: Calories 100; Total Fat 8g (Saturated Fat 4g); Sodium 40mg; Total Carbohydrate 8g (Dietary Fiber 0g); Protein 0g. Exchanges: 1/2 Other Carbohydrate, 1-1/2 Fat. Carbohydrate Choices: 1/2.

Betty's Kitchen Tip

Use any chocolate you like in this tasty toffee— dark, milk, white; it's your call!

sugar cookie macaroon sandwiches

Prep Time: 1 Hour 20 Minutes
Start to Finish: 2 Hours
Servings: 24 sandwich cookies

- 1 pouch (1 lb 1.5 oz) Betty Crocker® sugar cookie mix
- 1/2 cup butter, softened
- 3 cups flaked coconut
- 1 egg
- 1 bar (4 oz) semisweet baking chocolate, chopped
- 2 tablespoons whipping cream

1 Heat oven to 350°F. Spray cookie sheets with cooking spray.

2 In a medium bowl, beat the cookie mix, butter, coconut and egg with an electric mixer on medium speed until a soft dough forms. Shape the dough into 48 (1-inch) balls. On the cookie sheets, place the balls 2 inches apart; flatten slightly.

3 Bake 12 minutes or until the bottoms are golden. Cool 5 minutes. Remove from the cookie sheets to cooling racks; cool completely.

4 In a small microwavable bowl, microwave chocolate and whipping cream uncovered on High 30 seconds; stir. Microwave 30 seconds longer, stirring every 15 seconds, until the chocolate can be stirred smooth.

5 For each sandwich cookie, spread about 1 teaspoon chocolate mixture on the bottom of 1 cookie. Top with the second cookie, bottom side down; gently press together. Let cookies stand until the chocolate is set.

Nutritional Info: 1 Sandwich Cookie: Calories 206; Total Fat 11g (Saturated Fat 7g); Sodium 115mg; Total Carbohydrate 24g (Dietary Fiber 1g); Protein 2g. Exchanges: 1/2 Starch, 1 Other Carbohydrate, 2 Fat. Carbohydrate Choices: 1-1/2.

Betty's Kitchen Tip

Crunched for time? Skip step 4. Omit the baking chocolate and whipping cream and substitute a can of Betty Crocker® Rich & Creamy chocolate frosting instead.

salty caramel peanut brittle bars

Prep Time: 15 Minutes
Start to Finish: 2 Hours 5 Minutes
Servings: 48 bars

EASY

- 1 pouch (1 lb 1.5 oz) Betty Crocker® sugar cookie mix
- 1/4 cup packed brown sugar
- 3/4 cup cold unsalted or regular butter, cut into pieces

- 2 cups salted cocktail peanuts
- 1 cup semisweet chocolate chips (6 oz)
- 1 jar (12.25 oz) caramel topping
- 1/2 teaspoon coarse sea salt

1 Heat oven to 350°F. Spray a 15x10x1-inch pan with cooking spray.

2 Reserve 3 tablespoons cookie mix. In a large bowl, stir the remaining cookie mix and the brown sugar. Cut in butter, using pastry blender or fork, until the mixture is crumbly. Press into the bottom of the pan. Bake 18 minutes.

3 Immediately sprinkle peanuts and chocolate chips over the partially baked cookie crust. In a small microwavable bowl, microwave the caramel topping on High about 30 seconds or until it is of drizzling consistency. Add the reserved cookie mix; blend well. Drizzle the mixture evenly over the peanuts and chocolate chips. Sprinkle evenly with salt.

4 Bake 12 to 14 minutes or until caramel is bubbly. Cool completely on a cooling rack, about 1 hour. Refrigerate 15 minutes to set the chocolate. Cut bars into 8 rows by 6 rows. Store covered at room temperature.

Nutritional Info: 1 Bar: Calories 150; Total Fat 8g (Saturated Fat 3g); Sodium 130mg; Total Carbohydrate 17g (Dietary Fiber 0g); Protein 2g. Exchanges: 1/2 Starch, 1/2 Other Carbohydrate, 1-1/2 Fat, Carbohydrate Choices: 1.

Betty's Kitchen Tip

For sweet and salty items that can be used in addition to chocolate chips and salted peanuts, consider marshmallows, candy-coated peanut butter candies, pretzels or crumbled peanut butter cookies.

pear-apple chutney

Prep Time: 15 Minutes
Start to Finish: 1 Hour 15 Minutes
Servings: 26 (1/4 cup each)

2	lb Bartlett pears, peeled and chopped (5 cups)
2	lb Gala apples, peeled and chopped (7 cups)
1	cup chopped sweet onion (1/2 medium)
3/4	cup golden raisins
1	cup cider vinegar
3	cups sugar
4-1/2	teaspoons grated gingerroot
3	tablespoons fresh lemon juice
1/2	teaspoon salt
1-1/2	teaspoons apple pie spice

1 In a 6-quart Dutch oven, combine all of the ingredients. Heat to boiling over high heat. Reduce the heat to medium-low; simmer 1 hour, stirring occasionally, until mixture has thickened.

2 Pour the chutney into containers with tight-fitting lids. Store in the refrigerator.

Nutritional Info: 1 Serving: Calories 143; Total Fat 0g (Saturated Fat 0g); Sodium 48mg; Total Carbohydrate 37g (Dietary Fiber 2g); Protein 0g. Exchanges: 1 Fruit, 1-1/2 Other Carbohydrate. Carbohydrate Choices: 2-1/2.

Betty's Kitchen Tip

If you want Pear-Apple Chutney to have a longer shelf life, process the jars in a boiling water bath for 10 minutes.

coconut-macadamia nut brittle

Prep Time: 20 Minutes
Start to Finish: 1 Hour 20 Minutes
Servings: 32 pieces

- 2 cups sugar
- 1 cup light corn syrup
- 1 cup chopped macadamia nuts, toasted
- 3/4 cup flaked coconut, toasted
- 1/2 cup chopped dried pineapple
- 3 tablespoons butter, cut into pieces
- 1 teaspoon baking soda
- 1 teaspoon vanilla

1 Grease a 17x12-inch half-sheet pan or 15x10x1-inch pan with butter.

2 In a large microwavable bowl, combine the sugar and corn syrup. Cover with microwavable plastic wrap; microwave on High 4 minutes. Uncover; microwave 7 to 8 minutes or until light golden brown. Stir in the nuts, coconut and pineapple. Microwave 1 minute longer or until boiling. Stir in 3 tablespoons butter, the baking soda and vanilla.

3 Immediately pour into the pan and spread evenly with a lightly greased offset spatula. Cool 1 hour or until completely cooled. Break into 2-inch pieces. Store tightly covered at room temperature.

Nutritional Info: 1 Piece: Calories 134; Total Fat 5g (Saturated Fat 2g); Sodium 65mg; Total Carbohydrate 24g (Dietary Fiber 1g); Protein 0g. Exchanges: 1-1/2 Other Carbohydrate, 1 Fat. Carbohydrate Choices: 1-1/2.

Betty's Kitchen Tip

Toasting coconut greatly enhances its flavor. To do so, bake uncovered in an ungreased shallow pan at 350°F for 5 to 7 minutes, stirring occasionally, until it becomes golden brown.

hot buttered rum sauce

Prep Time: 15 Minutes
Start to Finish: 15 Minutes
Servings: 32 (1 tablespoon each)

1/2	cup packed brown sugar
1/2	cup butter or margarine
2/3	cup whipping cream
1/4	cup rum

1 In a 1-1/2-quart saucepan, combine all ingredients. Heat to boiling over medium heat, stirring constantly. Boil 3 to 4 minutes, stirring constantly, until sauce is slightly thickened. Serve warm. Store covered in the refrigerator.

Nutritional Info: 1 Serving: Calories 75; Total Fat 6g (Saturated Fat 4g); Sodium 30mg; Total Carbohydrate 5g (Dietary Fiber 0g); Protein 0g. Exchanges: 1/2 Other Carbohydrate, 1 Fat. Carbohydrate Choices: 1/2.

Betty's Kitchen Tip

Drizzle this sauce over fresh fruit, ice cream or pound cake. If you prefer, you can use 2 teaspoons rum extract instead of the rum.

maple-walnut shortbread cookies

Prep Time: 1 Hour 40 Minutes
Start to Finish: 4 Hours
Servings: 48 cookies

1	cup butter, softened	1	teaspoon baking powder
1/3	cup sugar	1/4	teaspoon salt
1/2	cup finely chopped toasted walnuts	1	teaspoon maple flavor
1	egg yolk	1	cup semisweet chocolate chips (6 oz)
2	cups Gold Medal® all-purpose flour		

1 In a large bowl, beat the butter and sugar with an electric mixer on medium speed 30 seconds or until smooth. Add 1/2 cup of the walnuts and the egg yolk; beat until blended. On low speed, beat in the flour, baking powder, salt and maple flavor until a stiff dough forms. Shape the dough into a ball. Wrap in plastic wrap; refrigerate 45 minutes.

2 Heat oven to 350°F. Divide the dough into 8 equal parts. On a lightly floured surface, shape each part into a rope 12 inches long and 3/4 inch thick. Cut into 2-inch lengths. On ungreased cookie sheets, place cookies about 2 inches apart; flatten slightly.

3 Bake 15 to 17 minutes or until edges begin to brown. Cool 2 minutes; remove from cookie sheets to cooling racks. Allow cookies to cool completely.

4 In a small microwavable bowl, microwave the chocolate chips uncovered on High 1 minute 30 seconds, stirring every 30 seconds, until the chips can be stirred smooth. In another small bowl, place the remaining 1 cup walnuts. Dip 1/2 inch of 1 long side of each cookie into the chocolate, then coat the chocolate-covered edge with walnuts. Place on waxed paper; let stand about 2 hours until the chocolate is set.

Nutritional Info: 1 Cookie: Calories 100; Total Fat 7g (Saturated Fat 3.5g); Sodium 50mg; Total Carbohydrate 8g (Dietary Fiber 0g); Protein 1g. Exchanges: 1/2 Starch, 1-1/2 Fat. Carbohydrate Choices: 1/2.

Betty's Kitchen Tip

To toast walnuts, spread whole nut pieces in an ungreased shallow pan; bake at 350°F 5 to 8 minutes, stirring occasionally, until aromatic. Finely chop when cooled.

chipotle honey-roasted peanuts

Prep Time: 5 Minutes
Start to Finish: 5 Minutes
Servings: 10 (1/4 cup each)

EASY QUICK

- 1   container (12 oz) honey-roasted peanuts
- 1/2   teaspoon ground cinnamon
- 1/8   teaspoon chipotle chile pepper powder
- Dash salt
- Dash ground nutmeg

1. In a large bowl, place the peanuts. In a small bowl, mix the cinnamon, chile pepper powder, salt and nutmeg.

2. With a large spoon, scoop the peanuts up and over while sprinkling with the spice mixture, coating the nuts completely. Store in a jar, a sealed plastic bag or a container with a tight-fitting lid.

Nutritional Info: 1 Serving: Calories 195; Total Fat 16g (Saturated Fat 2g); Sodium 148mg; Total Carbohydrate 8g (Dietary Fiber 3g); Protein 7g. Exchanges: 1/2 Other Carbohydrate, 3-1/2 Fat. Carbohydrate Choices: 1/2.

Betty's Kitchen Tip

Start with honey-roasted peanuts, toss with any complementary spices you like, and you'll have a homemade-tasting snack in minutes.

gingerbread caramels

Prep Time: 25 Minutes
Start to Finish: 24 Hours
Servings: 36 caramels

1-3/4	cups whipping cream		1-3/4	cups sugar
1/2	cup unsalted butter		1/4	cup water
3/4	cup light corn syrup		10	gingersnap cookies, crumbled (3/4 cup)
1	teaspoon coarse sea salt		1/2	cup chopped crystallized ginger
1	piece (2 inch) gingerroot, peeled			

1 Line the bottom and sides of an 11x7-inch pan with foil, leaving the foil overhanging at 2 opposite sides of the pan; spray the foil with cooking spray. In a 2-quart saucepan, heat the whipping cream, butter, corn syrup, salt and gingerroot over medium heat to simmering, stirring often. Remove from heat; cover to keep warm.

2 In a 3-quart saucepan, cook sugar and water over medium heat until sugar melts and is amber in color. Remove from heat. Discard the gingerroot from the cream mixture. Slowly add cream mixture to the melted sugar, stirring constantly with a wire whisk. Cook over medium-high heat, stirring constantly to dissolve any sugar. Boil uncovered about 36 minutes, until a candy thermometer reads 246°F or a small amount of the mixture dropped into a cup of very cold water forms a firm ball that holds its shape until pressed.

3 Remove from the heat; stir in the crushed cookies. Immediately pour the mixture into the pan; sprinkle with crystallized ginger, pressing down slightly. Cool completely overnight. Use the foil to lift the caramel out of the pan. Cut into 9 rows by 4 rows. Wrap the caramels individually in waxed paper. Store up to 1 week.

Nutritional Info: 1 Caramel: Calories 136; Total Fat 7g (Saturated Fat 4g); Sodium 72mg; Total Carbohydrate 20g (Dietary Fiber 0g); Protein 0g. Exchanges: 1 Other Carbohydrate, 1-1/2 Fat. Carbohydrate Choices: 1.

Betty's Kitchen Tip

Making old-fashioned candies from scratch is much easier when you know what to look for during cooking. Here, the caramel reaches the Firm Ball Stage, 242°F to 248°F.

divine caramel sauce

Prep Time: 15 Minutes
Total Time: 45 Minutes
Servings: 40 (1 tablespoon each)

EASY

1	cup light corn syrup
1-1/4	cups packed brown sugar
1/4	cup butter or margarine
1	cup whipping cream

1. In a 2-quart saucepan, heat the corn syrup, brown sugar and butter to boiling over low heat, stirring constantly. Boil 5 minutes, stirring occasionally.

2. Stir in the whipping cream; heat to boiling. Remove from heat. Cool about 30 minutes. Serve warm.

3. Store covered in the refrigerator up to 2 months. Reheat slightly before serving, if desired.

Nutritional Info: 1 Serving: Calories 80; Total Fat 3.5g (Saturated Fat 2g); Sodium 25mg; Total Carbohydrate 13g (Dietary Fiber 0g); Protein 0g. Exchanges: 1 Other Carbohydrate, 1/2 Fat. Carbohydrate Choices: 1.

Betty's Kitchen Tip

To make Divine Toasted Pecan-Caramel Sauce, stir in 1 cup chopped toasted pecans after the sauce has cooled in step 2.

chocolate-drizzled lace brittle

Prep Time: 25 Minutes
Start to Finish: 1 Hour 45 Minutes
Servings: 24 pieces

1/4 cup butter or margarine	1/2 cup finely chopped almonds
1/2 cup sugar	1 teaspoon vanilla
1/4 cup light corn syrup	1/2 cup semisweet chocolate chips
1/3 cup Gold Medal® all-purpose flour	

1 Heat oven to 375°F (350°F for dark or nonstick pan). Line a cookie sheet with cooking parchment paper.

2 In a 2-quart saucepan, melt the butter over medium heat. Stir in sugar and corn syrup. Heat to boiling over medium-low heat, stirring constantly, until the sugar is dissolved. Remove from heat. Stir in the flour, almonds and vanilla until blended. Quickly spread the mixture into an 11x10-inch rectangle on the cookie sheet.

3 Bake 10 minutes or until the brittle spreads thin and is deep golden brown. Cool 5 minutes; remove from the cookie sheet to a cooling rack. Cool completely, about 15 minutes.

4 In a small resealable plastic freezer bag, place chocolate chips; seal the bag. Microwave on High about 1 minute or until softened. Gently squeeze the bag until the chocolate is smooth; cut off a tiny corner of the bag. Squeeze the bag to drizzle chocolate over the brittle. Let stand 1 hour or until the chocolate is firm. Break into irregular pieces.

Nutritional Info: 1 Piece: Calories 84; Total Fat 4g (Saturated Fat 2g); Sodium 20mg; Total Carbohydrate 12g (Dietary Fiber 1g); Protein 1g. Exchanges: 1 Other Carbohydrate, 1/2 Fat. Carbohydrate Choices: 1.

Betty's Kitchen Tip

This delicate brittle is much easier and quicker to make than the traditional nut candy.

fruitcake granola

Prep Time: 10 Minutes
Start to Finish: 1 Hour 10 Minutes
Servings: 18 (1/2 cup each)

EASY

4	cups old-fashioned oats
1	cup chopped walnuts
1/2	cup packed brown sugar
1/4	teaspoon ground cinnamon
1/4	teaspoon ground nutmeg
1/4	teaspoon salt
1/3	cup vegetable oil
1/4	cup honey
2	tablespoons granulated sugar
1	tablespoon spiced rum
	or 1/2 teaspoon rum extract
1	cup dried fruit bits
1/2	cup diced dried pineapple
1/4	cup diced candied orange peel
1/4	cup diced candied lemon peel

1 Heat oven to 300°F. In a large bowl, mix the oats, walnuts, brown sugar, cinnamon, nutmeg and salt; set aside.

2 In a 1-quart saucepan, heat the oil, honey and granulated sugar to simmering, stirring constantly, until the sugar has dissolved. Remove from heat; stir in the rum. Pour the hot liquid over the oat mixture, stirring until the dry ingredients are moistened. Spread in an ungreased 15x10x1-inch pan.

3 Bake 30 minutes, stirring occasionally, or until golden brown. Cool completely in the pan on a cooling rack, about 30 minutes.

4 Stir the granola to break it apart. Stir in the fruit bits, pineapple, orange peel and lemon peel. Store tightly covered.

Nutritional Info: 1 Serving: Calories 241; Total Fat 10g (Saturated Fat 1g); Sodium 53mg; Total Carbohydrate 37g (Dietary Fiber 3g); Protein 3g. Exchanges: 1 Starch, 1 Other Carbohydrate, 1/2 Fruit, 1-1/2 Fat. Carbohydrate Choices: 2-1/2.

Betty's Kitchen Tip

Kitchen scissors work well for cutting the dried pineapple and candied citrus peel in this recipe.

mexican-spiced fudge brownies

Prep Time: 10 Minutes
Start to Finish: 2 Hours
Servings: 16 brownies

EASY

. . . .

1-1/3	cups Gold Medal® all-purpose flour
2	cups sugar
1/2	cup unsweetened Dutch processed baking cocoa
1/2	teaspoon salt
1/4	teaspoon ground cinnamon

1/4	teaspoon ground red pepper (cayenne)
1	cup butter
6	oz Mexican chocolate (from 18.6-oz box), chopped
4	eggs
1	teaspoon vanilla

. . . .

1 Heat oven to 325°F. Spray an 8-inch square pan with cooking spray.

2 In a medium bowl, mix flour, sugar, cocoa, salt, cinnamon and red pepper; set aside.

3 In a large microwavable bowl, microwave butter and chocolate uncovered on High 2 minutes, stirring after 1 minute, or until melted and the mixture can be stirred smooth. Stir in the flour mixture, eggs and vanilla. Pour into the pan.

4 Bake 50 minutes or until a toothpick inserted in the center comes out almost clean. Cool completely on a cooling rack, about 1 hour. Cut into 4 rows by 4 rows.

Nutritional Info: 1 Brownie: Calories 312; Total Fat 15g (Saturated Fat 9g); Sodium 194mg; Total Carbohydrate 43g (Dietary Fiber 1g); Protein 4g. Exchanges: 1/2 Starch, 2-1/2 Other Carbohydrate, 2-1/2 Fat. Carbohydrate Choices: 3.

Betty's Kitchen Tip

Mexican chocolate is laced with cinnamon, almond and vanilla flavors. You can find it at Latin grocery stores and at some supermarkets.

cranberry-pistachio bark

Prep Time: 10 Minutes
Start to Finish: 40 Minutes
Servings: 32 pieces

EASY

2	lb white chocolate-flavored candy coating, coarsely chopped
1-1/2	cups dried cranberries or cherries
1-1/2	cups salted pistachio nuts
1	teaspoon grated orange peel

1 Spray a cookie sheet with cooking spray; line with waxed paper. In a large microwavable bowl, microwave the candy coating on Medium (50%) 1 minute; stir. Microwave 1 minute longer, stirring after 30 seconds, or until smooth.

2 Stir in cranberries, nuts and orange peel. Spread on the cookie sheet. Refrigerate 30 minutes. Break into 2-inch pieces. Store tightly covered at room temperature.

Nutritional Info: 1 Piece: Calories 201; Total Fat 11g (Saturated Fat 8g); Sodium 25mg; Total Carbohydrate 26g (Dietary Fiber 1g); Protein 1g. Exchanges: 1-1/2 Other Carbohydrate, 2 Fat. Carbohydrate Choices: 1-1/2.

Betty's Kitchen Tip

This is a perfect long-lasting recipe to keep on hand for last-minute gift-giving! Simply place the candy pieces in a decorative bag and tie with colorful ribbon.

jumbo coffeehouse muffins

Prep Time: 10 Minutes
Start to Finish: 1 Hour 40 Minutes
Servings: 6 muffins

EASY

3/4 cup chocolate milk	1 container (8 oz) mascarpone cheese or 1 package (8 oz) cream cheese, softened
1/4 cup vegetable oil	1 tablespoon sugar
2 tablespoons instant espresso coffee powder or granules	1/2 teaspoon instant espresso coffee powder or granules
2 eggs	3 tablespoons coarsely crushed chocolate-covered coffee beans
1 box (16.4 oz) Betty Crocker® chocolate chip muffin mix	

1 Heat oven to 425°F (400°F for dark or nonstick pan). Place a jumbo foil baking cup in each of six jumbo muffin cups; spray foil cups with cooking spray.

2 In a medium bowl, mix chocolate milk, oil, 2 tablespoons coffee powder and the eggs with a whisk until blended. Gently stir in the muffin mix just until blended (batter may be lumpy). Divide the batter evenly among the muffin cups, filling each one about two-thirds full.

3 Bake 22 to 24 minutes or until browned and the tops spring back when touched lightly. Cool 5 minutes (if you did not use foil baking cups, run a knife around edges of the cups before removing); carefully remove muffins from pan to a cooling rack. Cool completely.

4 In a medium bowl, mix the cheese, sugar and 1/2 teaspoon coffee powder until blended. Spoon about 1 tablespoon cheese mixture on top of each muffin. Sprinkle crushed coffee beans over the cheese topping. Store in the refrigerator.

Nutritional Info: 1 Muffin: Calories 645; Total Fat 40g (Saturated Fat 16g); Sodium 692mg; Total Carbohydrate 61g (Dietary Fiber 2g); Protein 10g. Exchanges: 1-1/2 Starch, 2-1/2 Other Carbohydrate, 7-1/2 Fat. Carbohydrate Choices: 4.

Betty's Kitchen Tip

To lower the fat in this recipe, replace whole eggs with 1/2 cup fat-free egg product or 4 egg whites—you'll save more than 20 grams of fat and 200 calories.

GLUTEN-FREE GOODNESS

p. 338

337

336

330

double chocolate-cherry cookies

Prep Time: 1 Hour 10 Minutes
Start to Finish: 1 Hour 50 Minutes
Servings: 32 cookies

1 box Betty Crocker® Gluten Free chocolate chip cookie mix
1 box (4-serving size) chocolate instant pudding and pie filling mix
1 cup dried cherries
1/2 cup coarsely chopped pecans

1/2 cup butter, melted
2 eggs
1 teaspoon vanilla
1 cup semisweet chocolate chips (6 oz)
1/4 cup whipping cream

1 Heat oven to 350°F. In a large bowl, mix the cookie mix, dry pudding mix, cherries and pecans. Add the melted butter, eggs and vanilla; stir until a soft dough forms.

2 Onto an ungreased cookie sheet, drop dough by rounded tablespoons; flatten slightly. Bake 9 to 11 minutes or until set. Cool 2 minutes; remove from the cookie sheet to a cooling rack. Cool completely.

3 Meanwhile, in a small microwavable bowl, microwave the chocolate chips and whipping cream uncovered on High 30 to 45 seconds; stir until smooth. Spoon a generous teaspoonful on each cookie; spread over the cookies. Allow the chocolate to set until firm, about 1 hour.

Nutritional Info: 1 Cookie: Calories 190; Total Fat 8g (Saturated Fat 4g); Sodium 150mg; Total Carbohydrate 26g (Dietary Fiber 0g); Protein 2g. Exchanges: 1 Starch, 1 Other Carbohydrate, 1-1/2 Fat. Carbohydrate Choices: 2.

Betty's Kitchen Tip

Always read labels to be sure recipe ingredients are gluten free. Product and ingredient sources can change.

apple crisp

Prep Time: 15 Minutes
Start to Finish: 1 Hour
Servings: 12 (3/4 cup each)

Apples

6	large tart cooking apples, thinly sliced
1	teaspoon ground cinnamon

Topping

1	box Betty Crocker® Gluten Free yellow cake mix
1/2	cup chopped nuts
1/2	cup butter, softened
1	teaspoon ground cinnamon
1	egg, beaten

Gluten-free ice cream, if desired

1 Heat oven to 350°F. In a large bowl, toss apples and 1 teaspoon cinnamon. Spread apples evenly in ungreased 13x9-inch pan.

2 In a large bowl, mix the cake mix and nuts. Cut in butter, with a pastry blender or fork, until crumbly. Add 1 teaspoon cinnamon and egg; mix well. Sprinkle evenly over the apples.

3 Bake about 45 minutes or until the topping is light brown. Serve warm with ice cream.

Nutritional Info: 1 Serving: Calories 300; Total Fat 11g (Saturated Fat 5g); Sodium 250mg; Total Carbohydrate 46g (Dietary Fiber 2g); Protein 2g. Exchanges: 1 Starch, 1/2 Fruit, 1-1/2 Other Carbohydrate, 2 Fat. Carbohydrate Choices: 3.

Betty's Kitchen Tip

To help keep Apple Crisp's crunchy topping intact, use a wide spatula to lift slices of the dessert out of the pan.

apple streusel cheesecake bars

Prep Time: 20 Minutes
Start to Finish: 3 Hours 30 Minutes
Servings: 24 bars

1 box Betty Crocker® Gluten Free yellow cake mix	1 teaspoon vanilla
1/2 cup cold butter	1 egg
2 packages (8 oz each) gluten-free cream cheese, softened	1 can (21 oz) apple pie filling
1/2 cup sugar	1/2 teaspoon ground cinnamon
	1/3 cup chopped walnuts

1 Heat oven to 350°F. Spray the bottom and sides of a 13x9-inch pan with cooking spray (without flour).

2 Place cake mix in large bowl. Cut in the butter, with a pastry blender or fork, until the mixture is crumbly and coarse. Remove 1-1/2 cups crumb mixture for the topping. Press the remaining mixture into the pan. Bake 10 minutes.

3 Meanwhile, in a large bowl, beat cream cheese, sugar, vanilla and egg with electric mixer on medium speed until smooth.

4 Spread the cream cheese mixture evenly over partially baked crust. In a medium bowl, mix the pie filling and cinnamon. Spoon evenly over the cream cheese mixture. Sprinkle the reserved crumbs over top. Sprinkle with walnuts.

5 Bake 35 to 40 minutes longer or until light golden brown. Cool on a cooling rack about 30 minutes. Refrigerate until chilled, about 2 hours. Cut into 6 rows by 4 rows. Store covered in refrigerator.

Nutritional Info: 1 Bar: Calories 230; Total Fat 12g (Saturated Fat 6g); Sodium 190mg; Total Carbohydrate 28g (Dietary Fiber 0g); Protein 2g. Exchanges: 1-1/2 Other Carbohydrate, 1/2 Milk, 1-1/2 Fat. Carbohydrate Choices: 2.

Betty's Kitchen Tip

A great snack for fall and winter, a tray of these tasty bites is the perfect contribution to Thanksgiving and Christmas celebrations.

carrot cake

Prep Time: 15 Minutes
Start to Finish: 1 Hour 55 Minutes
Servings: 12

EASY

1	box Betty Crocker® Gluten Free yellow cake mix
2/3	cup water
1/2	cup vegetable oil
1/2	teaspoon ground cinnamon
1/4	teaspoon ground nutmeg
2	teaspoons vanilla
3	eggs
1	cup finely shredded carrots (2 medium)
1	cup Betty Crocker® Whipped cream cheese frosting (from 12-oz container)
1/4	cup toasted flaked coconut, if desired

1 Heat oven to 350°F. Grease the bottom only of an 8- or 9-inch square pan with shortening or plain cooking spray.

2 In a large bowl, beat cake mix, water, oil, cinnamon, nutmeg, vanilla and eggs on low speed 30 seconds. Beat on medium speed 2 minutes, scraping bowl occasionally. With a spoon, stir in the carrots. Spread in the pan.

3 Bake an 8-inch pan 36 to 41 minutes or a 9-inch pan 33 to 38 minutes, or until a toothpick inserted in the center comes out clean. Allow to cool completely in the pan on a cooling rack, about 1 hour. Spread frosting over the cake and top with toasted coconut.

Nutritional Info: 1 Serving: Calories 420; Total Fat 16g (Saturated Fat 9g); Sodium 310mg; Total Carbohydrate 66g (Dietary Fiber 0g); Protein 3g. Exchanges: 1 Starch, 3-1/2 Other Carbohydrate, 3 Fat. Carbohydrate Choices: 4-1/2.

Betty's Kitchen Tip

Finely shredding the carrots spreads their goodness through the whole cake and makes it easier to cut, too.

impossibly easy french apple pie

Prep Time: 25 Minutes
Start to Finish: 1 Hour 15 Minutes
Servings: 6

Filling

3	cups thinly sliced peeled apples (3 medium)
1	teaspoon ground cinnamon
1/4	teaspoon ground nutmeg
1/2	cup Bisquick® Gluten Free mix
1/2	cup granulated sugar
1/2	cup milk

2	tablespoons butter or margarine, melted
3	eggs

Streusel Topping

1/3	cup Bisquick® Gluten Free mix
1/3	cup chopped nuts
1/4	cup packed brown sugar
3	tablespoons cold butter or margarine

1 Heat oven to 325°F. Spray a 9-inch glass pie plate with cooking spray.

2 In a medium bowl, mix apples, cinnamon and nutmeg; place in the pie plate. In the same bowl, stir the remaining filling ingredients until well blended. Pour over the apple mixture.

3 In a small bowl, mix all the topping ingredients with a fork until crumbly; sprinkle over the filling.

4 Bake 45 to 50 minutes or until a knife inserted in the center comes out clean. Store in the refrigerator.

Nutritional Info: 1 Serving: Calories 370; Total Fat 17g (Saturated Fat 8g); Sodium 250mg; Total Carbohydrate 48g (Dietary Fiber 2g); Protein 6g. Exchanges: 2-1/2 Starch, 1/2 Other Carbohydrate, 3 Fat. Carbohydrate Choices: 3.

Betty's Kitchen Tip

Bring your cell phone to the grocery store in case you need to call a manufacturer to double check a confusing ingredient or need to verify that processing methods are truly gluten-free.

peanut butter cookies

Prep Time: 40 Minutes
Start to Finish: 2 Hours 40 Minutes
Servings: 30 cookies

- 1/2 cup granulated sugar
- 1/2 cup packed brown sugar
- 1/2 cup peanut butter
- 1/4 cup shortening
- 1/4 cup butter, softened
- 1 egg
- 1-1/4 cups Bisquick® Gluten Free mix

1 In a large bowl, mix granulated sugar, brown sugar, peanut butter, shortening, butter and egg. Stir in the Bisquick mix. Cover; refrigerate about 2 hours or until dough is firm.

2 Heat oven to 375°F. Shape the dough into 1-1/4-inch balls. On ungreased cookie sheets, place the balls about 3 inches apart. With a fork dipped in sugar, flatten the balls in crisscross pattern.

3 Bake 9 to 10 minutes or until light golden brown. Cool 5 minutes; remove from cookie sheets to cooling racks.

Nutritional Info: 1 Cookie: Calories 100; Total Fat 6g (Saturated Fat 2g); Sodium 80mg; Total Carbohydrate 11g (Dietary Fiber 0g); Protein 1g. Exchanges: 1/2 Other Carbohydrate, 1 Fat. Carbohydrate Choices: 1.

Betty's Kitchen Tip

Want the perfect bumpy top on peanut butter cookies? Wipe off any excess dough and sugar that may collect between the tines of the fork.

fruit swirl coffee cake

Prep Time: 20 Minutes
Start to Finish: 45 Minutes
Servings: 18

Coffee Cake

- 4 eggs
- 3/4 cup milk
- 1/2 cup butter, melted
- 2 teaspoons gluten-free vanilla
- 1 box Bisquick® Gluten Free mix (3 cups)

- 2/3 cup granulated sugar
- 1 can (21 oz) fruit pie filling (any flavor)

Glaze

- 1 cup gluten-free powdered sugar
- 2 tablespoons milk

1 Heat oven to 375°F. Grease 1 (15x10x1-inch) pan or 2 (9-inch) square pans with shortening or cooking spray.

2 In a large bowl, stir all the coffee cake ingredients except pie filling until blended; beat vigorously 30 seconds. Spread 2/3 of the batter (about 2-1/2 cups) in the 15x10-inch pan or 1/3 of the batter (about 1-1/4 cups) in each of the square pans.

3 Spread pie filling over the batter (filling may not cover batter completely). Drop the remaining batter by tablespoonfuls onto the pie filling.

4 Bake 20 to 25 minutes or until golden brown. Meanwhile, in a small bowl, mix the glaze ingredients until smooth. Drizzle glaze over the warm coffee cake. Serve warm or cool.

Nutritional Info: 1 Serving: Calories 240; Total Fat 7g (Saturated Fat 4g); Sodium 280mg; Total Carbohydrate 41g (Dietary Fiber 0g); Protein 3g. Exchanges: 1 Starch, 1-1/2 Other Carbohydrate, 1-1/2 Fat. Carbohydrate Choices: 3.

Betty's Kitchen Tip

This easy fruit-filled coffee cake is ripe for any flavor of filling—take your pick! Try apple, cherry, blueberry, peach or apricot pie filling. Or use lemon curd for a luscious citrus twist.

harvest pumpkin-spice bars

Prep Time: 15 Minutes
Start to Finish: 2 Hours 40 Minutes
Servings: 49 bars

EASY

Bars

1	box Betty Crocker® Gluten Free yellow cake mix
1	can (15 oz) pumpkin (not pumpkin pie mix)
1/2	cup butter, softened
1/4	cup water
2	teaspoons ground cinnamon
1/2	teaspoon ground ginger
1/4	teaspoon ground cloves
3	eggs
1	cup raisins, if desired

Frosting

1	container (1 lb) Betty Crocker® Rich & Creamy cream cheese frosting
1/4	cup chopped walnuts, if desired

1 Heat oven to 350°F. Lightly grease the bottom and sides of a 15x10x1-inch pan with shortening or cooking spray.

2 In a large bowl, beat all bar ingredients except raisins with an electric mixer on low speed 30 seconds, then on medium speed 2 minutes, scraping bowl occasionally. Stir in the raisins. Spread in the pan.

3 Bake 20 to 25 minutes or until light brown. Cool completely in the pan on a cooling rack, about 2 hours.

4 Spread frosting over the bars. Sprinkle with walnuts. Cut into 7 rows by 7 rows. Store in the refrigerator.

Nutritional Info: 1 Bar: Calories 90; Total Fat 3.5g (Saturated Fat 1.5g); Sodium 85mg; Total Carbohydrate 14g (Dietary Fiber 0g); Protein 0g. Exchanges: 1/2 Starch, 1/2 Other Carbohydrate, 1/2 Fat. Carbohydrate Choices: 1.

Betty's Kitchen Tip

Add a bit of zing to the cream cheese frosting by stirring in 1 teaspoon grated orange peel.

brownie ganache torte with berries

Prep Time: 15 Minutes
Start to Finish: 1 Hour 55 Minutes
Servings: 12

EASY

- 1 box (16 oz) Betty Crocker® Gluten Free brownie mix
- 1/4 cup butter, melted
- 2 eggs

- 1/3 cup whipping cream
- 1/2 cup semisweet chocolate chips
- 1 cup fresh raspberries or sliced strawberries

1 Heat oven to 350°F. Spray the bottom only of an 8-inch springform pan with cooking spray (without flour).

2 In a medium bowl, stir brownie mix, butter and eggs until well blended. Spread in pan.

3 Bake 26 to 29 minutes or until a toothpick inserted 2 inches from the side of the pan comes out almost clean; cool 10 minutes. Run a knife around the edge of the pan to loosen; remove the side of the pan. Cool completely in the pan on a cooling rack, about 1 hour.

4 In a 1-quart saucepan, heat the whipping cream over medium-low heat until hot. Remove from heat; stir in the chocolate chips until melted and smooth. Let stand 15 minutes to thicken. Carefully pour the chocolate mixture onto the top center of the brownie; spread just to the edge. Slice into wedges. Garnish with berries.

Nutritional Info: 1 Serving: Calories 270; Total Fat 11g (Saturated Fat 7g); Sodium 110mg; Total Carbohydrate 38g (Dietary Fiber 1g); Protein 2g. Exchanges: 1 Starch, 1-1/2 Other Carbohydrate, 2 Fat. Carbohydrate Choices: 2-1/2.

Betty's Kitchen Tip

In addition to the fresh raspberries, top these fudgy wedges with a small dollop of whipped cream and a few toasted slivered almonds.

cinnamon-streusel coffee cake

Prep Time: 10 Minutes
Start to Finish: 40 Minutes
Servings: 6

EASY

Streusel Topping

1/3	cup Bisquick® Gluten Free mix
1/2	cup packed brown sugar
3/4	teaspoon ground cinnamon
1/4	cup cold butter or margarine

Coffee Cake

1-3/4	cups Bisquick® Gluten Free mix
3	tablespoons granulated sugar
2/3	cup milk or water
1-1/2	teaspoons vanilla
3	eggs

1 Heat oven to 350°F. Spray a 9-inch round or square pan with cooking spray.

2 In a small bowl, mix 1/3 cup Bisquick mix, the brown sugar and cinnamon. Cut in butter, using pastry blender or fork, until the mixture becomes crumbly.

3 In a medium bowl, stir all the coffee cake ingredients until blended. Spread in the pan; sprinkle with topping.

4 Bake 25 to 30 minutes or until golden brown. Store tightly covered.

Nutritional Info: 1 Serving: Calories 360; Total Fat 11g (Saturated Fat 6g); Sodium 460mg; Total Carbohydrate 58g (Dietary Fiber 1g); Protein 6g. Exchanges: 2-1/2 Starch, 1-1/2 Other Carbohydrate, 2 Fat. Carbohydrate Choices: 4.

Betty's Kitchen Tip

Contributing to a bake sale? Individually wrapped slices of this coffee cake would be a welcome addition. People with gluten-free diets generally have few choices at such events.

café au lait cake

Prep Time: 30 Minutes
Start to Finish: 3 Hours 30 Minutes
Servings: 10

Cake

1	tablespoon instant espresso coffee powder or granules
1	cup water
1	box Betty Crocker® Gluten Free devil's food cake mix
1/2	cup butter, softened
3	eggs

Frosting

2	teaspoons instant espresso coffee powder or granules
1	tablespoon cool water
1	cup Betty Crocker® Whipped milk chocolate frosting (from 12-oz container)
1-1/2	cups frozen (thawed) whipped topping

1 Heat oven to 350°F (or 325°F for dark or nonstick pan). Grease bottom only of an 8- or 9-inch round cake pan with shortening. Dissolve 1 tablespoon coffee in 1 cup water. In a large bowl, beat coffee mixture, cake mix, butter and eggs with electric mixer on low speed 30 seconds, then on medium speed 2 minutes, scraping the bowl constantly. Pour into the pan.

2 Bake 43 to 48 minutes or until a toothpick inserted in the center comes out clean. Cool 10 minutes. Run a knife around the side of pan to loosen cake; remove to a cooling rack. Cool completely, about 1 hour.

3 Dissolve 2 teaspoons coffee powder in 1 tablespoon water. Stir 2 teaspoons of coffee mixture into the frosting. In a medium bowl, mix whipped topping and remaining coffee mixture; gently stir in 1/4 cup frosting mixture. Cut cake in half horizontally. Place 1 cake layer, cut side up, on serving plate. Spread with half of whipped topping mixture (about 3/4 cup) to within 1/4 inch of edge. Top with the second cake layer, cut side down. Frost side and top of cake with frosting. Pipe remaining whipped topping mixture around top of cake. Refrigerate 1 hour or until chilled.

Nutritional Info: 1 Serving: Calories 370; Total Fat 17g (Saturated Fat 10g); Sodium 370mg; Total Carbohydrate 51g (Dietary Fiber 1g); Protein 3g. Exchanges: 1-1/2 Starch, 2 Other Carbohydrate, 3 Fat. Carbohydrate Choices: 3-1/2.

Betty's Kitchen Tip

The espresso flavor develops more fully as the cake continues to chill, and if served the next day, the flavor will be stronger.

chocolate crinkles

Prep Time: 1 Hour
Start to Finish: 5 Hours
Servings: 72 cookies

1/2	cup vegetable oil
4	oz unsweetened baking chocolate, melted, cooled
2	cups granulated sugar
2	teaspoons vanilla
4	eggs
2-1/2	cups Bisquick® Gluten Free mix
1/2	cup powdered sugar

1 In a large bowl, mix the oil, chocolate, granulated sugar and vanilla. Stir in the eggs, one at a time. Stir in the Bisquick mix until dough forms. Cover; refrigerate at least 3 hours.

2 Heat oven to 350°F. Grease the cookie sheets with shortening or cooking spray (without flour). Drop the dough by teaspoonfuls into the powdered sugar; roll around to coat and shape into balls. Place about 2 inches apart on cookie sheets.

3 Bake 10 to 12 minutes or until almost no imprint remains when touched lightly in the center. Immediately remove from cookie sheets to cooling racks.

Nutritional Info: 1 Cookie: Calories 60; Total Fat 2g (Saturated Fat 0g); Sodium 50mg; Total Carbohydrate 10g (Dietary Fiber 0g); Protein 0g. Exchanges: 1/2 Other Carbohydrate, 1/2 Fat. Carbohydrate Choices: 1/2.

Betty's Kitchen Tip

Parchment paper is your best friend in the kitchen. From cookies and cake to buns and brownies, parchment offers stick-free release, and is often a good alternative to cooking spray. And cleanup is a breeze—you'll never scrub your baking pans again.

strawberry truffle brownies

Prep Time: 30 Minutes
Start to Finish: 2 Hours 30 Minutes
Servings: 20 brownies

Brownies

1   box (16 oz) Betty Crocker® Gluten Free
    brownie mix

Melted butter and eggs called for on brownie mix box

Strawberry Truffle Topping

1   cup white vanilla baking chips (6 oz)
1/4   cup butter, cut into pieces
1/2   cup powdered sugar

1/2   cup strawberry jam
3   to 4 drops gluten-free red food color,
    if desired

Chocolate Glaze

1/2   cup semisweet chocolate chips
2   tablespoons butter
2   tablespoons light corn syrup

Additional powdered sugar, if desired

1   Heat oven to 350°F. Spray the bottom only of a 9-inch square pan with cooking spray. Make brownie mix as directed on the box, using melted butter and eggs. Spread batter into pan. Bake 26 to 30 minutes or until a toothpick inserted comes out almost clean. Cool on a cooling rack 30 minutes.

2   In a microwavable bowl, microwave the white chips and 1/4 cup butter on Medium-High (70%) 1 to 2 minutes, stirring once, until the butter is melted. Stir until smooth. Add 1/2 cup powdered sugar and jam; stir until smooth. Stir in the food color. Spread over the brownies. Chill 30 minutes.

3   Melt the chocolate chips and 2 tablespoons butter. Stir in the corn syrup. Drizzle over the topping; spread gently to cover. Chill 30 minutes or until set. Sprinkle with powdered sugar. Cut the brownies into 5 rows by 4 rows. Store tightly covered in the refrigerator.

Nutritional Info: 1 Brownie: Calories 260; Total Fat 12g (Saturated Fat 7g); Sodium 115mg; Total Carbohydrate 37g (Dietary Fiber 1g); Protein 2g. Exchanges: 1/2 Starch, 2 Other Carbohydrate, 2 Fat. Carbohydrate Choices: 2-1/2.

Betty's Kitchen Tip

Measure out what you need from the jar of strawberry jam and let it come to room temperature so it will blend into the white chocolate mixture more easily.

general index

alphabetical index